Synthetic, Insurance and Hedge Fund Securitisations

Head Office: 100 Harris Street PYRMONT NSW 2009
Tel: (02) 8587 7000 Fax: (02) 8587 7100
For all sales inquiries please ring 1800 650 522
(for calls within Australia only)

INTERNATIONAL AGENTS & DISTRIBUTORS

CANADA
Carswell Co
Ontario, Montreal,
Vancouver, Calgary

HONG KONG
Sweet & Maxwell Asia
Hennessy Road, Wanchai

Bloomsbury Books Ltd
Chater Road, Central

MALAYSIA
Sweet & Maxwell Asia
Petaling Jaya, Selangor

NEW ZEALAND
Brooker's Ltd
Wellington

SINGAPORE
Sweet & Maxwell Asia
Albert Street

UNITED KINGDOM & EUROPE
Sweet & Maxwell Ltd
London

UNITED STATES
Wm W Gaunt & Sons, Inc
Holmes Beach, Florida

William S Hein Co Inc
Buffalo, New York

JAPAN
Maruzen Company Ltd
Tokyo

Synthetic, Insurance and Hedge Fund Securitisations

A Guide to Structuring Innovative Securitisations

Paul U Ali
Senior Lecturer, Faculty of Law
University of Melbourne

Principal, Stellar Capital

and

Jan Job de Vries Robbé
Lawyer*
Minter Ellison, Melbourne
* admitted in the Netherlands

with contributions by
Cynthia T M Teo and Alan C H Chang

THOMSON

2004

Published in Sydney by

Lawbook Co.
100 Harris Street, Pyrmont, NSW

First edition 2004
National Library of Australia
    Cataloguing-in-Publication entry

Ali, Paul Augustine Usman.
    Synthetic, insurance and hedge fund securitisations: a
    guide to structuring innovative securitisations.

    Includes index.
    ISBN 0 455 21993 1.

    1. Security (Law) - Australia. 2. Securities - Australia.
    I. De Vries Robbé, Jan Job. II. Title.

    346.94092

© 2004 Paul Ali and Jan Job de Vries Robbé. Reproduced under exclusive licence
by Thomson Legal & Regulatory Limited ABN 64 058 914 668 trading as Lawbook Co.

This publication is copyright. Other than for the purposes of and subject to the conditions
prescribed under the Copyright Act, no part of it may in any form or by any means (electronic,
mechanical, microcopying, photocopying, recording or otherwise) be reproduced, stored in a
retrieval system or transmitted without prior written permission. Inquiries should be addressed
to the publishers.

Acknowledgment: The publisher and authors wish to thank the International Swaps and Derivatives
Association (ISDA) for kindly permitting the reproduction of the materials in the Appendix.

This edition current to 24 October 2003

Product Developer: Trina-Louise Berry
Editor: Melanie Eslick
Indexer: Madeleine Davis

Designed by Voss Design
Typeset in Century Schoolbook by Paula Kelly

Printed by Ligare Pty Ltd, Riverwood, NSW

Foreword

STEVEN L SCHWARCZ*

Despite its now well-established role as a funding source for corporations and financial institutions worldwide, securitization (or, as it's known outside the United States, securitisation) remains one of the most innovative tools of corporate finance. Securitization enables companies to obtain low cost funding from investors in the capital markets, compared to traditional funding sources, such as bank loans. Even for companies that can readily access the capital markets directly, securitization may provide the additional benefits of off-balance sheet funding; for financial institutions, securitization also can reduce the regulatory capital burden.

In a typical securitization transaction, a company raises funds by selling receivables or other financial assets to a bankruptcy-remote special-purpose corporation, trust or other vehicle or entity (SPV). The SPV finances its acquisition of receivables by issuing securities to capital market investors, who look to the receivables for repayment. Dr Ali and Mr de Vries Robbé have combined their considerable legal and banking expertise to focus, in this clearly written and well-documented book, on the latest innovations in securitization transactions. One such innovation is the extension of securitization beyond traditional classes of receivables (such as trade receivables or residential and commercial mortgage-backed loans) to a diverse range of assets. Chapters 6 to 8 of this book examine the securitization of such non-traditional receivables as investment-portfolio and hedge-fund rights, intellectual-property rights, and the cashflows of entire business enterprises.

The second innovation discussed, which goes hand-in-hand with the exponential growth of the global derivatives markets, is the considerable flexibility of derivatives to break receivables down into their component risks. Chapters 2 to 5 of the book examine the increasingly common replacement in financial-institution securitizations of the sale of receivables to an SPV with the derivatives-based transfer of the credit or other risks on those receivables to the SPV. These derivatives-based or so-called "synthetic" securitizations represent one of the fastest-growing areas of securitization globally.

Foreword

Dr Ali and Mr de Vries Robbé also provide in this book a practical compendium of innovative securitization transactions. Their analysis of the key legal, structural, and business features of these transactions should make the book an even more valuable and accessible guide — useful for both legal practitioners and scholars — to what the authors have called the "next generation" of securitization transactions.

October 2003
Durham, North Carolina

---

* Professor of Law, Duke University School of Law; Founding Director, Duke Global Capital Markets Center; Adj. Professor of Business Administration, The Fuqua School of Business. Contact: Schwarcz@law.duke.edu.

About the Authors

Paul Ali is a senior lecturer in the Faculty of Law, University of Melbourne and a principal of Stellar Capital, Sydney, a private investment firm. Paul has worked as a finance lawyer in Sydney, including as a senior associate in a Sydney law firm, and also in the securitisation group of a US bank. He has worked on one of the first Australian CDOs and the first Australian equity securitisation. Paul is the author of Chapters 1, 5 and 6 and the co-author of Chapter 7 (with Alan Chang). Paul wishes to thank Kanako Yano (Clifford Chance Tanaka Akita & Nakagawa, Tokyo), Douglas Lucas (UBS, New York) and Christian Ochsenbein (Capital Dynamics, Zug). Paul can be contacted at p.ali@unimelb.edu.au.

Jan Job de Vries Robbé is a lawyer (admitted in the Netherlands) with Minter Ellison, Melbourne. Prior to joining Minter Ellison in early 2003, Jan Job worked for nine years as a finance lawyer in private practice in the Netherlands with top firm De Brauw Blackstone Westbroek and also as senior legal counsel at pioneering Dutch investment bank NIB Capital Bank. He has extensive experience in derivatives and has advised on the structuring and documentation of a wide range of securitisations, from true sale RMBSs to synthetic CDOs. Jan Job is a guest lecturer on credit derivatives at both the University of Melbourne Law School and Sydney Law School and a permanent observer of AFMA's Credit Derivatives Committee. He is the author of Chapters 2, 3 and 4. Jan Job wishes to thank Fred Tinsley and Ralph Ayling of Minter Ellison for their continued support in this initiative. Mention of thanks is also due to Christian Kepel, Sjoerd Wegener Sleeswijk, Frenk van der Vliet and Johan Jol of NIB Capital Bank and Greg Wakelin of ANZ Bank for their comments, suggestions or other support.

Alan Chang is the co-author of Chapter 7. Alan is currently completing the requirements for admission as a barrister and solicitor in Victoria. He was previously the general counsel of a major semi-conductor company and a major pharmaceuticals conglomerate in Taiwan.

Cynthia Teo is the author of Chapter 8. Cynthia has recently completed the degree of Master of Banking and Financial Services Law in the Faculty of Law, University of Melbourne. She was previously a senior associate in a Singapore law firm.

The authors welcome any suggestions readers may have on this book.

The authors intend to make available updates and further information on the transactions discussed in this book. For details, visit Paul Ali's staff-page at http://www.law.unimelb.edu.au/db/profile/staff-list.cfm.

DISCLAIMER

This book is intended to provide general information about synthetic securitisations and selected cash securitisations. The information contained in this book does not constitute legal advice or investment advice (including recommendations to buy, sell or hold any of the instruments discussed in this book). The authors may, from time to time, be employed by or associated with entities that advise on, structure, market, deal in, invest in, or otherwise have a pecuniary interest in the instruments discussed in this book. Readers should assume that the authors will receive compensation for such services. In addition, any views expressed in this book are the personal views of the respective author, not of the employer.

Table of Contents

Foreword by Professor Steven L Schwarcz	v
About the Authors	vii
Abbreviations	x
1 Securitisation: an Introduction	1
2 Credit Derivatives: the Gateway to Synthetic Securitisation	5
3 Synthetic Securitisation: Should Every Bank Have One?	41
4 Synthetic Arbitrage: Merger of Credit Derivatives, Securitisation and Asset Management	91
5 Insurance Securitisation: Convergence of the Insurance and Capital Markets	131
6 Hedge Fund Securitisation: Repackaging Funds of Hedge Funds	145
7 Intellectual Property Securitisation: Crystallising the Value of Brand Names and Ideas	161
8 Whole of Business Securitisation: Unlocking the Wealth Within	171
Appendix	182
Index	209

Abbreviations

1999 Definitions	1999 Credit Derivatives Definitions
2003 Definitions	2003 Credit Derivatives Definitions
ABS	Asset backed securities
APRA	Australian Prudential Regulation Authority
BBA	British Bankers' Association
BIS	Bank for International Settlements
CAD3	Third capital adequacy directive
CAT bonds	Catastrophe-linked securities
CDO	Collateralised debt obligations
CDS	Credit default swap
CFO	Collateralised fund of hedge fund obligations
CLO	Collateralised loan obligations
CMBS	Commercial mortgage backed securities
CP3	Consultation Document, The New Basel Capital Accord
CSA	ISDA Credit Support Annexes
CSO	Managed arbitrage synthetic CDO
FSA	Financial Services Authority, UK
GIC	Guaranteed investment contract
IC	Interest coverage
IPO	Initial public offering
ISDA	International Swaps and Derivatives Association
LIBOR	London Inter Bank Offered Rate
MTN	Medium term note
OC	Over-collateralisation coverage
OTC	Over-the-counter
PAI	Publicly available information
QIS3	Quantitative Impact Study
Repo	Repurchase agreement
RMBS	Residential mortgage backed securities
SPV	Special purpose vehicle
WAR	Weighted average recovery rate
WAS	Weighted average spread
WOBS	Whole of business securitisation

Chapter 1

SECURITISATION: AN INTRODUCTION

About this book
[1.10] This book is a practitioner-oriented guide to the key legal and structuring issues that arise in the so-called "next generation" of securitisation transactions. These are transactions that involve the securitisation of non-traditional assets (eg the securitisation of hedge funds and intellectual property rights) or the disaggregation of financial assets into their component risks and the synthetic securitisation of discrete risks (the prime example being the securitisation of credit risk).

Securitisation has attracted much attention following the collapse of Enron Corporation in 2001 and revelations relating to the use by Enron of off-balance sheet special purpose vehicles to "window dress" its accounts.[1] It is commonly believed that the transactions involving these vehicles contributed materially to Enron's demise.[2] One result has been that securitisations and, more particularly, the special purpose vehicles at the heart of all securitisations have begun to be viewed with some degree of suspicion or, at least, concern by persons outside the securitisation industry.

In the US, these concerns have been manifested, for example, in the denial of a statutory safe harbour from bankruptcy legislation for the sale of the securitised assets from the transaction sponsor to the special purpose vehicle issuer and proposals to enact legislation conferring on the courts the specific power to recharacterise such sales as secured transactions.[3] In addition, regulators, such as the UK Financial Services Authority, are becoming increasingly apprehensive about the use of credit derivatives (and synthetic securitisations involving the issuance of securities backed by such derivatives) to transfer credit risk from banks to insurance companies and other non-bank investors in the capital markets and the potential for such cross-sector transfers of risk to result in the accumulation of credit risk in the hands of parties without the necessary expertise to evaluate, monitor and manage properly the risks being assumed.[4]

It is hoped that this book will, by stripping down synthetic securitisations and other exotic securitisations to their "bare bones", go some way to convincing readers that securitisations are no different to more conventional financial transactions, in that both are designed to achieve legitimate financial objectives, and consequently dispel many of the misconceptions associated with securitisations. This necessarily raises two questions: What is securitisation? How do the securitisation transactions discussed in this book differ from conventional securitisations?

What is securitisation?

[1.20] "Securitisation" is the label given to the generic process by which generally illiquid or lumpy assets (principally, income-producing assets for which no ready secondary market in which those assets can be readily bought and sold exists) are converted into instruments that can be traded in a market, typically the bond market. In the case of cash securitisations, this is achieved by issuing debt securities to investors that are serviced by the cash flows derived from the securitised assets. Virtually any asset with a medium to long-term duration that generates a relatively regular cash flow and is of adequate credit quality can be securitised. The assets that have been the subject of successful cash securitisations range from vanilla assets, eg residential mortgages, commercial mortgages, credit card debts, car loans, bank loans and student loans, to more exotic assets, such as aircraft, champagne, diamonds, films, hedge funds, kimonos, life insurance, music albums, ships, sports stadiums and tobacco litigation proceeds.

Types of securitisation transactions

[1.30] This book focuses on two broad categories of securitisation transactions. The first category relates to synthetic securitisations, which, in contrast to the examples of cash securitisations detailed at **[1.20]**, involve the issuance of debt securities backed by derivatives or other risk transfer mechanisms, as opposed to cash flow-generating assets. Synthetic securitisations, in essence, break down assets into their component risks and effect a transfer of certain risks independent of those assets to investors in the capital markets. This book is concerned with two particular risks that have been transferred to investors via these structures: credit risk (the risk of default or insolvency) and catastrophic risk (the risk of an earthquake or other natural disaster occurring).

The second category of transactions examined in this book relates to the new classes of assets that are forming the basis of cash securitisations, including life insurance policies, hedge funds, copyrights, patents and trademarks and entire business enterprises.

Chapter breakdown

[1.40] Chapter 2 deals with credit derivatives, the building blocks of synthetic securitisations. It explains the different types of credit derivatives (credit default swaps, total return swaps and credit spread transactions), provides a detailed guide to the new ISDA Credit Derivatives Definitions and examines the key legal issues arising out of the transfer of credit risk via credit derivatives, including the potential application of insurance laws.

Chapter 3 is concerned with synthetic collateralised debt obligations (CDO). It explains the legal structure of synthetic CDOs, contrasts synthetic securitisations with cash securitisations, examines fully funded and partly funded synthetic CDOs and discusses the key legal and regulatory issues arising out of the securitisation of credit risk, including the potential application of insurance laws and the application of capital adequacy rules.

Chapter 4 covers managed arbitrage synthetic CDOs (CSO). It explains the legal structure of CSOs and contrasts CSOs with other synthetic CDOs. It aims to demystify these increasingly complex and rapidly evolving structures to both legal practitioners and investors.

Chapter 5 examines insurance securitisations. It explains the legal structure of catastrophe-linked securities (the dominant class of insurance securitisations, involving the synthetic securitisation of catastrophic risk) and discusses the key legal issue, that of the potential application of insurance laws, arising out of the securitisation of catastrophic risk. Chapter 5 also examines the emerging class of life insurance securitisations, including "open block", "viatical settlement" and "life settlement" securitisations.

Chapter 6 discusses collateralised fund of hedge fund obligations (CFO). It explains the legal structure of CFOs, including the use of total return swaps to obtain exposure to hedge funds, examines the underlying assets of CFOs, funds of hedge funds, and provides an overview of the legal structure and investment strategies of hedge funds.

Chapter 7 examines intellectual property securitisations. It explains the legal structure of intellectual property securitisations, discusses the key legal issues involved in creating security interests over intellectual property rights and examines four ground-breaking intellectual property securitisations (involving the securitisation of copyrights, trademarks and software).

Chapter 8 is concerned with whole of business securitisations. It explains the legal structure of whole of business securitisations, contrasts whole of business securitisations with conventional cash securitisations and discusses the key legal issues involved in creating the "security package" that forms the basis of whole of business securitisations.

[1] See Powers Jr WC, Troubh RS and Winokur Jr HS, *Report of Investigation by the Special Investigative Committee of the Board of Directors of Enron Corp* (1 February 2002) pp 36-40. See further Schwarcz SL, "Enron and the Use and Abuse of Special Purpose Entities in Corporate Structures" (2002) 70 U Cincinnati L Rev 1309.

[2] See, for example, Klee KN and Butler BC, "Asset-Backed Securitization, Special Purpose Vehicles and Other Securitization Issues" (2002) 35 UCCLJ 23 at 31-33; "Enron Ties itself in Knots, then Falls Over", *Financial Times* (29 January 2002); cf Partnoy F, "A Revisionist View of Enron and the Sudden Death of 'May'" (2003) 48 Villanova L Rev 1245 who argues that "the most prominent SPE transactions were largely irrelevant to Enron's collapse, and that most of Enron's deals with SPEs were arguably legal, even though disclosure of those deals did not comport with economic reality" (at 1245).

[3] See Schwarcz SL, "Securitization Post-Enron" (Duke University School of Law, May 2003) p 3.

[4] See Financial Services Authority, *Cross-Sector Risk Transfers* (May 2002) at [3.87]-[3.96] and [3.120]-[3.126]; Evans D, "Credit Swaps, High Risks, Few Rules", *Bloomberg Markets* (August 2003). The FSA is also concerned about the use of catastrophe-linked securities to transfer catastrophic risks from insurance companies to investors in the capital markets: see Financial Services Authority, *Cross-Sector Risk Transfers* (May 2002) at [4.59]-[4.66] and [4.71]-[4.72].

Chapter 2

CREDIT DERIVATIVES: THE GATEWAY TO SYNTHETIC SECURITISATION

CREDIT DERIVATIVES: DEFINITION AND TYPES

Credit derivatives: an introduction
[2.10] Credit derivatives are an increasingly popular tool in credit risk management.[1] They are also essential building blocks for synthetic securitisations. An analysis of credit derivatives should therefore precede a discussion of synthetic securitisation.

The global credit derivatives market has shown strong, if not explosive, growth. Its market volume in 1997 of US$180 billion compares thinly to the US$1,952 billion in 2002. It is expected that this growth will continue to around US$4,800 billion in 2004.[2] In the first half of 2003, credit derivatives continued their strong growth at 25% to US$2,690 billion.[3]

The documentation of credit derivatives is based upon the Credit Derivatives Definitions 1999 (1999 Definitions), published by the International Swaps and Derivatives Association (ISDA). ISDA is active in drafting and updating standard documentation for derivatives. ISDA recently published a new set of definitions for credit derivatives (2003 Definitions).[4]

This chapter introduces credit derivatives and focuses on credit default swaps. It addresses the drivers and risks of credit default swaps, with emphasis on the documentation and legal aspects. A discussion of recently incorporated 2003 Definitions is also provided. Its purpose is to familiarise market participants with the concepts of credit derivatives as far as necessary to facilitate the discussion of synthetic securitisation structures.[5]

What is a credit derivative?
[2.20] A credit derivative is a bilateral agreement that allows one party to transfer the credit risk of a "reference entity" to another party.[6] Credit risk is the risk that a counterparty will not meet its obligations (in whole or in part) as and when due. Some credit derivatives (such as the credit default swap) do not cover other risks, such as loss in value of the underlying as a result of market conditions. Also, credit risk is not default risk. Only defaults caused by the inability of the payer to perform are covered by credit risk.

Credit derivatives have a number of characteristics. Primary among these is that they entitle market participants to transfer the credit risk of a reference entity to a third party without the need to transfer the underlying assets, the "reference obligations".

Secondly, the reference entity is usually a third party. The party seeking protection, the "buyer", may have exposure to the reference entity it is trying to hedge, eg if it has provided a loan facility. However, this is not a requirement.[7] Thirdly, credit derivatives are (as yet) off-balance instruments.[8] Fourthly, they are non-funded, ie the buyer of protection will not receive any funds up front. Consequently, credit derivatives are leveraged investments.

The fact that the referenced asset (or "underlying") does not need to be legally transferred has been cardinal in the development of the credit derivatives market in general and of the credit default swap market in particular. It has been instrumental in opening up the market to new participants, such as investors with limited access to the capital markets. Taking a position in credit derivatives may enable these investors to obtain the desired exposure without recourse to capital markets. Furthermore, credit derivatives enable market participants to trade the credit risk of entities that have no listing on a particular stock exchange or those that are not publicly traded at all.

Types of credit derivatives

[2.30] There are three basic types of credit derivatives: the total return swap, the credit spread and the credit default swap.

In a *total return swap* one party transfers all the cash flow it receives from a referenced asset, such as a bond or a loan, to the other party, which in return pays an up-front agreed-upon cash flow, based on, for example, the London Inter Bank Offered Rate (LIBOR). The respective obligations of the parties do not depend upon the occurrence of a specific event, such as a credit event. The total return swap can be regularly marked to market: its value is adjusted based on the current market value of the underlying asset. A total return swap transfers not only credit risk, but also market risk.

In a *credit spread transaction* the payments of the respective parties are based upon the spread of an underlying security as compared to either a (theoretically risk-free) benchmark (in the case of an *absolute* spread) or the spread of another security (in the case of a *relative* spread). As with total return swaps, the payment obligations of the respective parties do not depend upon the occurrence of a credit event. A credit spread only transfers credit risk.

The most common credit derivative is the *credit default swap*. With this instrument one party, the buyer of protection, or buyer, transfers the credit risk on a third party, the reference entity, to the seller of protection, or seller. The buyer pays a (regular) protection fee. The seller commits to making a contingent payment to the buyer, to pay the settlement amount upon the occurrence of any credit event, with respect to the reference entity.

Generally, these types of credit derivatives relate to the transfer of credit and/or market risk on a *single* reference entity. In basket or portfolio transactions, however, this transfer relates to the credit risk on *multiple* reference entities. These are often referred to as "multi-name swaps". Unlike a single-name credit default swap, a portfolio credit default swap does not terminate upon the occurrence of a single credit event. Strictly speaking, portfolio transactions are not a type of credit derivative. Each of the abovementioned types can take the form a portfolio product.

The credit linked note combines funding and credit derivative technology. It is an on-balance instrument and, as such, it is the funded equivalent of the credit default swap. Whereas in a credit default swap the seller's payment obligation is triggered by the occurrence of a credit event, in a credit linked note the occurrence of a credit event affects the amount repayable to the protection seller. The buyer of protection will set off its claim for the credit event payment against its obligation to repay the notes. A credit linked note may reference a single entity or (more commonly) a portfolio of reference entities.

Credit default swaps

Credit default swaps: an introduction
[2.40] A credit default swap enables a buyer of protection, or simply "buyer", to transfer the credit risk on a reference entity (or entities) to a seller of protection, or simply "seller". The buyer pays a (regular) protection fee against the consideration of which the seller commits to pay the settlement amount to the buyer after the occurrence of a credit event and any other conditions to settlement being met.

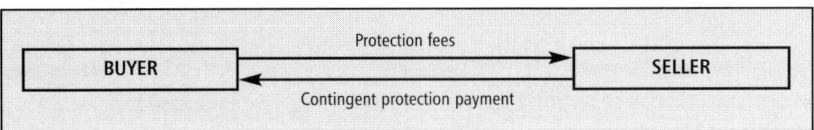

A credit default swap revolves around credit events (see **[2.50]**), obligations (of which there are different types: see **[2.60]**), the conditions to settlement (see **[2.70]**) and the types of settlement (see **[2.80]**). To facilitate the discussion of these concepts for readers not familiar with credit derivatives, reference is made to the standard credit default swap published by ISDA, reproduced in the Appendix.[9]

Credit events

[2.50] The occurrence of a credit event is a precondition for settlement of the transaction. In the global over-the-counter (OTC) market, three credit events are customary: bankruptcy, failure to pay and (different kinds of) restructuring.[10] Due to concerns over restructuring (discussed at **[2.130]**), some market participants in the US and Japan have taken to trading in two credit event risks only: bankruptcy and failure to pay.

Main credit events
The three main credit events can be described as:
- *Bankruptcy*: the bankruptcy or dissolution of a reference entity, it becoming insolvent, seeking or becoming subject to a trustee or similar official, or an analogous effect under applicable jurisdictions.
- *Failure to pay*: failure by a reference entity to make payments when and where due in an aggregate amount of not less than the *payment requirement*[11] after the expiration of any applicable grace period.
- *Restructuring*: a reduction or deferral in the rate or amount of interest payable or principal, a change in the ranking in priority of payment or change in the currency of any payment of interest or principal, provided such event directly or indirectly results from a deterioration in the creditworthiness or financial condition of the reference entity.

Other credit events
The three other credit events are: obligation acceleration, obligation default and repudiation/moratorium.[12] These are the so-called "soft" credit events and are rarely used with respect to corporate reference entities. They can be described as:
- *Obligation acceleration*: obligations in an aggregate amount of not less than the payment requirement have become due and payable before they would otherwise have been due and payable on the basis of an occurrence of a default or similar event other than a failure to make any required payment.
- *Obligation default*: one or more obligations in an aggregate amount of not less than the default requirement have become capable of being declared due and payable before they would otherwise have been due and payable as a result of the occurrence of a default or similar event other than a failure to make any required payment.
- *Repudiation/moratorium*: the repudiation in whole or in part of obligations in an aggregate amount of not less than the default requirement or declaring the imposition of a moratorium or similar event, and a failure to pay without regard to the payment requirements.

Caution
As is apparent, these definitions do not necessarily coincide with a layperson's understanding. For example, bankruptcy not only covers the obvious bankruptcy court order, it covers a variety of similar, but not equal, occurrences. The definition of "bankruptcy" even used to contain a "catch-all" clause, which covered all kinds of actions taken (or not taken) by the reference entity which could be construed as agreeing to its dissolution or filing for its bankruptcy.

This is relevant for market participants if they try to hedge exposure arising from credit derivatives. It can also be relevant in the context of hedging exposure from synthetic collateralised debt obligations (CDOs). For that reason the transaction year or "vintage" of a credit derivative or synthetic CDO is a key element in understanding its risk profile.

Types of obligations
[2.60] The second essential element in understanding the credit default swap is the different types of obligations: reference obligations, obligations and deliverable obligations.[13]

Reference obligations are obligations in respect of which protection is purchased and sold.

The term *obligations* covers a group of different obligations of the reference entity. In order to qualify as an obligation, an obligation must meet the requirements of the *obligation category* and the *obligation characteristics*,[14] both of which are specified in the confirmation. The most common obligation category is borrowed money.[15] Although generally similar, some differences remain between the applicable characteristics in the various regional markets.[16] Obligations are tied to the occurrence of a credit event.

Deliverable obligations are relevant only if physical settlement (discussed at **[2.80]**) is opted for. After the occurrence of a credit event, the buyer of protection is obliged to deliver certain obligations to the seller, against which the seller pays to the buyer the physical settlement amount that corresponds with the deliverable obligations delivered.[17] The buyer may choose to deliver obligations provided they fit the definition of "deliverable obligations" and its category[18] and characteristics.

In other words, the parties to a credit derivatives transaction may agree to buy and sell protection on a specific bond (the reference obligation). Settlement of this transaction is not only triggered if a credit event occurs with regard to that reference obligation, but also if a credit event occurs with respect to any other obligation that would fit the requirements of obligations in the confirmation.[19]

Conditions to settlement

[2.70] The occurrence of a credit event does not in itself trigger settlement of the credit derivatives transaction. Several "conditions to settlement" must be met,[20] including the delivery of a credit event notice, a notice of publicly available information and, in respect of physical settlement, a notice of physical settlement by the buyer to the seller.[21]

The *credit event notice* must contain a description in reasonable detail of the facts relevant to the determination that a credit event has occurred.

The *notice of publicly available information* (PAI) confirms the occurrence of a credit event citing PAI. "Publicly available information" is defined to include information:
- published in (usually two) public sources, eg Bloomberg and the Wall Street Journal;
- received from or published by a reference entity not party to the relevant transaction or a trustee;
- contained in any petition for bankruptcy; or
- contained in any order, however described, filed with a court or similar administrative regulatory or judicial body.[22]

The *notice of physical settlement* is a notice from the buyer to the seller, which confirms that the buyer will settle the transaction in accordance with the physical settlement method and contains a detailed description of the deliverable obligations that the buyer will deliver to the seller, including the principal outstanding balance and the due and payable amount.

To facilitate the use of standard notices in the market, ISDA has published templates of these notices on its website (http://www.isda.org) as exhibits to the 2003 Definitions[23]. The credit event notice and the notice of PAI are usually combined in a single notice.

In the context of back-to-back credit default swaps entered into by various financial institutions, the (fall-back) requirement of two public sources for PAI is not without merit. In a rare case of litigation on credit derivatives, Deutsche Bank as buyer of protection sought judgment against ANZ for failing to pay out under a credit default swap referencing bonds of the city of Moscow.[24] Deutsche Bank had sold protection on these bonds to Daiwa. Requiring only one public source (in this case, IFR) did not give ANZ protection against the possibility that Daiwa was the sole source of PAI.[25]

Settlement

[2.80] Fourth, but by no means least, the various settlement methods of a credit default swap should be discussed. Settlement of the transaction can be either in cash or physical form.[26]

In the *cash settlement* method, the seller of protection pays the buyer an amount (defined as the "cash settlement amount"[27]) that is typically derived from the loss in value of the reference obligation over time, from when the transaction was entered into and the occurrence of the credit event.

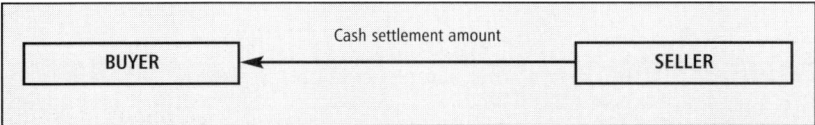

In the *physical settlement* method, the buyer of protection delivers (a portfolio of) deliverable obligations against full payment of the original price.[28] The deliverable obligations should have an outstanding principal balance (or, if not borrowed money, a due and payable amount) in the aggregate amount of the physical settlement amount.[29] So, when making a delivery, the market value of the deliverable obligations is not relevant for the purpose of the calculation of the settlement amount.

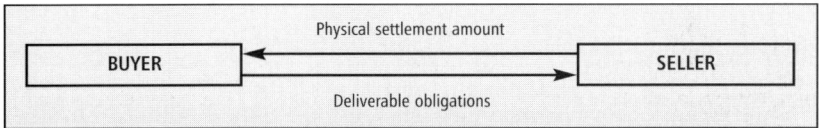

In the over-the-counter (OTC) market, *physical settlement* is the customary method of settlement. This is because banks are generally comfortable with the process of "working out" the defaulted assets to maximise the recovery. In addition, ownership of the delivered obligations may be useful to the seller of protection in the context of restructuring the reference entity. The seller may be able to block a restructuring from going forward using the rights contained in the deliverable obligations. Others may prefer a cash settlement, eg because this sidesteps any problems of suitability. After all, one of the reasons for a market participant to enter into a credit derivative might have been its inability to accept delivery of the underlying asset.

A typical credit default swap has a maturity of five years and a currency notional amount of US$10 million. However, other maturity trades are available as well.

Drivers and risks

Drivers for credit derivatives

[2.90] So, if these products are so popular, what are the drivers for the use of credit derivatives (and default swaps in particular)? The primary driver is credit risk management. Credit default swap users can hedge or gain exposure to specific risks more effectively using credit default swaps than through the cash bond market. The number of traded cash bonds is limited, while the terms of a credit default swap are freely negotiable. A second objective is portfolio diversification. A third reason for the use of credit default swaps (for banks) is regulatory capital relief. Simply, by buying protection on a reference entity from another bank, a bank is able to substitute the credit risk weighting of the reference obligation with that of its counterparty, the seller of protection. However, regulatory capital relief is rarely a motivation on its own. Rather, it is a side effect of the use of credit derivatives for credit risk management purposes. A further and important driver has been the opportunity for market participants to use credit derivatives to "short" a bond. In the cash bond market this is hardly a possibility. Relying on a repo tends to be expensive. Credit derivatives fill this gap. Last but not least, credit derivatives offer substantial opportunities for arbitrage (see Ch 4 for discussion in the context of synthetic securitisations).

Credit derivatives are often thought of as instruments primarily suitable for use by banks and other financial institutions. However, in terms of hedging credit risk or portfolio diversification, credit derivatives offer the same potential to the corporate sector. For instance, a corporate entity active within a specific industry, such as aircraft or energy, may face a concentration of risk in that industry, perhaps because almost all of its contracting parties are active in that same industry. This entity could benefit from the use of credit derivatives by buying protection on competitors to mitigate exposure.

Risks in derivatives
[2.100] No new products are without risks. This is no different with credit default swaps. It is crucial for new market participants to fully understand the risks involved. The caution also applies to experienced market players. As discussed at **[2.230]**, credit derivatives are increasingly standardised and traded as commodities. Although this development facilitates a further growth of the market and a more efficient distribution of credit risk, it presumes users continue to address these underlying risks.

The legal risks in derivatives, such as whether the parties have the power and capacity to enter in the transaction,[30] have been widely debated.[31] To discuss all in any detail would fill a separate book.[32] Instead, note that the impact of legal risks may differ across jurisdictions. For example, a counterparty may not have the power or capacity to enter into a (credit) derivatives transaction. This is referred to as *ultra vires*. The effect is mostly similar across different jurisdictions: contracts designated as ultra vires are subject to nullification by the entity the powers of which were exceeded. However, the scope of counterparties to which ultra vires potentially applies may differ. Under different common law jurisdictions, ultra vires is generally limited to non-private entities or other entities with limited powers, such as trusts. Under other jurisdictions,[33] however, ultra vires does apply to private entities. Needless to say, this may have an impact on the due diligence required before entering into a cross-border credit derivative.

It is presumed the parties to a credit derivative transaction have entered into an ISDA Master Agreement and Schedule, that they had the capacity and authority to do so and that their respective obligations under such a transaction are enforceable.[34] Furthermore, parties need to reassure themselves that netting between the different (credit) derivative transactions is permitted under all relevant jurisdictions. Members of ISDA benefit from the legal opinions that have been issued to ISDA by law firms in practically all relevant jurisdictions. However, these opinions relate to netting under the ISDA Master Agreement in general and do not address credit default swaps in any detail.

Derivatives exposure is increasingly curtailed through the use of automated collateral management systems. Parties may enter into a credit support document, such as the Credit Support Annex under English law, to facilitate weekly or ever more often daily valuation of portfolios. Collateral management can be efficiently used to limit any derivative exposure, including credit derivatives exposure.[35]

Risks in credit derivatives

[2.110] Credit derivatives may incur a variety of risks. Within the context of this chapter, which is a prelude to understanding synthetic securitisations, rather than a fully fledged analysis of every detail of credit derivatives, only some of the main risks are discussed.[36] These include counterparty risk, basis risk, liquidity risk and market risk.

Buying protection by means of an uncollateralised credit derivative transaction results in *counterparty risk* (on the protection seller paying the settlement amount). This counterparty risk is defined as the risk that the counterparty fails to perform according to the terms and conditions of the financial contract. In addition, there may be *correlation risk*. This is the risk that the reference entity and the protection seller default at the same time. Typically, the joint probability of default should be low.[37]

In fact, the counterparty risk is more concentrated than it may appear on first sight. The major players in credit derivatives are few, particularly in the US market.[38]

Basis risk is incurred when the credit derivative used does not adequately match the characteristics of the underlying asset being hedged. Basis risk can take various forms, such as a maturity mismatch, currency mismatch or asset mismatch. Basis risk is also present in terms of spread volatility between a physical and a derivative position.

Credit markets can be illiquid. Credit derivatives are subject to the same factors that affect liquidity in the cash market. If cash settlement is used, the value of the credit derivative could be distorted if the reference obligation is illiquid. Where protection is purchased against an underlying asset that is shorter in maturity, the buyer carries the risk that it cannot replace or roll over the hedge (if needed) when the contract matures.

Fourth is *market risk*. This can take two forms. First, movements in interest rates affect the discounted value of the expected future cash flows under the credit derivatives, affecting market values. This is insignificant for unfunded products, such as credit default swaps, but is significant for funded instruments, such as credit linked notes and total return swaps. Second is spread risk. These are movements in the market spread due to systematic factors, such as supply of physical credit, demand for protection, industry trends and so on.

Regulatory risk refers to the need for credit derivative users to remain abreast of the appropriate regulatory rules and to correctly report risk positions. Misunderstanding or mismanagement may result in more capital than is necessary being ultimately allocated to a position.

A particular documentation issue is the "cheapest-to-deliver" risk, detailed at **[2.130]** and **[2.180]**. The enhanced standardisation of credit derivatives documentation has significantly reduced documentation risk. The 2003 Definitions and other initiatives undertaken by ISDA (see **[2.220]**) have contributed to that. Various regulators or financial market authorities have issued market conventions for credit derivatives, which has also facilitated the documentation issue.[39]

Finally, the parties to a credit derivatives transaction should take particular care that the name of the reference entity is correct. This may be of concern if different names within a group could be referenced. Also, the exact name used by Bloomberg may not necessarily be fully up to date.

Early documentation of credit derivatives

1999 Definitions
[2.120] Within ISDA, a separate working group deals with credit derivatives market practice. Through this forum ISDA consults with its members and distributes drafts of new publications. The first standard confirmation for credit derivatives, the ISDA Long Form Credit Swap Confirmation, was published in January 1998. It is on the basis of this document that subsequently the 1999 Definitions were published.

Market use has stress-tested these definitions to a significant degree and the working group has primarily focused on solving the issues that arose as a result of market use. In order to provide swift relief, ISDA has acted to publish bandaids on specific issues, by publishing "supplements" to the 1999 Definitions, respectively the Convertible, Successor and Restructuring Supplement (see **[2.130]**). Under the 1999 Definitions, the parties to a credit derivative transaction were free to choose whether to apply (any of) these supplements to the transactions entered into between them.

Restructuring Supplement

[2.130] The Restructuring Supplement has given rise to most debate. At issue was the definition of the credit event "restructuring". Credit events, and hence their definition, play a cardinal role in the buying or selling of protection under credit default swaps. It is based upon the definition of credit events that a buyer claims payment of the settlement amount. Generally, most problems have arisen as a result of subjective terms or vague references leading to different interpretations in the definition of respective credit events. For example, restructuring is specified not to cover events occurring that do not directly or indirectly result from a deterioration in the creditworthiness or financial condition of the reference entity.[40] This language was added to avoid events that were not considered true defaults from triggering settlement.

However, as is apparent from the Conseco case, it is sometimes difficult to ascertain whether a "true" restructuring has occurred.

> **Conseco Inc.**
> Conseco was a solvent company, but faced a shortage in liquidity. There had been no events of default in its outstanding loans. In order to redress the shortage in liquidity some maturing loans were refinanced. The provisions of the refinancing provided that repayment was deferred.[41]
>
> Financing banks had hedged their exposure on Conseco by credit default swaps. Physical delivery, as the market standard, had been agreed to. These banks decided that it was preferable to restructure the loans, rather than force Conseco into bankruptcy.
>
> The conditions of the restructured loans were better (from a lender's point of view) than the old loans. They profited from an additional guarantee and earned higher margins. As a consequence, the different types of Conseco debt traded at substantially different levels. The restructured loans traded at 92% of its outstanding principal amount, while the senior bonds with a long maturity traded at 68%.[42]

> As the provisions of the confirmation did not set any relevant limitations on the deliverable obligations, the banks were in a position to choose those deliverable obligations that were cheapest in the market – the ones with a very long maturity and which had not been restructured – and deliver these to their counterparties, handing them a profit (some would argue a windfall profit) in the process. The option for the buyer to choose which deliverable obligation to deliver to the seller is referred to as the "cheapest-to-deliver" option.
>
> A further concern was that the refinancing banks were only few, held large stakes in the reference obligation and their positions were aligned as each had hedged its exposure in the credit default swap market. Consequently, they had a parallel interest in negotiating the restructured loans so that they would be able to maximise any cheapest-to-deliver option. Also, they were in a position to block any other restructuring as their votes as creditors were needed,[43] while their credit default swap counterparties had no clue whether a credit event would occur.[44]

In order to alleviate these concerns, ISDA published the Restructuring Supplement in May 2001.[45] By declaring this supplement applicable, the parties to a credit default swap can substantially limit the impact of the cheapest-to-deliver option. In summary, the seller would only be entitled to transfer obligations of the reference entity with a final maturity not exceeding 30 months after the scheduled termination date. Additionally, only fully transferable obligations would qualify, ie no consent would be required for such transfer.

The second concern related to the parallel interest of the financing banks. This issue has been addressed by providing that only "multiple holder obligations" can qualify as a deliverable obligation in the case of a restructuring credit event. That is an obligation that, at the time the credit event notice is delivered, is held by more than three holders that are not affiliates of each other, and with respect to which a percentage of holders at least equal to 66⅔% is required to consent to the event, which would otherwise constitute a restructuring credit event.[46]

In practice, the Restructuring Supplement is commonly applied with respect to trades in US names and this is commonly known as "Mod R". However, this supplement has not been accepted in the European market, a practice known as "Old R".[47] The limitations imposed under Mod R were too strict for the European market. Most European loans tend to be transferable only with the consent of the debtor (not to be unreasonably withheld). Under the Mod R regime, these loans would not qualify as fully transferable and, hence, not as deliverable obligations.

Successor Supplement

[2.140] The two other supplements, the Successor and Convertible Supplements, have been far less contentious. The driver behind the Successor Supplement[48] has been the demerger of National Power in England.

> **National Power PLC**
>
> Market participants had traded in National Power credit risk. When National Power demerged into several other entities, it was unclear which of these entities was or were the successor entity or entities. The 1999 Definitions only referred to the successor as the entity that had acquired "all or substantially all" of the obligations of the demerging entity. When an entity demerged into various others, which percentage would suffice to constitute "substantially" all? Also, to which obligations of National Power would any percentage test have to be applied?
>
> In order to overcome these issues, ISDA has chosen a more objective, numerical approach by means of thresholds. Depending on the respective percentage of obligations that has been acquired by the emerging entities, a table specifies which of these is or are the successor reference entity or entities.[49] Also, this supplement defines the "relevant obligations" that should be taken into consideration when applying the numerical test to the emerging entities.

Despite this supplement, it still is not always easy to identify the best available information,[50] the relevant obligations or the proper successor entity. With respect to sovereigns, for instance, how is devolution in the UK explained?[51] In Australia, the demerger of WMC Limited into WMC Resources Limited and Alumina Limited caused AFMA to publish a legal opinion to advise the market as to the successor issues.[52]

Convertible and Bankruptcy Supplements

[2.150] The Convertible Supplement[53] addresses the interpretation of the definition of the deliverable obligation characteristic "not contingent". It is standard practice to include this characteristic in OTC credit default swap transactions. The seller includes this characteristic because it wants to avoid delivery of obligations the repayment of which is subject to the occurrence of an event over which it has no control. Otherwise, the realised value could be substantially affected.

> **Railtrack PLC**
>
> In the receivership of UK rail company Railtrack buyers of Railtrack credit risk wanted to deliver convertible bonds as deliverable obligations. In discussion was whether these bonds constituted "not contingent" obligations. The supplement differentiated between the parties entitled to convert or exchange (in the case of exchangeable bonds). If the noteholder had the

option, this was not deemed a true contingency, as it has full control over the option's exercise. However, if the conversion or exchange option is bestowed upon a third party (such as the issuer), then such obligations would be considered contingent and, hence, would not qualify as deliverable obligations.

Some market participants refused to take delivery of convertible bonds, under the terms of which the trustee (on behalf of the noteholders) had the option to convert. This case was litigated in and provides a rare example of credit derivatives case law. In summary, the interpretation contained in the supplement was upheld.[54]

In its judgment the court recognised that the definition of "not contingent" is broadly formulated (repayment in respect of which is not subject to *any* contingency). However, it emphasised that this definition cannot be intended to cover a contingency in the event of which the noteholder has control over the execution. This is not any different in the event that the execution of the right to convert on the basis of the provisions of the trust deed is in the hands not of the noteholder, but of a trustee who acts on the noteholder's behalf. A trustee acting in the interests of the noteholder was not deemed to be an extraneous factor as it would only be exercising the option to convert the bonds into equity if that were in the commercial interests of the noteholder.

If the parties have agreed to the characteristic not contingent, it is therefore legitimate to deliver vanilla convertible notes.

This supplement is usually declared to be applicable by market participants. Its provisions have therefore been incorporated in the 2003 Definitions.[55]

This judgment is not without criticism.[56] It is apparent that the judgment was based on the specific conditions of the convertible notes. Different conditions of the notes may yield a different result.

Bankruptcy
[2.160] The Successor Supplement also details an amendment to the credit event bankruptcy. As noted, the definition of the credit event is crucial. Provided the conditions to payment have been met – such as the service of a notice of publicly available information – the occurrence of a credit event triggers settlement and payout by the seller.

The definition of "bankruptcy" is another example of the fact that the definitions of credit events are not what they would appear prima facie.

The definition of the credit event "bankruptcy" in the 1999 Definitions[57] is derived from the "bankruptcy" definition of the 1992 ISDA Master

Agreement.⁵⁸ This is remarkable, given that bankruptcy in the ISDA Master Agreement is an event of default. An event of default functions as an early warning signal for the counterparty, enabling it to undertake timely action to secure its claims. It is exactly for that reason that bankruptcy has been construed to have a broad meaning under the ISDA Master Agreement. However, in a credit default swap a credit event is a trigger for payment. The broad definition used in the ISDA Master Agreement need not apply per se in that context.⁵⁹

Considering this origin, it is understandable that bankruptcy covers more than the court judgment rendering the reference entity bankrupt. Bankruptcy also covers any action in furtherance of, or indicating its consent to, approval of or acquiescence in any of these acts. This catch-all provision has provoked most resistance from market participants. First, it could be argued that even merely discussing the possibility of submitting a request for bankruptcy by the reference entity with its legal advisers would attribute to a bankruptcy.⁶⁰ Secondly, the rating agencies have argued that the definition of "bankruptcy" was far too broad and did not fit their own definition of default.⁶¹ Given these concerns, the catch-all provision has been deleted in the Successor Supplement.⁶² This amendment has been incorporated into the 2003 Definitions.⁶³

2003 Definitions and beyond

Major changes to 1999 Definitions
[2.170] Originally, the 2003 Definitions only intended to incorporate the supplements referred to at **[2.120]** – **[2.160]**. In the process of the consultations, however, market participants have seized the opportunity to improve the 1999 Definitions for a range of issues.

The 2003 Definitions include a number of substantial changes and improvements to the 1999 Definitions. Its impact has been discussed in various articles by both rating agencies and legal commentators.⁶⁴ The focus here is on changes that are relevant for credit default swaps in (arbitrage) synthetic securitisations. Basically, these new definitions contain three major changes, yet another restructuring regime, clarification of the treatment of guarantees and an extended timeframe for settlement.

Restructuring (again)
[2.180] After Conseco (see **[2.130]**), the various regional markets have gone their separate ways. The North American market embraced the restructuring supplement (Mod R), while the European market has stuck with the old definitions (Old R). This bifurcation appears due to the different banking practices in the US and in Europe. In Europe it is much more common to restructure loans along the way, while in the US this is

more often associated with the bankruptcy event and, therefore, categorised into a credit risk sensitive area.

The drafters of the 2003 Definitions tried to reach a compromise and establish a single market standard. This goal has not been reached. However, the 2003 Definitions provide for an additional regime next to Old R and Mod R.[65] That new standard now specifically addresses the limitation in transferability of European loans and also substantially limits the cheapest-to-deliver option to obligations with a final maturity not exceeding 60 months after the scheduled termination date. This third regime, tailored upon the Loan Market Association documentation, is already referred to as "Mod Mod R". Its adoption by the European markets will substantially reduce the divisions in the global market.[66]

The markets in Japan, Singapore and the rest of Asia trade under Old R, while the standard in Australia and New Zealand is Mod R.[67] Given this divergence in the regional markets, it is understandable that some market participants have opted for the two credit event trades.

Bonds or loans not delivered
[2.190] The 1999 Definitions allowed a buyer to take advantage of market fluctuations of deliverable obligations. For instance, a buyer may have an incentive to play for time if it anticipates that the obligations to be delivered will decline in value. This is more valuable still if the range of deliverable obligations is larger. In order to protect the seller against this exploitation, the 2003 Definitions now provide rules to ensure timely delivery of the deliverable obligations.[68]

The 2003 Definitions effectively provide two regimes, one for bonds and one for loans. In the case of bonds, if the buyer has not delivered written notice five business days after the physical settlement date,[69] the seller may exercise a right to close out all or a portion of the credit derivative transaction by purchasing bonds (a "buy-in"). The seller will have to give the buyer two or more business days notice of the intention to buy in, specifying the date of the anticipated buy-in, the bonds to be subject to the buy-in and the principal amount thereof to be bought in. The provisions contain rules to which the seller must adhere when obtaining quotes for the buy-in. Ultimately, the buyer will be deemed to have delivered a principal amount of the deliverable obligations specified in the notice of physical settlement for which a buy-in price was determined and the seller may reduce the payment of the settlement amount to the buyer of protection with the buy-in price.[70]

The rules for loans that are not delivered in time are similar in set-up. However, a specific arrangement is made to cover the event that the buyer of protection has not been able to obtain the required consent in order for the loans to be delivered. In that case, the buyer is entitled to deliver other loans, provided that they meet specific conditions, in addition to obviously satisfying the requirements of the deliverable obligations agreed to in the confirmation. The rules also provide for a solution in the event that the buyer drags its feet. In that event, the seller may require the buyer to deliver a bond that is transferable and not bearer or a loan that is assignable, in either case selected by the seller. It must have on the delivery date each of the deliverable obligation characteristics (if any) specified in the related confirmation and must otherwise satisfy the requirements of the deliverable obligation agreed.

Clarifying guarantees

[2.200] Another area in which the 2003 Definitions have progressed is that of the guarantees.

The 1999 Definitions did not distinguish between the situation in which the reference entity acted as principal or as surety with respect to an obligation. As a result, if physical settlement applied, a buyer was entitled to deliver an obligation of the reference entity in its capacity as guarantor as a deliverable obligation.

It was not clear which types of "guarantees" were acceptable. The 2003 Definitions have tried to alleviate this concern by allowing the parties the possibility to specifically agree to several types of guarantees. The 2003 Definitions introduced several new definitions of which the qualifying guarantee is the main one. A *qualifying guarantee* is an arrangement pursuant to which a reference entity irrevocably agrees to pay all amounts due under an obligation for which another party is the obligor and that is not subordinated. Letters of credit, surety bonds and financial guarantee insurance policies do not qualify as qualifying guarantees.[71] These instruments have been excluded because of doubts as to the legal consequences of the transferring of credit risk in these legal instruments.

A separate category has been introduced in the event that a parent company would extend a guarantee for the obligations of a subsidiary, the *qualifying affiliate guarantee*.[72] Other guarantees, such as upstream or side-stream guarantees, have not yet been included in the definitions, although this was a matter of discussion during the consultations.[73] The primary reason therefore is again that doubts have arisen as to the enforceability of these instruments within the concept of the credit default swap.[74]

The new definitions not only served clarification purposes, but also encompassed the different trading practices in various regional markets. In the US, the ability to deliver guarantees was frowned upon, presumably because it increased the cheapest-to-deliver option. As a result, the US market only accepts delivery of the narrowest definition, the qualifying affiliate guarantee. In Europe and Asia trading in third party guarantees is more widely accepted and standard trades allow for delivery of qualifying guarantees.[75] This is effected in the confirmation by specifying that "all guarantees" is applicable.[76]

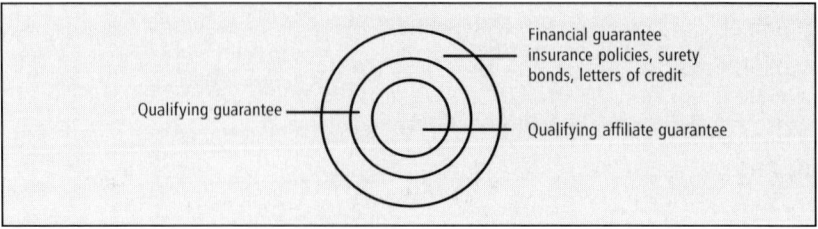

Other changes under the 2003 definitions

[2.210] Several other changes to the 1999 Definitions were prompted by market demands to deal with "mechanical" issues that had arisen in the market.

The first issue relates to the notice of physical settlement. Once the conditions to payment have been met, the buyer must specify the deliverable obligations to be delivered to the seller. Under the 1999 Definitions, some buyers only described these obligations in terms of their obligation category (eg bond or loan), leaving the seller guessing what was going to be delivered. Under the 2003 Definitions, it is expressly provided that the buyer must provide a detailed description of the deliverable obligations, including the outstanding principal balance or due and payable amount and, if available, the CUSIP or ISIN number or, if that is not available, the rate and tenor of each of the deliverable obligations.[77]

The definition of "effective date" and "scheduled termination date" have been made more precise. Unless the parties agree otherwise, these dates cannot be changed as a result of the choice for a specific business day convention.[78] Also, the criteria for delivering notices has been clarified. In the 2003 Definitions it is now specifically provided that a notice that has been issued before 4 pm in the city of the calculation agent is valid as having been issued on that specific day. This provision is of particular importance because of the fact that a credit event occurring does not in itself result in settlement of the transaction. Specific notices need to be issued (on time).[79] Also note the change in the definition of the characteristics pari passu and not subordinated.[80] As regards trading protection on sovereigns, the changes to the credit event repudiation/moratorium are relevant.

Transfer by novation of credit derivatives transactions has also been facilitated under the 2003 Definitions by novation provisions in Chapter

X and a separate novation agreement and novation confirmation (annexed to the Definitions). As a result, a transaction can now be novated by executing the novation confirmation, which incorporates both the novation provisions and the agreement.

Further developments
[2.220] The credit derivatives market continues to evolve quickly. The publication of the 2003 Definitions has been followed by various publications, in particular the May Supplement, the master credit derivatives confirmations[81] (see **[2.230]**), additional provisions for monoline insurers (see **[2.240]**) and a 60-day cap on settlement (see **[2.250]**).

Master confirmations
[2.230] A recent development that has substantially contributed to the standardisation of credit derivatives transactions is the publication by ISDA of the Master Credit Derivatives Confirmation (Master Confirmation). This template of confirmation effectively splits the full confirmation in two parts. The first is the General Terms Confirmation, which contains almost all of the terms and conditions that parties would otherwise negotiate, such as the categories and characteristics of obligations and deliverable obligations, the applicable credit events and payment requirements, as well as the public sources that are relevant for the notice of PAI. These details will apply in respect of all credit derivatives transactions entered into between the parties, just like a Schedule under an ISDA Master Agreement would apply to all swap transactions. The second part is the Transaction Supplement, which contains the terms which are less sensitive from a negotiation point of view, such as the details of the reference entity and the trade and effective date. The advantage of this approach is that it enables the parties to negotiate these terms once and for all and thereafter rely on a very short confirmation supplement, which contains basic information like the effective date of the transaction as well as the reference obligation.

The contents of the Master Confirmation are driven by market conventions. As these conventions may differ between regional markets, ISDA has published different templates for the different relevant legal markets, including the European, North American, Australian, Japanese and Asian markets. The North American and European Master Confirmations and the Asia-Pacific Master Confirmations are reproduced in the Appendix.[82]

The publication of these Master Confirmations is a sound contribution to the further standardisation of the credit derivatives market, provided that market participants will use this type of document. The advantage of the Master Confirmation is to a certain degree offset by legal risk. To clarify:

with respect to the ISDA Master Agreement and the Credit Support Annex, legal opinions are published and regularly updated, made available to ISDA's members, confirming that netting (or the posting of collateral, respectively) in different transactions will be enforceable in a particular jurisdiction. A similar structure as to credit derivatives so far is noticeably absent. The concern here is that credit derivatives continue to be a very strong and growing market and market participants should have comfort on a continuous basis that these transactions are not impeded by recharacterisation or other legal issues.[83]

The different Master Confirmations for the relevant markets clearly identify the differences between these markets. Noticeable differences continue to exist in respect of the business day convention, the conditions to settlement, payments requirements, the use of modified restructuring and multiple holder obligations, as well as the obligation categories and obligation characteristics.

Though not all market participants have yet switched to using Master Confirmations, this document has the potential to further reduce any operational burden of credit default swaps.

Additional provisions for monoline insurers

[2.240] In a step to assist the broadening of the credit derivatives market, ISDA has published additional provisions for physically settled default swaps in which the reference entity is a monoline insurer.[84] The provisions could be added to the Master Confirmation. These additional provisions are reproduced in the Appendix.[85]

Monoline insurers are restricted to writing guarantees or insurance policies related to a single type of risk ("wraps"). They do not have outstanding bonds that would be fit for delivery as a deliverable obligation under a physically settled credit derivatives contract. The purpose of the provisions is to ensure that these guarantees may be delivered for the purpose of settling a credit derivatives contract. A failure to pay under a financial guarantee insurance policy or similar financial guarantee will thus constitute a credit event. The monoline provisions are essentially another illustration of the cheapest-to-deliver risk in physically settled credit derivatives contracts.

Sixty business days cap on (physical) settlement

[2.250] The latest addition to the spectrum of credit derivatives documents is the publication of a letter agreement relating to a 60 business days cap on physical settlement.[86] The purpose of this agreement is to have the parties to a transaction work towards settlement within a limited finite period, thus limiting the opportunity for the buyer to profit from market developments in choosing the deliverable obligations. The agreement incorporates the cap into the Master Confirmation. It also allows the parties to apply or disapply the cap to transactions within the various regional markets. The 60-day cap is reproduced in the Appendix.

Unwinding credit default swaps

[2.260] Credit default swaps can be unwound in three different ways: by termination, assignment or offsetting trades. Each of these has different legal implications. Simply terminating an existing credit default swap is the cleanest option from a legal point of view. By paying the mark to market value of the swap, both parties are fully released from their obligations. Alternatively, a party can transfer by novation its interest in a credit derivatives transaction to a third party against payment or receipt of the mark to market value. As mentioned at **[2.210]**, the novation confirmation and agreement annexed to the 2003 Definitions facilitate this. From a practical perspective, this transfer requires the consent of the "remaining party". Less preferable from a legal perspective would be to unwind by entering into an offsetting transaction: it results in two (continuing) legal relationships and bearing credit risk on both counterparties. On the other hand, this option does not necessitate payment of the market value of the transaction.[87]

Legal framework

Recharacterisation: an introduction

[2.270] Credit derivatives in general, and the credit default swap in particular, bear resemblance to more established legal concepts, such as an agreement of insurance, a guarantee or even gambling. These concepts are governed by specific regulations or statutes, which, if applied to the context of a credit default swap transactions, might have adverse consequences for one or both of the parties to that transaction. Credit derivatives users might argue that this issue is brought up by lawyers eager to pursue a merely theoretical question. They would point to the growth of the credit derivatives market and, particularly, to the unmistakable position credit derivatives have taken globally. In their reasoning, the point of no return has long since passed. The consequences of a recharacterisation would simply be too far-reaching for any court to contemplate.

There is no denying the role that credit derivatives have come to play in the global financial market. The publication by the Bank for International Settlements on global risk transfer is tantamount to that.[88] However, neither can the similarities with, in particular, an agreement of insurance be denied. Insurers and reinsurers are aware of this and are major players as sellers of protection in the credit derivatives market. In addition, case law on this issue is sporadic at best. In this environment, best described as "not fully resolved", an analysis of recharacterisation and the possibilities to limit this risk is essential.

Insurance

[2.280] The recharacterisation discussion focuses on insurance. This is not surprising, as applicability of insurance rules to credit default swap contracts may have several undesired effects, depending on the applicable jurisdictions. The first is that the seller of protection may be deemed to have sold an insurance policy without the proper licence or authorisation from the relevant regulator, thus exposing the seller to fines or other penalties.[89] A second effect might be that insurance tax is payable by the protection buyer. Thirdly, in a nightmare scenario, the entire transaction might be declared void as a result of this offence. That would leave the buyer of protection unhedged, which for banks would also affect regulatory capital treatment. If the contract is declared null and void, the buyer will want to recoup the protection fees paid. Whether it will be able to do so depends on the applicable jurisdiction. Generally, the prospect of recharacterisation is deemed a highly unlikely and remote prospect across jurisdictions.

Last but not least, recharacterisation as an insurance contract would affect the contractual positions of the respective parties to a credit derivative transaction. Under most common law jurisdictions, insurance contracts impose upon both parties the duty of utmost good faith and, as a result, any party with knowledge of any material facts would be under an obligation to disclose these facts to the other party. This would be contrary to the intentions of a credit default swap; the reason for entering into it is likely to have been the material knowledge by a party. Under the 2003 Definitions, neither party is obligated to disclose such information to the other.[90] Bearing in mind these potential consequences of the recharacterisation as an insurance contract, further analysis of this risk, however remote, is indispensable.

Authorised insurers

[2.290] In Australia, a person who conducts an "insurance business" must be authorised to do so by the Australian Prudential Regulation Authority.[91] Non-compliance carries criminal penalties.[92] It remains unclear what the position is with regard to insurance contracts entered into by an unauthorised insurer (in contrast to life insurance contracts, there is no statutory safe harbour for contracts of general insurance made by an unauthorised insurer). There is some judicial support for the enforceability of such contracts,[93] but nonetheless there remains a real risk that where a credit default swap has been recharacterised as a contract of insurance and the protection seller is not an authorised insurer, that a credit default swap may be unenforceable under Australian law.

Jurisdiction

[2.300] This analysis is primarily based on common law. However, the recharacterisation discussion is not per se limited to English (or New York) law (as the two most prevalent laws governing ISDA documentation in general). Some countries prefer (credit) derivatives to be governed by local law under their local equivalent to ISDA Masters (eg Germany, France). Also, international private law may dictate that the rules of another jurisdiction(s) apply, eg if a number of relevant indicators (such as the domicile of both transaction parties) point to such jurisdiction. Last but not least, the statutes of insurance law usually are of public order. The mere choice of the parties to apply English law to a credit default swap transaction does not necessarily avoid this issue. It would therefore be wise for the parties to a credit derivatives transaction to verify the position of local regulators in cross-border transactions.

Legal opinion

[2.310] In an Australasian or European environment English law will often be the starting point of the analysis. Shortly after the emergence of the credit derivatives market, ISDA has swiftly moved to address recharacterisation. ISDA obtained a legal opinion,[94] concluding that credit derivatives do not qualify as an insurance under the *Insurance Companies Act 1982* (Cth) (the regulation of insurance companies in the UK has now been subsumed within the *Financial Services and Markets Act 2000* (UK)).

The legal opinion built on two main arguments. The first is that a credit derivative, as opposed to an insurance, does not intend to compensate the buyer for damages incurred. The payout under an insurance is based upon the notion of indemnity. Credit derivatives link the payout of the settlement amount to the occurrence of a credit event with respect to a reference entity. Whether the buyer has in fact incurred any damages is considered irrelevant. More often than not, the buyer is not the owner of the reference asset and therefore is not in a position to claim damages.

Across jurisdictions, it is the obligation to indemnify which separates an insurance contract from a credit derivative transaction. The litmus test is whether the obligation by the seller of protection is linked to actual loss incurred by the buyer of protection. That test would appear to be passed if, for instance, the payout is linked to the value of the assets in the books of the buyer. In most credit default swap transactions, however, the payout is linked to the difference in market value of an underlying asset. It is the objective value the market attributes to the asset, rather than the subjective value of the individual buyer, which is decisive.[95] In addition, incurring loss on the asset presumes the buyer actually holds it from the effective date of the transaction to the date the credit event occurred. In most cases, that requirement will not be met.

Insurable interests

[2.320] Under English law, it is a feature of a contract of insurance that it must protect an insurable interest of the beneficiary in the contract. Insurance contracts under English law possess three characteristics:

1. The insurer has agreed, for valuable consideration, to pay the beneficiary an amount on the occurrence of a stipulated event.
2. There is uncertainty as to whether or when that event will occur.
3. The beneficiary must have an insurable interest in the subject matter of the contract.[96]

Traditional legal commentary suggests that the requirement for an insurable interest means that the beneficiary must have a proprietary (ie legal or equitable) interest in the subject matter of the insurance contract.[97] However, the English courts have in recent times taken a more liberal view of the requirement, accepting that a pecuniary interest, rather than a formalistic proprietary interest, may amount to an insurable interest.[98] This liberal interpretation has by no means been unanimously accepted: for example, it has been flatly rejected by the authors of one of the leading English insurance law texts.[99] What this means is that, at the very least, the payment obligation under the contract of insurance must be conditional on the buyer suffering a loss.

Within the context of a credit default swap, the conditions to payment do not stipulate that it is required for the buyer to have suffered a loss. To emphasise this point, the 2003 Definitions stipulate as a separate representation that "the parties will be obligated to perform ... irrespective of the existence or amount of the parties' credit exposure to a Reference Entity, and Buyer need not suffer any loss, nor provide evidence of any loss as a result of the occurrence of a Credit Event".[100]

In addition, in a recently published discussion paper the English financial markets supervisor, the Financial Services Authority (FSA), has addressed the question whether the dividing line between credit derivatives and insurances is sufficiently clear.[101] Following up on the responses to this discussion paper the FSA has indicated that it does not intend to undertake further initiatives on this issue. It may therefore be concluded that the FSA feels this topic sufficiently clear to market participants and no further action on its part is yet required.[102] In summary, there are sound reasons to support the argument that a credit default swap transaction should not be recharacterised as an insurance contract under different common law jurisdictions.

Australian law

[2.330] The analysis and the potential consequences of recharacterisation may differ across jurisdictions. The concept of "insurable interest", for example, has been substantively modified by statute in Australia (in the case of all contracts of general insurance other than marine insurance).[103] However, the defining characteristic of an insurance contract under Australian law is, in common with English law, that the beneficiary of the insurance contract must have suffered a loss through physical damage to, or a diminution in the value of, the subject matter of the contract due to the occurrence of the insured event, and that the payment made to the beneficiary under the contract is designed to indemnify the beneficiary for that loss.[104] Again, as is the case under English law, the decoupling of the payment to be made to the protection buyer under a credit default swap on the occurrence of a credit event from the loss suffered by the protection buyer as a result of the credit event occurring should render it unlikely that an Australian court would recharacterise the credit default swap as an insurance contract.

In addition, a statutory safe harbour is potentially available for certain credit default swaps under Australian law. Even in the unlikely event that a credit default swap is recharacterised as an insurance contract under Australian law, the parties to that contract may be shielded from the adverse effects of such recharacterisation by the "pecuniary loss insurance" exception under the *Insurance Act 1973* (Cth), where the protection seller is an "authorised deposit-taking institution" under the *Banking Act 1959* (Cth) (which term comprises Australian licensed banks, building societies and credit unions). The Insurance Act provides that an authorised deposit-taking institution that carries on pecuniary loss insurance (which is defined as the business of insuring persons against the risk of loss due to the insolvency or default of their debtors – and which business is economically equivalent to that of selling protection under credit default swaps) solely in the course of its banking business will not be considered to be carrying on an insurance business.[105] This exception should be available to Australian licensed banks but will be of little comfort to other protection sellers, such as life insurance companies.

Gaming
[2.340] Under some jurisdictions, credit derivatives transactions may resemble gaming or gambling contracts. That would expose the transactions to the risk of being declared void, as contrary to public policy. It is generally assumed that these risks are not significant when dealing with credit default swaps.[106]

The differences between a credit default swap and a guarantee are substantial as well. Across jurisdictions, the effect of a guarantor paying out under a guarantee is that the guarantor is subrogated in the rights of the party the debt of which the guarantor is paying. This is tantamount to establishing a legal relationship between the guarantor, on the one hand, and the creditor, on the other. Also, the guarantor would have a recourse claim on the party on whose behalf it has paid out. Essential in a credit derivatives transaction is that such a transaction does *not* create any rights or impose any obligations in respect of any third party. There is no legal relationship with the reference entity, nor is there intended to be one.[107]

Structured transactions

[2.350] When credit derivatives are used in structured transactions, the effect of local law may have to be considered as well, notwithstanding the choice of the parties to have their documentation governed by, for example, English law. Under local jurisdictions, statutory provisions may prevail as a matter of public order and may be given effect irrespective of the governing law elected. Insurance law provisions are often considered a matter of public order under local international private law. Also, relevant rules or guidelines of applicable local supervisory bodies may have to be taken into account. In structured transactions involving credit derivatives concepts, it is therefore advisable to have local counsel verify whether the transaction could be affected.

Confidentiality

[2.360] Credit derivatives raise several issues regarding confidentiality.[108] The first issue is whether a bank is allowed to divulge information regarding the reference entity to its counterparty, in particular when the reference entity is a client of the bank. This issue is also relevant in the context of balance sheet synthetic transactions and is further explored in Ch 3. In terms of a standard credit default swap, two issues remain. First, as mentioned at **[2.90]**, the motive for a protection buyer to enter into a credit default swap with a third party as protection seller with respect to a reference entity may be that it has more knowledge than its counterparty on the credit position of the reference entity. In that context it is important that this party does not owe any obligation to the other party to disclose such information. The 2003 Definitions underline this point. They explicitly state that that each party may be in possession of information in relation to a reference entity or any underlying obligor that is or may be material in the context of the transaction and that may or may not be publicly available or known to the other party, and that such a transaction does not create any obligation on the party to disclose to the other party any such relationship or information (whether or not confidential).

The second confidentiality issue relates to consequences of disclosure to a counterparty. The counterparty is not in a position to verify whether the information disclosed to it is in breach of any duty of confidentiality on the part of the disclosing party. Realising this, the 2003 Definitions stipulate that unless a party is otherwise bound by or subject to a confidentiality obligation or agreement, a party receiving any information from the other party with respect to such transaction shall not become subject to any obligation of confidentiality in respect of that information and the transferor of such information shall indemnify the transferee.[109]

Integration with ISDA Master
[2.370] Several terms found in the 2003 Definitions, most notably that of "close-out amount", are referenced to their meaning in the (new) 2002 ISDA Master Agreement.[110] It is therefore recommended, but not strictly necessary, that market participants using the 2003 Definitions upgrade to the 2002 ISDA Master Agreement. Presumably this will cease to be relevant in the near future as most market participants will upgrade to the 2002 Master Agreement and adhere to the recently published 2002 Master Agreement protocol, available from ISDA's website (http://www.isda.org).

A related issue is that users of credit derivatives will want to ensure that it is possible to net their exposures under credit derivative transactions with other transactions with the same counterparty. Though this may be possible under English law,[111] in international transactions relevant local law will have to be taken into consideration as well.

A final legal consideration is insider trading. A full analysis is beyond the scope of this publication. In brief, insider trading provisions are relevant if one of the parties to the transaction has knowledge regarding the reference entity that is price sensitive and not publicly available. In the context of a credit default transaction, a party might have material knowledge from its banking relationship with the reference entity.

Capital adequacy

Basel I and II
[2.380] Capital adequacy treatment for banks in most industrialised countries is based upon the Basel capital accord (the Accord), laid down by the Bank for International Settlement (BIS) in 1988. This Accord does not specifically address capital adequacy for credit derivatives. Faced with the strong emergence of credit derivatives in recent years, local regulators have filled this vacuum to provide guidance to the market. As a result, different regulators have differing views on the operational requirements that credit derivatives must meet in order for the hedged exposure to be recognised for capital relief.

In its time the Accord proved a step forward towards harmonisation of capital adequacy regulations. However, its regulations were very basic and did not fit the sophistication of current structured finance transactions. A framework for a revised accord (Basel II) is in its latest stages of negotiation. The BIS has issued a third consultative paper (CP3) on its contents, widely assumed to be the blueprint of the new accord.[112] The latest proposals for this revised Accord specifically address credit derivatives, as well as synthetic securitisation. The main issues affecting capital treatment of credit derivatives are highlighted in this chapter.

The BIS intends to have Basel II in force by the end of 2006. This timetable, already twice delayed, may be ambitious. The legislative process in both the EU and the US must run its course. In Europe, a separate directive, the third capital adequacy directive (CAD3) is to be implemented first. A complicating factor is that the global markets will want to maintain (or establish) a level playing field, applying the same capital adequacy regulations to all banks at the same time. This ideal is already under threat, as regulators in the US have indicated that the new rules will only apply to a selected group of approximately ten international banks.[113] This is of particular concern, as these banks would be adopting the advanced regime for capital adequacy, the internal ratings based approach (IRB). Research on the expected impact of the new rules (the Quantitative Impact Study, or QIS3) has shown that banks adopting this advanced approach will profit and will have to hold less capital against assets.[114]

These are but a few of the concerns raised by the financial industry. After the British Bankers' Association flagged serious concerns in the implementation of Basel II, particularly with respect to the level playing field, it was suggested that the implementation should be delayed further, perhaps even to 2010.[115] Few market participants expect the new rules to be implemented by the current deadline of ultimo 2006.

In essence, the new Accord applies risk weights that are much more finely tuned to the actual risk profile of the assets concerned than under the basic approach of its predecessor. Also, it substantially increases the assets that qualify as eligible financial collateral, eg by incorporating senior structured finance securities.[116]

Capital adequacy and credit derivatives
[2.390] Only credit default swaps and total return swaps that provide credit protection equivalent to guarantees will be eligible for recognition.

Generally, the capital treatment for credit derivatives has been and continues to be based upon that of a guarantee. This capital treatment follows the substitution approach. For example, a bank buying protection through a credit default swap can obtain regulatory capital relief by replacing the risk weight of the underlying asset with the risk weight of the credit default swap counterparty, the seller of protection.[117] According to CP3, a credit derivative must represent a direct claim on the protection provider and must be referenced to specific exposures, so that the extent of the cover is clearly defined. Furthermore, the credit protection contract must be irrevocable; there must be no clause in the contract that would allow the protection provider unilaterally to cancel the credit cover or that would increase the effective cost of cover as a result of the deteriorating credit quality enhanced exposure. It must also be unconditional. There should be no clause in the protection contract outside the direct control of the bank that could prevent the protection provider from being obliged to pay out in a timely manner in the event that the original counterparty fails to make the payments due.[118]

The third consultative paper furthermore provides for additional operational requirements specific to credit derivatives. These requirements relate to the credit events required and address several mismatches. According to the CP3, a credit derivative should at least contain the credit events failure to pay, bankruptcy and restructuring.[119] Given the controversial events surrounding the credit event restructuring, the industry has lobbied BIS to remove restructuring as a precondition to granting capital relief.

In the current proposals, a compromise has been worked out that allows a bank not to include restructuring and to still obtain full capital relief, provided it has "complete control" over the decision of whether there will be a restructuring of the underlying obligation. This would, for example, be the case when a bank can prevent restructuring by withholding its consent. However, local regulators may nevertheless require the bank to acquire restructuring protection in order to have the protection recognised for capital adequacy purposes if, notwithstanding the legal form, the economic reality of the transaction is such that the bank will not be able to prevent a restructuring.

Alternatively, some capital relief may be granted even if there is no "complete control". In the light of ongoing concerns regarding the effectiveness of the hedge provided by a credit derivative that does not include restructuring, the Basel Committee is investigating alternative regulatory capital treatments. A "discount approach" is currently being explored.[120] In a letter to the Basel Committee, ISDA and the Bond Market Association have suggested a discount factor of 35%.[121] This is relevant as some market participants have switched to trades with only bankruptcy and failure to pay as credit events, and such trades could be further facilitated.

A number of factors may affect the amount of protection (and capital relief). For example, some credit default swaps incorporate a materiality threshold. Losses realised below that threshold do not trigger a credit event. The payout may be structured in a fixed amount. The protection is then only limited to that specified amount.

When a bank uses the credit default swap to hedge exposure, it should ensure that the reference obligation for which it purchases protection is the same asset as the one on its balance sheet. If not (an "asset mismatch"), protection may still be granted provided both assets are of the same obligor, rank pari passu and are cross-defaulted.[122] Another factor affecting the amount of protection is the maturity of the credit derivative compared with the underlying asset. If the credit default swap has a maturity less than that of the underlying asset, recognition of the protection depends on the residual maturity of the credit derivative. Furthermore, the CP3 requires a robust valuation process to estimate loss reliably in the event of cash settlement.[123]

Further developments and conclusion

ISDA User Guide
[2.400] ISDA may work towards the completion of a user's guide for the 2003 Definitions in the course of 2003.[124] Given the fact that such a user's guide for the 1999 Definitions has never been published and has been overtaken by the consultations for the 2003 Definitions, it is likely that the market participants will have to be patient. It will be interesting to see whether ISDA can fulfil its promise or whether its intentions will be overtaken by the drafting of additional supplements or, for instance, the desire in the market to change the 2003 Definitions to incorporate trades in basket products. At this stage the focus appears to be on harmonising global markets first.

The challenge for the global credit derivatives market will be in the further standardisation of terms. Modified restructuring and the application of guarantees in credit derivatives contracts differ across regional markets, proving that complete harmonisation is a bridge yet to be crossed.

Effects of standardisation
[2.410] The standardisation of credit default confirmations has commodotised credit risk. It has enhanced the ability of the market to trade in an ever-increasing number of names in credit risk. As credit derivatives are essentially about a more efficient distribution of credit risk, this is quite a milestone. The data available suggests that the market continues to embrace credit derivatives.

Some words of caution may be added in this strong, some would say bubbling, market. The sophisticated nature of credit derivatives has led to a situation in which a relatively small number of market players dominate. To alleviate the concentration risk, a further diversification of this market would be preferable. This in turn would help enhance investors' acceptance of credit derivatives even further.

The increased level of standardisation is impressive, particularly given the limited timeframe. This swift development of the market towards trading credit risk as a commodity does, however, require substantial efforts on the part of the market players to not only implement, but also monitor, compliance with the underlying risks. This issue may be particularly relevant to new players in the credit derivatives market. The challenge for the global credit derivatives market seems to be in the diversification of the market players, as well as in increased investor acceptance. This is an ongoing process.

Sound alternative for credit risk management

[2.420] A credit derivative is a new kid on the block of credit risk management. Notwithstanding its young age, it has matured remarkably fast.[125] Market data (see **[2.10]**) prove that the market has accepted credit derivatives as a sound alternative to the bond market and syndicated lending for credit risk management.

Like all innovations, credit derivatives have had their ups and downs. However, market participants have reacted swiftly to address issues. ISDA has played a premier role in this process. To ensure a continued success story for credit derivatives-based instruments, such as synthetic securitisation, a thorough understanding of credit derivatives remains of the essence.

[1] Bank for International Settlements, *Credit Risk Transfer* (report submitted by a Working Group established by the Committee on the Global Financial System, January 2003) p 5. It provides an overview of the different instruments by means of which credit risk can be transferred, from loan trading to synthetic collateralised debt obligations. The report is posted at http://www.bis.org.

[2] British Bankers Association Credit Derivatives Report 2001-2002, *FSA Discussion Paper 11, Cross-Sector Risk Transfers* (May 2002) pp 3 and 15. Also refer to Bank for International Settlements, *Credit Risk Transfer* (report submitted by a Working Group established by the Committee on the Global Financial System, January 2003) p 10, discussing the credit derivatives market.

[3] ISDA, "ISDA Announces 2003 Mid-Year Market Survey Results" (23 September 2003) posted at http://www.isda.org, viewed September 2003.

[4] The 2003 Definitions were implemented on 20 June 2003.

[5] For a detailed analysis of derivatives generally, refer to Firth S, *Derivatives Law and Practice* (Sweet & Maxwell, 2003).

[6] Gooch AC and Klein LB, *Documentation for Derivatives* (Vol 1, 4th ed, Euromoney Books, 2002) p 639.

[7] However, in some credit derivatives the credit risk transferred relates to one of the parties to the credit derivatives transaction. These are so-called "self-referencing" credit default swaps. This particular type of credit derivative may give rise to bankruptcy issues, such as fraudulent conveyance. Any party should carefully consider these issues before entering into such a transaction.

[8] Note that the accountancy treatment of credit derivatives generally is receiving scrutiny as a result of the Enron debacle. The accountancy aspects of credit derivatives are not discussed here.

[9] A template of a credit default swap confirmation, published by ISDA as Exhibit A to the 2003 Credit Derivatives Definitions, is available as a free download from http://www.isda.org.

[10] See ss 4.2, 4.5 and 4.7 of the 2003 Definitions for the full definitions of these credit events.

[11] Section 4.8(d) of the 2003 Definitions.

[12] See ss 4.3, 4.4 and 4.6 of the 2003 Definitions for the full definitions of these credit events.

[13] See ss 2.3, 2.14 and 2.15 of the 2003 Definitions for the full definitions of these terms. In relation to the determination of a successor the 2003 Definitions use the term "relevant obligations": see s 2.2(f) of the 2003 Definitions.

[14] See s 2.19 of the 2003 Definitions for a full description of all obligation categories and obligation characteristics. As both are increasingly standardised in the over-the-counter credit default swap market, these various options are not further discussed. Refer to the use of the Master Confirmation, which is discussed at **[2.230]**.

[15] Section 2.19 of the 2003 Definitions. "Borrowed money" is defined to include, without limitation, deposits and reimbursement obligations arising from drawings pursuant to letters of credit.

[16] Refer to the Master Credit Derivatives Confirmation Agreements published by ISDA for the various regional markets, including North America, Europe, Japan, Singapore, (rest of) Asia, Australia and New Zealand, posted at http://www.isda.org.

[17] See ss 2.15 and 8.1 of the 2003 Definitions.

[18] The deliverable obligation category is usually bonds or loans: see s 2.19(a)(iv) and (v) of the 2003 Definitions. Bonds include bonds, notes, certificated debt securities and other debt securities. Loans include both revolving and terms loans.

[19] See ss 2.14 and 2.19 of the 2003 Definitions.

[20] Refer to s 3.2 of the 2003 Definitions.

[21] Refer to ss 3.3, 3.4 and 3.6 of the 2003 Definitions respectively for the full description of these notices.

[22] See s 3.5 of the 2003 Definitions.

[23] The 2003 Definitions, including these templates, may be downloaded for a fee.

[24] *Deutsche Bank AG v ANZ Banking Group* (unreported, 28 May 1999).

[25] Lentile T and Harris G, "Credit Derivatives and Documentation Issues: Deutsche Bank AG v ANZ Banking Group Ltd" (2000) 11 (No 1) *Journal of Banking and Finance Law and Practice* ? at 52-56.

26 Though in certain circumstances *partial* cash settlement is also possible: see ss 9.3 to 9.8 of the 2003 Definitions.

27 See ss 7.3 and 7.4 of the 2003 Definitions. The cash settlement amount (when not otherwise specified in the confirmation) is defined as the greater of (a)(i) the floating rate payer calculation amount multiplied by (ii) the reference price minus the final price and (b) zero.

28 See ss 8.1 and 8.2 of the 2003 Definitions.

29 Section 8.1 of the 2003 Definitions.

30 In particular, the landmark case of *Hazell v Hammersmith London Borough Council* (1991) All ER 545 at 553-554.

31 Conlon SD and Aquilino VM, *Principles of Financial Derivatives US & International Taxation* (WESTLAW) Ch A4, http://www.westlaw.com.au viewed July 2003.

32 Conlon SD and Aquilino VM, *Principles of Financial Derivatives US & International Taxation* (Westlaw) Ch A4, http://www.westlaw.com.au viewed July 2003.

33 The Netherlands for one: see s 2:7 of the *Dutch Civil Code*.

34 Most financial institutions do not allow derivative transactions to be entered into without an ISDA Master Agreement being agreed to first.

35 The use of cross-border collateral carries additional risks. For instance, the parties need to ensure that the transfer of collateral under a CSA is effective and enforceable under all relevant jurisdictions. This may be a problem in civil law jurisdictions, which have a "closed" system of rights in rem, and may not recognise the transfer of collateral. Market participants are advised to consult the collateral opinions that ISDA has posted on its website for its members (http://www.isda.org). The use of CSAs in synthetic securitisations is briefly addressed in Chapter 4.

36 "Understanding the Risks in Credit Default Swaps" (Special Report, Moody's, March 2001).

37 Merryl Lynch, *Credit Derivatives Handbook 2003* (Merryll Lynch, 2003) p 109.

38 The five major credit derivatives houses in the global market together last year controlled 59% of the market, with JP Morgan leading at 26%. See Bloomberg Markets (August 2003) p 51-52.

39 For instance, in Australia, AFMA has published Financial Product Conventions for Credit Derivatives on its website (http://www.afma.gov.au).

40 Section 4.7(b)(iii) of the 2003 Definitions.

41 The first part of the "restructuring" definition was met. Some doubt remained as to whether the deferral of the loans resulted directly or indirectly from a deterioration in the creditworthiness or financial condition of Conseco. Ultimately, market consensus was that it had.

42 "Can a Growing Market Meet a Growing Challenge?", *Asset Securitization Report* (30 June 2003) 2003 WL 7469497.

43 JP Morgan, *Modified Restructuring* (JP Morgan Research, 25 May 2001), in which the particular circumstances to this transaction are further detailed. The windfall profit is detailed as follows: the restructured 15-month loan was trading around 92% of face (8% mark to market loss) and banks were receiving par in exchange for long-dated senior unsecured bonds that they had sourced for 68% of face in the secondary market (a 32% realised gain).

44 Gooch AC and Klein LB, *Documentation for Derivatives* (Vol 1, 4th ed, Euromoney, 2002) p 666.

45 All supplements are posted on ISDA's website (http://www.isda.org).

46 Section 4.9 of the 2003 Definitions.

47 Not to be confused with "Old Europe".

48 *Supplement Relating to Successor and Credit Events to the 1999 ISDA Credit Derivatives Definitions* (ISDA, 28 November 2002).

49 Section 2.2(f) of the 2003 Definitions.

50 Section 2.2(g) of the 2003 Definitions.

51 Clancy P, "ISDA Successor Rules Leave Derivatives Mismatch" (2003) July IFLR 35.

52 The opinion is posted at http://www.afma.com.au. Select "Market data and research" then "Demergers".

53 *Supplement Relating to Convertible, Exchangeable or Accreting Obligations* (ISDA,

9 November 2001).

54 *Nomura International Plc v Credit Suisse First Boston International* [2003] EWHC 160 (Comm).

55 Section 2.20 in relation to s 8.7 of the 2003 Definitions.

56 Henderson SK, "When is an Option not a Contingency" (2003) 18 *Journal of International Banking and Financial Law* 178.

57 Section 4.2 of the 1999 Definitions.

58 Section 5(a)(vii) of the 1992 ISDA Master Agreement.

59 *Commentary on Supplement Relating to Successor and Credit Events to the 1999 ISDA Credit Derivatives Definitions* (ISDA, 28 November 2002) p 2.

60 *Commentary on Supplement Relating to Successor and Credit Events to the 1999 ISDA Credit Derivatives Definitions* (ISDA, 28 November 2002) p 3.

61 "Understanding the Risks in Credit Default Swaps" (Special Report, Moody's, 2001) and *Moody's Approach to Rating Synthetic CDOs* (Moody's, 29 July 2003) p 13.

62 *Supplement Relating to Successor and Credit Events to the 1999 ISDA Credit Derivatives Definitions* (ISDA, 28 November 2002).

63 However, at the recent credit derivatives conference it was suggested that this clause be put back in.

64 Refer to "Fitch Examines Effect of 2003 Credit Derivatives Definitions" (Special Report, Fitch Ratings, 6 March 2003); see also Henderson SK, "2003 ISDA Credit Derivatives Definitions" (2003) 18 (No 4) *Journal of International Banking and Financial Law* 138. For a comparison between credit default swaps under the new definitions and cash bonds, see Vrij E, "Credit Default Swaps Versus Cash Bonds: More Exposed", 18 (No 7) *Journal of International Banking and Financial Law* (2003).

65 Sections 2.33 and 2.34 respectively of the 2003 Definitions.

66 O'Connor CM, "Synthetic CDOs Playing with New Option: Mod Mod R Takes Effect", *Asset Securitization Report* (30 June 2003) 2003 WL 7469489.

67 *2003 Master Credit Derivatives Confirmation Agreement (Asia-Pacific) and (European-North American)*, Pt 3.

68 Sections 9.9 and 9.10 of the 2003 Definitions.

69 Section 8.5 of the 2003 Definitions.

70 See "Fitch Examines Effect of 2003 Credit Derivatives Definitions" (Special Report, Fitch Ratings, 6 March 2003) p 7 for an overview in a time line.

71 Section 2.23 of the 2003 Definitions, as amended by the May Supplement to the 2003 Definitions.

72 Section 2.24 of the 2003 Definitions.

73 Section 2.14 of the 2003 Definitions.

74 "The 2003 ISDA Credit Derivatives Definitions" (JP Morgan Research, 13 June 2003) p 4.

75 *2003 Master Credit Derivatives Confirmation Agreement (Asia-Pacific) and (European-North American)*, Pt 1.

76 Section 2.15(a) of the 2003 Definitions.

77 Section 3.4 of the 2003 Definitions.

78 Sections 1.4 and 1.6 of the 2003 Definitions.

79 Refer to s 1.10 of the 2003 Definitions. For example, the credit event notice and the notice of publicly available information, for which the 2003 Definitions comprise a standard format: see Exhibit B of the 2003 Definitions.

80 Section 2.19(b)(i) of the 2003 Definitions.

81 As well as the Master Credit Derivatives Confirmation Agreements for Sovereigns.

82 These template Master Confirmations have been published by ISDA and may be freely downloaded from http://www.isda.org.

83 As to the issues such an opinion might cover, refer to Gooch AC and Klein LB, *Documentation for Derivatives* (Vol 1, 4th ed, Euromoney Books, 2002) p 661.

84 Published on 9 May 2003, available on the ISDA website (http://www.isda.org).

85 The Additional Provisions for Monoline Insurers have been published by ISDA and may be freely downloaded from http://www.isda.org.

[86] *Side Letter on the 60 Business Days Cap on Settlement* (published by ISDA on 5 August 2003 and freely downloaded from http://www.isda.org). The side letter consists of a letter agreement and two annexes. The letter agreement specifies two minor exceptions to the 60 business days cap.

[87] Along the same line: *Credit Derivatives Handbook 2003* (Merrill Lynch, 2003) pp 19-20.

[88] Bank for International Settlements, *Credit Risk Transfer* (report submitted by a Working Group established by the Committee on the Global Financial System, January 2003) p 5. It provides an overview of the different instruments by means of which credit risk can be transferred, from loan trading to synthetic collateralised debt obligations. The report is posted at http://www.bis.org.

[89] As to Australia, refer to the *Insurance Act 1973* (Cth), ss 9 and 10.

[90] Section 9.1(b)(iv) of the 2003 Definitions.

[91] *Insurance Act 1973* (Cth), s 12(1) and (2).

[92] *Insurance Act 1973* (Cth), ss 10(1) and 11.

[93] *Yango Pastoral Co Pty Ltd v First Chicago Australia Ltd* (1978) 139 CLR 410.

[94] ISDA counsel's opinion by Potts QC, which followed up on a guidance note from the Financial Law Panel on the same issue in 1997.

[95] Firth S, *Derivatives Law and Practice* (Sweet & Maxwell, 2003) at 16-030.

[96] *Prudential Insurance Co v Commissioners of Inland Revenue* [1904] 2 KB 658.

[97] For example, Macaura v Northern Assurance Co Ltd [1925] AC 619.

[98] For example, *Petrofina (UK) Ltd v Magnaload Ltd* [1983] 2 Lloyd's Rep 91.

[99] Legh-Jones N, Longmore A, Birds J and Owen D (eds), *MacGillivray on Insurance Law* (9th ed, Sweet & Maxwell, 1997) at [1-117].

[100] Section 9.1(b)(i) of the 2003 Definitions.

[101] "Discussion Paper 11 on Cross-Sector Risk Transfer" (FSA, May 2002).

[102] "Feedback on Responses to Discussion Paper 11 on Cross-Section Risk Transfer" (FSA, December 2002) p 11. Both articles can be downloaded from http://www.fsa.gov.uk.

[103] *Insurance Contracts Act 1984* (Cth), ss 16(1) and 17.

[104] *Insurance Contracts Act 1984* (Cth), s 17.

[105] See para (c) of the definition of "insurance business" in s 3(1) of the *Insurance Act 1973* (Cth).

[106] For a further discussion, see Ali PU, "Unbundling Credit Risk: the Nature and Regulation Of Credit Derivatives" (2000) 11 (No 1) *Journal of Banking and Finance Law of Practice* 73. In Australia, s 1101(i) of the *Corporations Act 2001* (Cth) provides a safe harbour from gaming and wagering legislation for all financial products, which definition includes (credit) derivatives. As to England, refer to s 412 of the *Financial Services and Markets Act 2000*.

[107] Section 9.1(b)(ii) of the 2003 Definitions. For a further analysis see Whitely C, "Credit Derivatives, Documentation and Legal Issues" in Das S (ed), *Credit Derivatives and Credit Linked Notes* (2nd ed, John Wiley & Sons, 2000) p 682.

[108] More generally, the handling and use of material non-public information may give rise to a number of legal and business issues. Refer to Joint Practices Forum, "Statement of Principles and Recommendations Regarding the Handling of Material Nonpublic Information by Credit Market Participants", published by ISDA at http://www.isda.org viewed October 2003.

[109] Section 9.1(b)(iv)(v) of the 2003 Definitions.

[110] Section 1.18 of the 2002 ISDA Master Agreement.

[111] Firth S, *Derivatives Law and Practice* (Sweet & Maxwell, 2003) at 16-061.

[112] In full: Basel Committee on Banking Supervision, *Consultative Document, The New Basel Capital Accord* (Bank of International Settlement, April 2003), in short: "CP3".

[113] Testimony of Roger W Ferguson, Vice Chairman of the Federal Reserve Board, before a House Subcommittee on Basel II, posted at http://www.federalreserve.gov viewed 29 September 2003.

[114] In England the FSA is consulting on the implementation of the new Basel and EU Capital Adequacy Standards, specifically on the IRB approach: see FSA Consultation Paper 189.

[115] The BBA's letter to the Basel Committee is posted on the BBA's website (http://www.bba.org.uk) and has been followed up by various articles in the *Financial Times*.

[116] CP3, no 116 ff.
[117] Financial Services Authority, *Interim Prudential Source Book for Banks* Ch CD, para 5.2, sub 5(b); APRA AGN 112.4, no 21, published at http://www.apra.gov.au, viewed August 2003.
[118] CP3, *Operational Requirements Common to Guarantees and Credit Derivatives*, no 160.
[119] CP3, no 162.
[120] ISDA and other industry organisations have recently supplied the BIS with industry data in this consultation process. Refer to this letter for more details.
[121] Letter to the Basel Committee on Banking Supervision from ISDA and the Bond Market Association, 31 July 2003, p 3.
[122] Financial Services Authority, *Interim Prudential Source Book for Banks* Ch CD, para. 5.4, sub 10; APRA AGN 112.4, no 29-32, published at http://www.apra.gov.au, viewed August 2003.
[123] CP3, no 163(d).
[124] In its press release of 11 February 2003, on occasion of the publication of the 2003 Definitions, ISDA informed that the User's Guide will be published in the course of 2003. A first draft is expected in the final quarter.
[125] For a general overview, refer to "Global Credit Derivatives, A Qualified Success" (Special Report, Fitch Ratings, 24 September 2003).

Chapter 3

SYNTHETIC SECURITISATION: SHOULD EVERY BANK HAVE ONE?

SYNTHETIC SECURITISATION: DEFINITION AND MARKET

Synthetic securitisation: an introduction
[3.10] True sale or "traditional" securitisation is widely accepted as an efficient means for banks to obtain both regulatory and economic capital relief, as well as an alternative source of funding. Innovative new structures have come to the fore to address drawbacks of traditional securitisation, most of all synthetic securitisation.

Definition
Synthetic securitisation is defined as a structure with at least two different stratified risk positions or tranches that reflect different degrees of credit risk, where credit risk of an underlying pool of exposures is transferred, whole or in part, through the use of funded (eg credit linked notes) or unfunded (eg credit default swaps) credit derivatives or guarantees that serve to hedge the credit risk of the portfolio. Accordingly, the investors' potential risk is dependent upon the performance of the underlying pool.[2]

This flexible structure has increasingly gained ground in the global market. There are encouraging signs that synthetic securitisation will soon take its rightful place in the Asia-Pacific market as a tool that alleviates most of the constraints of traditional securitisation and opens up promising opportunities for originators and investors alike.

This chapter discusses synthetic securitisation in general and, in particular, synthetic securitisations that were originated for capital relief purposes. This subject is covered as follows. First, the market for synthetic securitisation is discussed, along with a comparison of true sale and synthetic securitisations. The chapter then addresses the typical synthetic structure, its components and risks. The remainder of this chapter focuses on documentation and legal and regulatory issues. Finally, it discusses the latest trends and developments in this continuously evolving market.

The synthetic market
[3.20] Globally the synthetic market has shown strong growth, particular in the market of collateralised debt obligations (CDOs). A CDO is a

security backed by a pool of various types of debt, which may include corporate bonds sold in the capital markets, loans made to corporations by institutional lenders and tranches of securitisations.[2] While many of the innovations in the financial market have originated from the US, Europe and the UK, in particular, are the main drivers of the market for synthetic securitisations. This position is hardly surprising, as London is the global centre of the global derivatives market.[3] The European CDO market totalled a volume of US$182 billion in 2002 and it is almost entirely a synthetic market. According to one rating agency, approximately 96% of the deal volume and 85% of the number of deals in 2002 were issued in synthetic form.[4] In the US, traditionally a cash market, the trend towards synthetics continued, accounting for 30% of a CDO volume of US$65.1 billion in 2002.[5]

The Asia-Pacific market
[3.30] In the Asia-Pacific market, synthetic securitisation has only recently caught the public eye as a truly emerging securitisation market. In Asia, several high-profile transactions have closed since synthetics were introduced only a few years ago.[6] A recent rating agency's study sees the burst in synthetic CDO activity in Asia's structured finance market as a clear indication that Asian banks and investors are becoming increasingly aware of the untapped potential for such transactions.[7] By contrast, Japan's CDO market seems tepid at this time, but may be boosted by a decision of the Bank of Japan to purchase ABS and credit linked notes.[8]

The Australian market has traditionally focused on true sale securitisation of (residential and commercial) mortgage receivables. That market is very sophisticated and well matured. The number of publicly rated synthetic securitisations may be still small.[9] However, these transactions already have features that show the increased awareness of the market with this complex product, eg offerings have been made to retail investors.[10] Estimates put the Australian CDO market at 5% of total issuance and most of these transactions were privately placed, rather than public, deals. However, recent data indicate that the issuance of credit linked notes has picked up substantially, indicating that market participants are increasingly familiar with credit derivatives techniques so essential in synthetic securitisations.[11] It is therefore expected that the market for synthetic securitisations in Australasia will show healthy growth in the years to come.

TRADITIONAL AND SYNTHETIC SECURITISATION

Traditional securitisations: benefits and limitations

Traditional securitisation: benefits

[3.40] True sale or "traditional" securitisation offers a number of benefits to originating banks. By selling assets to a special purpose vehicle (SPV), which issues notes to finance the purchase of the assets, it provides an excellent means to obtain regulatory and economic capital relief. Next, it allows the originator to manage the balance sheet. In addition, the market for traditional securitisation is well developed and matured globally, allowing for tight coupons and thus relatively cheap funding for lower rated institutions.

So why worry? Because traditional securitisation does have its limitations (see **[3.50]** – **[3.80]**).

Limited choice of assets

[3.50] A traditional structure builds upon the sale of the assets.[12] A "true sale" opinion must be obtained. As a consequence, the entity that seeks to securitise (the "originator") is inherently limited in the choice of assets. Some assets cannot be legally transferred at all or only at prohibitive cost or effort.[13] The transfer of (bilateral) bank loans, and especially large tailor-made corporate loans, is often subject to borrower's consent. Even if the loan documentation provides that the borrower may not unreasonably withhold consent, the originator may not wish to approach the client, unwilling to put strain on the business relationship. There may even be regulatory or statutory constraints to effect the transfer of the assets. In particular, most regulators require the sale to qualify as a true sale and impose strict conditions on, for example, the recourse investors can seek on the originator.

Also, a true sale of assets may trigger adverse tax consequences that turn a true sale securitisation into an undesired option.

Inflexibility

[3.60] A second constraint on traditional or "cash-flow" securitisation is its relative inflexibility. The assets transferred serve both to generate the cash flow required to pay for the interest on the notes and as collateral for the repayment of principal on the notes. As a result, this cash flow (and thus also prepayments affecting it) must be relatively predictable; mortgage receivables are an excellent example.

The assets in a traditional securitisation tend to be more homogeneous and, as such, a pool is easier to transfer and is more easily assessable by rating agencies.

Delays and inflated cost

[3.70] A third limitation for traditional securitisations is timing and cost. These can, or will, critics would argue, get out of hand in a traditional structure for several reasons. First, in a true sale transaction, the proceeds of the issuance are needed to purchase the underlying assets. The cost of the issuance may, depending on the credit rating of the originator, very well be higher than the cost of funding. Secondly, as mentioned at **[3.50]**, the transfer of the assets should constitute a true sale under the relevant jurisdiction(s). This transfer may be subject to constraints. This is particularly true of loans, and due diligence is required to ensure that no contractual terms or other legal restrictions are broken.[14]

Thirdly, a true sale securitisation involves a substantial number of documents. Some of these may not be necessary in a synthetic structure, such as the asset purchase agreement and related documents. In a synthetic structure, for example, the protection premiums to be paid by the originator are often structured to match the interest rate payments due on the notes. A separate interest rate swap could thus be avoided.

Servicing the pool

[3.80] Traditional securitisation is not over after the closing. Servicing the pool will still require a significant amount of administrative effort. This is particularly true if the originator continues to service the pool. But even if that is not the case and a separate servicer is engaged, the input required from the originator during the full length of the securitisation, eg on streamlining payments, should not be underestimated.

SYNTHETIC SECURITISATIONS: OPPORTUNITIES

Diversity of transferable asset classes

[3.90] Given the constraints in the traditional securitisation market described at **[3.50]** – **[3.80]**, originators and investors alike have investigated alternative structures in order to reap the full fruits from securitisation technology. Synthetic securitisation goes a long way towards that goal for a number of reasons.

First and foremost, a synthetic structure entitles the originator to transfer the credit risk of substantially more asset classes than would be available under a traditional true sale structure. This is partly because the synthetic structure allows the originator to sidestep the requirements that exist for a true sale of the assets outlined at **[3.50]**. Only the *credit risk* of the assets is transferred to the investors by means of credit derivatives (or guarantees). There is no need to effect a legal transfer. As a result, asset classes that are not as easily transferable, or are not transferable at all for contractual or statutory reasons, are available. For instance, a portfolio of multi-jurisdictional loans in shipping or aircraft is likely to be more easily securitised in a synthetic format than in a true sale structure. The opportunity to securitise loans from a variety of jurisdictions has been particularly appealing in Europe.[15]

Cash flow

[3.100] A second benefit of synthetic securitisations is related to cash flow. In traditional securitisation the cash flow needed to service the interest payment on the notes issued is generated by the collateral. By contrast, in a synthetic structure the cash flow originates (at least partially) from the fee payments that the originating bank pays to the SPV under a credit default swap. This enables asset classes that do not generate as predictable a cash flow as mortgage receivables to be securitised as well.

In recent transactions, a variety of new asset classes has been securitised synthetically, such as shipping loans (Latitude), aircraft loans (Leonardo and Harrows), a combination of structured finance and synthetic securities (Jazz CDO II), repackaged securitisations, different types of loans and letters of credit (Verdi Synthetic), consumer loans (Golden Bar) and residential mortgages (Chalet).

Flexibility

[3.110] The third major benefit of synthetics is flexibility. While true sale securitisations transfer all risks and benefits associated with legal ownership to the investors, synthetic securitisations can be tailor-made to transfer credit risk to differing degrees. The flexibility is due to the fact that the structure is based upon credit default swap documentation. Market participants can use this swap to structure their transactions in a variety of ways by choosing either fully or partially funded structures, modifying the events upon which payout is conditioned (the "credit events") and choosing the form of settlement and even the calculation of payout upon settlement. Separate credit default swaps or tranches of credit linked notes can be issued to accommodate for varying investor risk appetite and wishes.

The flexibility also reflects on the term of a synthetic securitisation. The legal maturity of the transaction is not linked to the maturity of the underlying asset (which tends to be lengthy, particularly in the case of mortgage receivables). It can be tailored to market demands and to the standard term of a credit default swap, eg a five-year period. Also, the amount of credit protection taken out is flexible. The credit default swap may be defined to cover only a required part of the full exposure to the underlying asset.

Synthetic CDOs are significantly larger than their true sale counterparts (typically around US$1 billion or their equivalent). As a consequence, it is possible for the portfolios to have a higher degree of diversity, which may contribute to lower interest payable on the credit linked notes.

This flexibility enables originators to optimise their driver benefit, eg obtaining regulatory capital relief. Investors are aware of this flexibility and can therefore require amendments in the structure proposed and even reverse engineer transactions with a bank. Synthetic securitisation thus allows market participants to find the perfect match between supply and demand for risk transfer more easily than by the rough method of true sale.

Cheaper and faster
[3.120] A fourth advantage of synthetic securitisations relates to the timetable and associated cost. As discussed at **[3.210]**, synthetic securitisation does not require the aggregate amount of notes issued to mirror the full market value of the underlying assets. No assets are purchased. Only a limited amount of issuance is required to provide collateral or credit enhancement for the senior notes.

As the cost of the issuance is often higher than the originator's cost of funding, a partially funded structure is a substantial cost reduction. In addition, the due diligence in synthetic structures can be cut short. There is no check required to ensure the legal transfer of the asset. In synthetic structures, the crucial moment is when the originator buying protection claims that a credit event has occurred and the SPV is obliged to pay out the settlement amount. If at that stage it was established that a particular asset did not meet the eligibility criteria at the time of its inclusion in the portfolio, the buyer of protection would not receive a protection payment on that asset. As a result, the SPV does not need to ensure that the eligibility criteria have been met at closing. Rather, it is the originator that will want to do that check. As the originator has led the selection of the portfolio, this may be a much more forthright exercise.

A related issue is the selection of the (reference) assets. In a true sale transaction, this selection requires special attention, as the cash flow should match the interest payable on the notes. For that reason securities that allow a deferred payment of interest may have to be excluded. By contrast, in a synthetic securitisation the focus is merely on the reference entity.

Less administration and risk repackaging
[3.130] A fifth advantage of synthetic securitisations is that synthetic transactions are generally less administratively burdensome.[16] For example, unlike true sale securitisations for mortgage receivables, there is no need to inform the borrowers. Neither does the originator need to

ensure that the relevant payments will be diverted to the SPV. Also, monitoring hedging obligations requires input from the back office.

Synthetic transactions can also offer scope for risk repackaging. This can be achieved by using an intermediary, eg an OECD Bank, which takes the credit risk from the originating bank and sells part of it on the final investors while retaining other risks.[17] Alternatively, synthetics allow originators to take a proactive position in the selection of the assets of which the credit risk is hedged. By including reference entities in the portfolio to which the originator does not yet have any exposure (or not yet above a specific amount), the originator would be able to extend its business relationship while the increased exposure is already hedged.

Synthetic securitisations: limitations

Newness to Asia-Pacific market
[3.140] Naturally, it is not all gold that shines on the synthetic structure. There are drawbacks here as well that must be taken into account. There are issues associated with this particular kind of transaction that have to be specifically addressed in the documentation.[18]

Synthetic securitisations are still a relatively new phenomenon. Some investors may be reluctant to embrace a structure that is more or less unfamiliar. Others might be limited in their capacity or not be entitled to invest in these structures. As a result, spreads on synthetic structures may be slightly higher in the short term, in comparison with traditional structures. As the synthetic structure becomes more prevalent this difference is apt to disappear. Given the development of synthetic transactions in other major markets globally, this seems only a matter of time in the Asia-Pacific. The development of the global credit derivatives market, the increasing standardisation of credit default swaps and the growth of credit linked notes all point in that direction.

Balance sheet management
[3.150] Unlike true sales, synthetic securitisations do not allow the originator to manage the balance sheet. As the assets are not transferred, they remain on the originator's balance sheet.[19] Depending on the outcome of the current global reassessment of accountancy regulations in the wake of the Enron debacle, it is expected that originators will be required to provide more disclosure on, amongst others, synthetic securitisation.

Less capital relief
[3.160] The opportunity to obtain regulatory capital relief in synthetic structures is not as comprehensive as in traditional structures. In most synthetic deals, the originator buys protection on the unfunded part of the

reference portfolio by entering into a credit default swap, either directly with a super senior investor or indirectly with an OECD bank. As a consequence, the obligations of the obligors of the reference portfolio are substituted by an obligation of an OECD bank.

Under current BIS rules, this entitles the originating bank to apply a risk weighting of 20% instead of the full 100% to the applicable adequacy ratio.[20] In a traditional securitisation structure the originating bank would simply sell the receivables for cash and obtain full regulatory capital relief for that sale. The relevant capital adequacy considerations are discussed in detail at **[3.570] – [3.630]**.

Taking into account the limitations of traditional securitisation, synthetic structures do therefore offer substantial benefits in the form of an increased choice in assets and enhanced flexibility. Banks[21] can use the synthetic structure to their advantage to free up credit lines and increase their return on equity in the process.

Rating agencies

Rating process
[3.170] Just as in traditional securitisations, rating agencies play a pivotal role in synthetic securitisations. Like in other structured finance transactions, the credit rating addresses the likelihood of full payment of interest and ultimate repayment of principal. All relevant rating agencies have published criteria for structuring synthetic securitisations.[22]

Focusing on the rating process of a synthetic securitisation, the following steps can be distinguished:
- an examination of the motivation of the sponsoring institutions;
- a review of the reference portfolio (including the credit events and the reference obligations) to assess the probability of a credit event occurring;
- a review of the settlement mechanism (and if physical, the deliverable obligations) to assign recoveries in the event of a default;
- a calculation of the credit enhancement;
- in managed transactions the credit risk of the portfolio may change, which will require further monitoring during the life of the transaction; as well as
- a review of the manger's capabilities and the way the trading gains and losses are addressed in the transaction.[23]

The managed synthetic structure is explored in more detail in Ch 4.

Structure

Basic structures

[3.180] Two basic synthetic structures are distinguished: the balance sheet transaction and the arbitrage synthetic securitisation.[24]

Balance sheet securitisations are generally undertaken by banks that wish to transfer assets off their balance sheet. Synthetic securitisations do not affect the balance sheet. Instead, balance sheet synthetics deals refer to synthetic structures that are driven by the originator's desire to obtain regulatory capital relief.[25] Synthetic arbitrage transactions, on the other hand, intend to exploit a yield mismatch between the yield on the underlying assets and the (lower) cost of servicing interest on the notes issued.[26] This chapter primarily focuses on balance sheet synthetic structures. Chapter 4 addresses synthetic arbitrage securitisations.

The most common form of synthetic securitisation is the "green bottle" structure.[27] In such a structure, if a credit event occurs with respect to a reference obligation, only the loss with respect to that specific reference obligation is calculated. Protection is allocated proportionately among the assets in the basket. The remaining reference obligations (green bottles) are not affected (and continue to hang on the wall). This structure allows the buyer of protection to obtain regulatory capital relief for all reference obligations.[28] The diagram below shows a typical synthetic securitisation structure.

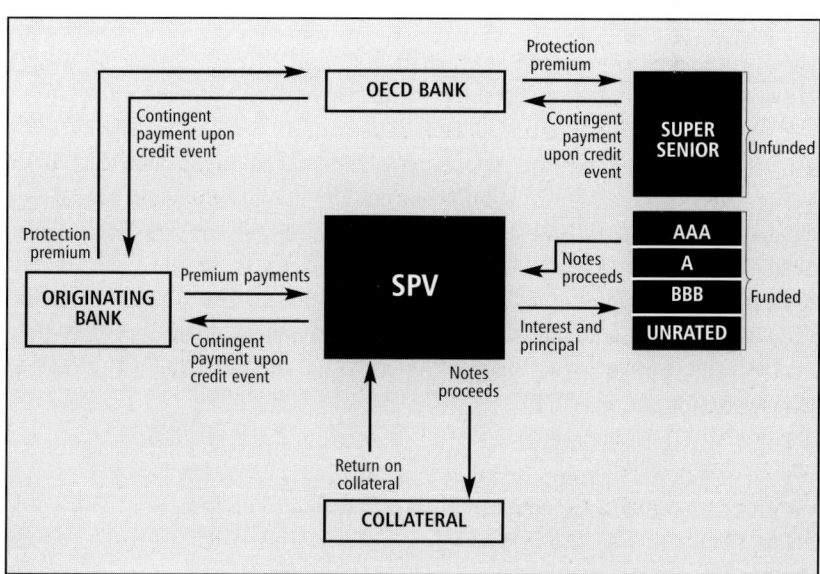

From this structure, the following building blocks can be distinguished:
- the credit default swap (between the originator and the SPV: see **[3.190]**);
- the credit linked notes issued by the SPV (see **[3.200]**);
- the super senior swap (see **[3.210]**); and
- the SPV (see **[3.220]**).

Credit default swap

[3.190] In synthetics, securitisation technology and credit derivatives are combined. The basic building block of a synthetic securitisation is the credit default swap. A proper understanding of credit derivatives and their inherent risks and benefits is thus needed.[29] The 2003 Definitions are based upon market conventions in trading over-the-counter (OTC) derivatives. These conventions do not apply per se to structured transactions such as synthetic securitisations.

Simulation of credit transfer
Credit default swaps entitle the isolated transfer of the credit risk of a portfolio of assets, the reference obligations. Specific definitions (such as credit events) and mechanisms (for settlement) are used to simulate the credit transfer of the relevant assets. This simulation is the key. It enables transaction parties to circumvent several drawbacks of traditional securitisation. However, it is fundamental that investors' understanding of what credit risk is and how it actually is drafted in the documentation may diverge. This divergence is most apparent in the selection of the relevant credit events and the details of the selected settlement method.

What happens in a credit default swap?
In a nutshell, in a credit default swap, the buyer of protection pays a periodic (usually fixed) amount to the seller of protection in consideration for the credit risk protection purchased. The seller agrees that upon occurrence of a credit event and other conditions to settlement being met, the seller will pay out the settlement amount agreed. In this method, the cash settlement method, the payout is usually structured as the diminution in value of the reference obligations. Alternatively, under physical settlement, the buyer is to deliver a specific amount of "deliverable obligations" against payment of the full face value of the reference obligations.

The credit default swap has an "all or nothing" structure.[30] Settlement is only triggered by the occurrence of specified credit events and meeting other conditions to payment. The choice of the credit events and the definition of the credit events selected determines the extent of risk transferred. In synthetic securitisations, the credit events selected are almost always different from the standard OTC definitions used in the

2003 Definitions. In addition, even if they are the same, their meaning may be very different. Only if such a credit event occurs may payment of the settlement amount be in order. There may be other events that adversely affect the creditworthiness of the reference entity. However, if such an event is not defined as a credit event in the transaction, the occurrence of such an event does not trigger payment of credit protection.[31]

Credit linked notes

[3.200] It takes two steps to change a credit default swap into a credit linked note. First, the unfunded credit default swap is modified to a funded transaction, in which the protection seller pays out the credit event payment up front. Secondly, the transaction is embedded in a note issued by an SPV. The up-front payment is the note purchase price, rather than the credit event payment. The seller becomes a noteholder. The overall effect is that the noteholder is insulated from the credit risk of the (ultimate) buyer of protection (the originator).

Upon the occurrence of a credit event, when cash settlement applies, the diminution in value of the reference obligations is calculated in accordance with the valuation provisions of the transaction. This calculated amount is subtracted from the notional amount of the notes in reverse order of seniority. The issuer as buyer of protection is released from its obligation to pay interest on or repay that part of the notes on maturity.[32]

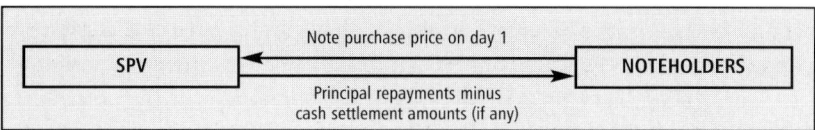

Synthetic CDOs may differ in the way that this write-down of principal is effected. In some transactions, this is an instant write-down, while other deals only write down at final maturity of the transaction. In the latter case, noteholders will continue to receive interest on the full amount of their investment until final maturity.

Tranching

The credit risk transferred is usually tranched, as in any other securitisation, using a series of loss thresholds to try to mirror credit enhancement as seen in traditional securitisation. The credit risk itself is also mirrored; the credit linked notes will reference the same credit events used in the credit default swap. In addition, the initial notional amount of the credit default swap will be equal to the initial aggregate amount of the notes. To streamline payments, the payment dates will mostly be identical.

Equity tranche

Just as in other note issuance, the credit linked notes in synthetic securitisations generally contain an unrated or equity tranche. This "first loss" piece serves as a threshold. The SPV will reduce the principal to be repaid to the noteholders only once the cumulative losses on the reference portfolio have exceeded this threshold. The losses upon each credit event are calculated in accordance with the settlement and valuation terms of the swap and recorded.

The equity note tends to be substantially smaller in synthetic CDOs than in comparable true sale deals, partly as a result of the higher rated assets that are usually included in a synthetic portfolio. As a result of the higher leverage, the occurrence of only a few credit events could suffice to wipe out the equity note.

Super senior swap

[3.210] The synthetic market has evolved from "fully funded" structures, in which the total amount of notes issued matches the aggregate amount of the reference portfolio, towards "partially funded" structures. Traditional securitisations are usually fully funded, as the proceeds of the notes are needed to purchase the underlying assets.

Advantages of partially funded structures

The advantage of a partially funded structure is twofold. It allows the originator to access a broader investment base and it is a lot cheaper. In a partially funded structure, only a limited number of notes are issued to investors.[33] The transfer of credit risk of the remainder of the portfolio is effected by means of a credit default swap. As the investors in the senior notes are subordinated to the seller of protection under this credit default swap, it is commonly referred to as the "super senior" swap.

As credit risk is transferred both in funded and unfunded form, the originator can access a broad investor base of both funded investors, such as pension funds, as well as unfunded investors, like insurance companies. In particular, monoline insurers play a major role in taking on credit risk in (synthetic) CDOs. It is estimated that their appetite for senior notes in funded (true sale) transactions and super senior tranches (in synthetic details) have helped sponsors originate volumes of US$180 billion since the mid-1990s.[34]

Better cost efficiency

The incorporation of a super senior swap is also cost efficient as it is cheaper for the originator to buy protection in unfunded form. The super senior swap capitalises on the limitations of the capital market: it is not possible for notes to be rated higher than AAA, and coupons payable have effectively reached their floor. The private market does not have such a constraint. Provided the AAA notes investors are subordinated to the super senior investor, the pricing of the premium payable on the super senior swap will reflect this smaller risk and be lower.

In effect, the inclusion of a super senior swap is a double-edged sword as it also reduces the amount of notes to be issued. Given that the coupons payable on these notes are generally higher than the originator's cost of funding, the super senior swap reduces negative carry. The AAA tranche serves as "proof" of the level of risk taken on by the super senior investor. Technically, this tranche could be as small as a single dollar.

Capital relief
As discussed at **[3.590]**, super senior swaps can provide capital relief as well. They therefore enable the originator to obtain capital relief relatively cheaply. These advantages are to an extent offset by the fact that no full credit risk transference is achieved. The originator has credit risk on the super senior investor's contingent obligation to pay the credit event payment. Generally, the super senior investor has a high credit rating, so that this concern is not substantial. However, as the *Mahonia case* has shown,[35] there may be other factors affecting a payout of the credit event payment.

Terms of swap
The terms of the credit default swap might, but do not necessarily, match those of the credit default swap between the originator and the SPV. For example, the originator and the super senior investor could agree a different maturity and a slightly amended credit risk transference might be negotiated to accommodate investors' requirements. Obviously, in a balance sheet transaction the bottom line for the originator is the level of risk transference the local regulator is comfortable with in allocating capital relief.[36]

Special purpose vehicles
[3.220] In a typical synthetic structure, the credit linked notes are issued by a "bankruptcy-remote" and "collateralised" SPV in order to insulate the investors from the credit risk of the originating bank.[37] The bankruptcy remoteness of the SPV is established, among other things, by the covenant that it must not undertake any business activities apart from those related to the securitisation transaction. The SPV is "collateralised" as its obligations towards the originator to pay out upon the occurrence of a credit event are secured by "eligible" collateral purchased by the SPV. The (principal) priorities of payments provide that the originator's claim on the SPV is first in priority. The tranches are

issued in the same notional amounts as the swap tranches and suffer losses in parallel with the associated swap tranche.

Alternatively, the structure may be trust-based in common law jurisdictions. In particular, the use of a master trust has facilitated the structuring of repeat transactions under ultimately the same vehicle, without the risk of commingling of underlying assets. In civil law jurisdictions, SPV holdings may be used to achieve the same effect.

Although the use of a collateralised SPV as issuing vehicle is most prevalent, some transactions alternatively use an MTN program as issuer or no SPV at all.[38] In the structure without an SPV, the highest rating assigned to the notes is typically capped at the credit rating of the issuer.[39]

Structural risks

Risk factors: an introduction
[3.230] Different structures incorporate different risks. Outlining all the risks for investors in synthetic securitisations is beyond the focus of this publication. A typical overview of the risk factors in a prospectus of a synthetic transaction may cover 20 pages. The focus is on those risks that appear most prevalent among the different structures, which are:
- credit risk on the referenced assets (portfolio risk: see **[3.240]**);
- credit risk on the originator (see **[3.250]**);
- termination risk (see **[3.260]**); and
- collateral risk (see **[3.270]**).

In comparison with the investor's risks in a traditional structure, the credit risk on the originator stands out. This additional risk is offset by the fact that other risks affecting traditional securitisations do not, or do not to the same extent, apply to synthetic securitisations. These include the prepayment risk and the possibility of structuring bullet maturity deals.

Portfolio credit risk
[3.240] Obviously, the quality of the pool referenced in the synthetic securitisation is a main consideration for investors. They will rely on their own assessment of the risk, as well as on the ratings assigned by the ratings agencies.

It is important to note that the reference portfolio of a balance sheet synthetic structure need not be static. In fact, an originating bank can maximise its capital relief if it is able to substitute reference obligations that are either repaid or prepaid. Generally, substitution is subject to the overall credit quality of the reference portfolio not deteriorating.

Originator credit risk

[3.250] A second risk is the *credit risk on the originator*. In traditional structures this is not a matter of concern. The SPV has no direct claim on the originator. In a synthetic securitisation, however, the originator and the SPV have entered into a credit default swap referencing a number of underlying credits. Under the terms of this credit default swap, the originator buys protection on these credits. As a result, the originator is obliged to pay to the SPV a (frequently quarterly) protection premium during the full life of the transaction. The SPV relies on this income flow to be able to service the interest on the notes.

Interposed bank

In some transactions another bank is interposed between the originator and the SPV. The respective credit default swaps (the one between the originator and this bank, and the one between this bank and the SPV) would mirror each other. To prevent the investors from bearing a double credit risk, the documentation in such transactions will provide that the obligations to pay the protection premium to the SPV are the obligations of the interposed bank itself. More specifically, these obligations will not be contingent upon the originator fully performing its payment obligations under its credit default swap with the interposed bank. This structure is the exception rather than rule.

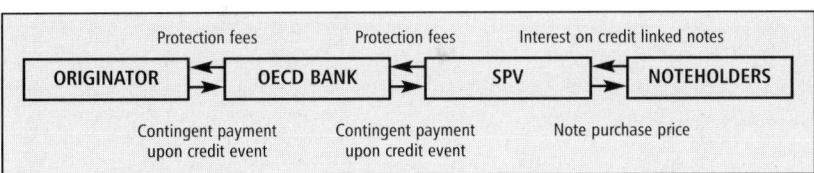

Without additional structuring, the fact that the investors take credit risk on the originator would make it very difficult to obtain a credit rating on the notes issued higher than the originator's credit rating.

Enhanced originator's credit risk

The originator's credit risk can be enhanced in several ways. Most common is to use either a funded reserve account and/or ratings downgrade triggers. A funded reserve account would be established at the outset of the transaction. Depending on the credit rating of the originator, this reserve account would have to be funded with either one or more periodic payments under the credit default swap. If insufficient, it would have to be replenished by the originating bank and failure to do so would constitute an event of default and result in early redemption of the notes. Alternatively, the structure could incorporate downgrade triggers that, when breached, require the swap counterparty to defease some or all of the future swap premium payments or post a satisfactory amount of collateral.[40]

55

Termination risk

[3.260] *Termination risk* is the third risk consideration. This is the risk that the swap counterparty will cause the credit default swap with the SPV to be terminated prior to the scheduled maturity of the notes. This risk has two components. First, the SPV would then not be able to generate cash flow from the credit default swap needed to service the interest payments on the notes. Secondly, the swap would have to be closed out and therefore marked to market upon termination. If the swap would be "out of the money" for the SPV, it would have incurred an additional financial obligation through no fault of its own. This, too, could cause the SPV to default on its obligations under the notes. To add insult to injury, the termination of the credit default swap could occur in a stressed market. Chances are, the spreads will then be even wider and the cost to the SPV higher as it may not be so easy to obtain quotes.

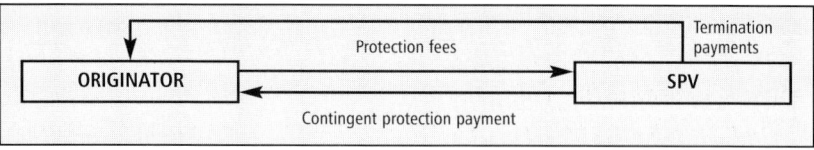

Termination provisions

In order to address the termination risk, rating agencies typically require specific provisions in the swap. These could involve the requirement that any payments to be made upon early termination of the swap would be subordinated to the obligations of the SPV to the noteholders in terms of priority of payment. Alternatively, the obligation to make any such payment could be eliminated by rendering s 6(e) of the ISDA Master Agreement "not applicable" at the outset of the transaction.[41]

Events related to termination

To minimise investors' credit risk exposure due to termination of the credit default swap, the number of applicable events of default and termination events under the ISDA Master Agreement is substantially reduced. This is also due to the nature of the SPV as a stand-alone vehicle, rather than a bank with a number of other outstanding obligations. Typically, events of default on the SPV's part, such as breach of agreement, misrepresentation, default under specified transaction and cross default, are not applied. The nature of the SPV also prompts the disapplication of the termination events tax event upon merger and credit event upon merger. On the other hand, the occurrence of an event of default under the notes is added as an additional termination event. Early termination is usually disapplied, as this could expose the SPV to the aforementioned termination risk.

In practice, rating agencies have accepted a number of termination events that accommodate originators. These include a failure to pay by either party to the credit default swap and certain insolvency-related events affecting such a party. In addition, certain tax events are common as termination events, eg the imposition of a new (or a change to) withholding tax.[42]

Collateral risk

[3.270] The fourth risk is *collateral risk*. The timely repayment of principal, as well as interest on the notes, depend on the way the SPV invests the proceeds of the notes in eligible collateral.[43] This risk has two components. First, if the proceeds of the notes are invested in securities or deposited with a bank, the repayment of these investments depends on the credit risk of the issuer or deposit bank. Secondly, if the collateral needs to be liquidated before its dated maturity, the sales proceeds will depend on the market value and the liquidity of the collateral. Proceeds may not be sufficient to cover all of the SPV's obligations under the notes.

Addressing collateral risk

Collateral risk is addressed in a variety of ways. These include investing in highly rated collateral (in combination with repurchase agreements, put options or total return swaps), entering into a guaranteed investment contract or the use of deposit accounts. The purpose of these mechanisms is the same: they are designed to ensure that collateral can be liquidated at par, at any time, and enable the SPV to fully comply with its payment obligations to (first) the originating bank, as well as (second) to repay the notes. The purpose of the collateral is thus primarily to absorb any losses on the reference portfolio as a result of the occurrence of credit events.

Investment in collateral

It is most common to invest the proceeds of the notes in highly rated (AAA) collateral. Such eligible collateral includes AAA government bonds, Pfandbriefe, financial institution bonds and certificates of deposits. These types of collateral are generally very liquid, providing a certain degree of comfort to investors that the payments to them will be made when due and in full. Some transactions have opted to invest in AAA structured finance securities (which qualify as eligible financial collateral under the current proposals for a revised Basel Accord). Though this investment insulates investors to a significant extent from a deterioration in value of the collateral, liquidity and maturity are then more of a concern. Rating agencies may require over-collateralisation (either at the outset of the transaction or during its course), depending on the issuer's credit rating. In addition, the originator may be required to substitute the collateral in the event of a collateral downgrade. If the collateral may be substituted under the terms of the transaction, rating agencies will require strict eligibility criteria for substitute collateral.

The investment in highly rated collateral should enable the SPV to repay principal on the notes when it is obliged to. To alleviate any concern about the ability of the SPV to repay interest, the return on the collateral needs to be ascertained in advance. To do this, the SPV may enter into a repurchase agreement (or "repo": see **[3.280]**), a put option or a total return swap (see **[3.290]**) or Guaranteed Investment Contract (see [**3.300**]). The relevant counterparty usually is, but need not be, the originator.

Repurchase agreement
[3.280] Under the terms of a repo, the SPV will use a portion of the proceeds of the notes to purchase certain eligible securities from the repo counterparty. To protect the SPV from market exposure, the repo counterparty would pay out a pre-agreed interest, while any interest on the collateral securities would be paid to the repo counterparty (Iliad, for instance). If the SPV were obligated to pay out a cash settlement amount to the originator, then the repo would be (partially) terminated and the purchased securities would be repurchased from the issuer to generate the required funds.

Put option or total return swap
[3.290] An SPV could purchase a put option from a third party (which usually has a high credit rating). Under the terms of the put option, the SPV would be entitled to put the collateral at par value to that counterparty. Another alternative would be for the SPV to enter into a total return swap with a third party. This would allow the SPV to transfer all proceeds from the collateral and in return receive a pre-agreed cash flow, matching (wholly or partially) the interest payments on the notes.

As additional protection, the documentation will commonly provide for certain "triggers", under which collateral must be substituted or additional collateral posted in the event the collateral issuer is downgraded. Or the originator is obligated to post additional collateral if its market value falls below a certain threshold. Finally, there may be a "make whole" provision, under which the counterparty will offset any yield shortfall between the original and substitute collateral.[44]

Guaranteed investment contract
[3.300] Investors may be protected from collateral risk by the SPV entering into a guaranteed investment contract (GIC). Under the terms of the GIC, the counterparty is obliged to repay a preset return on the collateral. In order to (at least partially) insulate the investors from the credit risk of the GIC counterparty, this agreement will include downgrade clauses, requiring a substitute bank to replace the original counterparty if downgraded below a specific short-term or long-term rating threshold. Varying on the same theme, the proceeds of the notes

could be put into a deposit with a bank, typically the originating bank. This deposit would then generate a base rate, such as LIBOR, and as such partially cover the costs of servicing the interest rate payments on the notes. As most of the credit linked notes are usually at a floating rate, the proceeds will typically be invested to match this profile to prevent a mismatch between assets and liabilities.

The choice of enhancement depends on various factors. Often, the originator's priority is to issue AAA notes that it finds easier to sell. In that case, the proceeds will typically be invested in highly rated securities, rather than deposited with a bank because, barring other protection, a ratings downgrade of the deposit bank would directly affect the ceiling rating of the most senior notes. On the other hand, depositing the proceeds with a bank (such as the originator) would provide this bank with cheap funding. To maximise this funding opportunity as deposit bank, the originator will invest only that part of the collateral required to safeguard the credit rating of the notes higher than its own.

Liquidity facility
Though by no means strictly necessary, a synthetic CDO can be structured in such a way that the credit event payments are funded through a liquidity facility.[45]

Risks: other considerations
[3.310] As indicated at **[3.230]**, the additional credit risk for investors in synthetics is offset by the elimination (wholly or partially) of several other features in synthetic structures. These include prepayment risk and possible bullet maturity.

In a traditional securitisation, prepayment risk is an important consideration that investors take into account. Securitised assets *may* allow (in the case of corporate loans) or *must* allow (in the case of mortgage receivables) the borrower to prepay (at least a part of) principal prior to maturity. In a synthetic securitisation this prepayment risk is generally eliminated. If a borrower/reference entity would prepay under its corporate loan, that prepayment would not trigger any credit event. The credit default swap does not reference a single loan. The credit default swap is therefore unaffected.

Another feature that sets synthetics apart from traditional securitisations is the possibility for bullet maturity. The use of credit default swaps and highly liquid collateral enable synthetic structures to mature on a single day. The cash market does not (yet) offer that benefit. Obviously, this is advantageous to investors.

Cash settled synthetic CDOs can reference assets that are denominated in a different currency than the SPV's liabilities. This may be overcome because the terms of the credit default swap can stipulate the settlement currency to be different to the referenced credit and match the currency of the notes.[46] In a true sale transaction a separate currency swap would be required.

The "vintage" of a CDO is relevant for the credit risk profile, given the rapid evolution of the credit derivatives definitions to the 2003 Definitions. An "older" CDO that builds upon the 1999 Definitions (with or without supplements) may fail to address risks that have subsequently surfaced. In addition, market conventions in the actual applications of these definitions may have changed.

DOCUMENTATION

Synthetics documentation: an introduction

[3.320] Given the differences in structure, it is not surprising that the documentation of a synthetic securitisation differs substantially from a traditional securitisation. The main issues are the use of a credit default swap between the originator and the SPV instead of an asset purchase agreement and the issuance of credit linked notes by the SPV to investors, rather than "ordinary" notes. Here we address these two elements from a documentation perspective. As the characteristics of the credit default swap are largely mirrored in the credit linked note, the emphasis is on the former.

Credit default swap

Credit default swaps: important documentation

[3.330] The two most important topics in the documentation of the credit default swap are:
1. the selection and definition of the credit events (see **[3.340]**); and
2. the documenting of the desired settlement method and valuation (see **[3.370]** – **[3.400]**).

Essentially, this is about the redefinition of the credit events and settlement mechanisms used in the single name credit default swap market for structured finance transactions, such as synthetic securitisations.

Two questions arise in respect of the use of credit events in synthetic securitisations:
- Which credit events are selected?
- Are the selected credit events similar to their definition in the 2003 Definitions or are they redefined to fit the purpose of the structured transaction?

Which credit events?
[3.340] The starting point is the selection of credit events in the relevant single name credit default swap market. As outlined in the Ch 2, the customary credit events in the North American, Asian and European markets are bankruptcy, failure to pay and (modified) restructuring. Within the context of a balance sheet structure, aimed at obtaining regulatory capital relief, the obvious limit on deleting any of these credit events is the regulator's confirmation that such relief will be granted. The regulators generally require bankruptcy and failure to pay as credit events.[47] If any of these is not included, the onus will be on the originator to substantiate that the significant risk transfer with respect to the referenced portfolio is nonetheless achieved.

Most recent synthetic balance sheet securitisations contained only bankruptcy and failure to pay. The focus of regulators seems to have shifted to the definition of these credit events and further analysis of the terms of the credit default swap to ensure that significant credit risk transfer is achieved.

In the Asia-Pacific some balance sheet transactions have closed that included additional credit events. In a particular transaction obligation acceleration and repudiation/moratorium were both included. In Australia, a transaction included obligation acceleration as a credit event. The bottom line is that obligation default is rejected by rating agencies, as it includes technical defaults that are not covered in their "default" definition. Market practice continues to evolve towards bankruptcy and failure to pay as the only credit events. The recent decision of APRA no longer to require either obligation default or obligation acceleration as a third credit event is proof of that.[48]

2003 Definitions or redefined?
[3.350] The second question about the use of credit events in synthetic securitisations (see **[3.330]**) regards the definition of the credit events selected. They are drawn from the credit derivatives definitions, tailored for the single credit default swap market. In synthetic securitisations, these credit events may be, and practically always are, modified. There are two reasons for the modification. First, the extent of credit risk transferred is negotiable between the originator and the investors, provided the originator is comfortable that it will obtain full capital relief from its regulator. Secondly, the credit events used in the 2003 Definitions presume the pool of assets referenced consists of bonds or loans. If other assets are referenced, such as credit derivatives or structured finance securities or even special types of loans, these standard credit events simply may not fit the bill. As structured finance securities or credit derivatives are mostly referenced in arbitrage transactions, these are discussed in Ch 4.

Tailored credit event: an example

[3.360] The tailoring of credit events is best illustrated by examples of the use of the credit event "failure to pay". In synthetic transaction referencing corporate bonds or loans, this credit event could be the standard failure to pay, after the expiration of any applicable grace period, when and where due, of any payments in the amount of not less than the payment requirement (or "threshold" amount).[49] Modifications may be made to the applicable grace period, as well as to the threshold amount. As to the first, under some transactions a credit event failure to pay is triggered without regard to any applicable grace period, substantially increasing the likelihood of a credit event occurring. At the other end of the spectrum, transactions failure to pay is only deemed to have occurred once an additional time period has elapsed on top of the grace period. This extra time may be up to 90 days if the referenced obligations are mortgage receivables or consumer loans (Chalet and Cibeles, for example), and even 180 days if the underlying assets are highly volatile loans (Latitude). Basically, the extra time added can be tailored to the recovery policies governing the referenced obligations.

Alternatively, the extent of the credit risk transferred can be tailored by changing (and particularly, lowering) the payment requirement threshold from the standard amount of US$1 million. In some transactions this threshold is reduced to as little as US$100,000 (or its equivalent in another currency). Bearing this in mind, most investors not only look at the credit risk profile of the reference obligations, but also analyse the definition of the applicable credit events very carefully.

As discussed in Ch 2, the occurrence of a credit event itself does not trigger settlement of the credit default swap. Additional "conditions to settlement" must be fulfilled, including the delivery of a credit event notice and of a notice of publicly available information (PAI). A notice of PAI relies on publication of facts substantiating the credit event in public sources, including (for the Asia-Pacific market) the Nihon Keizai Shinbun, Asahi Shinbun, Yomiuri Shinbun and the Australian Financial Review.[50] In a specific transaction, additional news sources could be added. Also, the number of public sources might be changed. To minimise subjectivity, information in which any of the parties to the credit default swap or their affiliates are cited as the sole source of information is usually carved out of the PAI.[51]

In this respect, proper attention should be given to the way in which the occurrence of a credit event is confirmed. A standard credit default swap relies on the notion of PAI and the accepted news sources. However, sole reliance on these may prevent an originator from triggering a settlement under a synthetic securitisation as the originator owes a duty of confidentiality to its clients.[52]

Settlement

[3.370] The documentation of the settlement method and the valuation process merit separate attention. Settlement of a credit default swap can be either in cash or in physical form. This choice decides the calculation of the payment, if any, and therefore the extent of the protection purchased. Both cash and physical settlement are acceptable to rating agencies. In practice, however, cash settlement is much the preferred settlement form in balance sheet synthetic structures. A ledger of loss on the reference portfolio is kept. This chapter focuses on the documentation of cash settlement, while Ch 4 addresses physical settlement in more detail, as that format is more prevalent in arbitrage transactions.

Cash settlement is usually defined as the difference in value of reference obligations at the outset of the transaction and at the time of the occurrence of a credit event.[53] However, in synthetic transactions, this value can be calculated in different ways. There are three ways to calculate the cash settlement amount:

1. rely on market valuation of the referenced asset (see **[3.380]**);
2. preset the calculation method in advance (see **[3.390]**); or
3. base it upon the recovery of the reference obligations (see **[3.400]**).

The first and the last are the most common.[54] Needless to say, investors carefully review this section, as it determines any reduction on the principal on their notes after the occurrence of a credit event. As outlined in the case studies at **[3.690]** – **[3.730]**, some asset classes may combine any of these options.

Market valuation

[3.380] The first method of calculating the cash settlement amount is to rely on the market. In order for this to work, the reference obligation needs to be in liquid form so that it is easily transferable in the market. If this method is used, it is important that market participants reassure themselves of the liquidity for the reference assets, so that an objective market quote is possible. Typically, the cash settlement amount is determined by a bidding process, taking market quotes a specified number of days after the credit event notice. Under ISDA standard terms, the default number of days is five. However, this valuation process is usually modified to take into account the fact that the market for credit instruments can be volatile immediately after a credit event and market and liquidity risk should be minimised.[55] Furthermore, the transaction documentation may limit the entities that could act as dealers from which bids may be obtained, eg carving out those affiliated with the originator.

Synthetic CDOs have seen a wide variety of valuation methods. The diversity relates to the minimum number of bids to be obtained (usually three to five), the time frame during which they are to be obtained (a specified number of days after the occurrence of the credit event, usually 45-60), which dealers' bids are eligible to be included (are affiliates of the originator included, only major dealers from a pre-agreed list?) and the way in which these bids are used to calculate the cash settlement amount (highest bid, average highest or otherwise[56]). In addition, the documentation may vary depending on what to do if not enough bids are obtained (will the process be repeated over and over or is there a cut-off date after which an independent accountant[57] determines the market value, rather than the sponsoring institution itself?[58]).

More recently, the variation in market valuation has been moving towards more standardised terms. This move is driven by rating agency research, identifying tweaks that affect investors (as the ultimate sellers of protection). Guidance on the market valuation is emerging: the bidding procedure is to start 30 days or more after the credit event and to include multiple dealers and valuation rounds as a back-up. Furthermore, the onus is increasingly on the sponsoring institution to disclose to investors which entities are eligible dealers (or may be so in the future).[59]

Preset the calculation method
[3.390] Reliance on the market can be circumvented by specifying the method for calculation of the cash settlement amount in advance. This can be done in the form of a lump percentage, based, for instance, on historical data. This approach is sometimes used in respect of unsecured loans.

Actual recovery
[3.400] Another way to calculate the cash settlement amount is to base it upon actual recovery. Simply, the amount payable by the protection seller (the SPV and ultimately the credit linked noteholders) would be the notional amount of the defaulted reference obligations less the recovery amounts. For example, in a transaction referencing mortgage receivables, the cash settlement amount was defined as the notional amount of the defaulted reference obligation plus accrued and unpaid interest plus foreclosure costs less recovery amounts.[60]

This option may be attractive if the recovery procedures are well established and relatively easy to carry out, as is the case with mortgage receivables. Typically the entire servicing and recovering of these assets is easily out-sourced and can be professionally and quickly handled. However, reliance on recovery values does introduce other issues; in particular, regulatory aspects of insolvency laws may affect the amount and timing of any proceeds by imposition of stays or moratoria. If the referenced assets are structured finance securities, this type of calculation is more cumbersome as these securities are not necessarily liquid.[61]

Cut-off date
An influential factor in the recovery process is the time allowed for the work out. This "cut-off date" may be anywhere between one or two years (for loans) or even longer (if the underlying are CDO and asset backed securities (ABS)) after the credit event notice has been delivered. The length of time depends on the liquidity of the underlying asset. Actual recovery may cause a moral hazard for the originating bank. The bank may have no incentive to maximise the recovery value of the defaulted assets as it will be repaid any reduced recovery value. This moral hazard is usually mitigated in the documentation, eg by involving an independent auditor or requiring a minimum recovery rate.

Calculation agent
It is important to note that the originator will often be the party calculating the cash settlement amount in its capacity as "calculation agent".[62] The calculation agent in a synthetic securitisation is usually held to fulfilling its obligations in good faith and in a commercially reasonable manner. As a result, it will not be easy for investors to object to or correct the calculations made. It would typically require inside knowledge to substantiate that the calculation agent did not act in good faith. As a result, there is a certain reliance by investors on the calculation agent.

A similar risk arises when the credit default swap is terminated and has to be marked to market. The 2002 ISDA Master Agreement builds upon the same notion of commercial reasonableness in the determination of the close-out amount.[63]

Other issues
Documentation of credit events and settlement is of the essence in a synthetic transaction. However, there is more to credit default swaps than these two topics. Other issues such as the (reference and deliverable) obligation category and characteristics do require review as well. Typically, borrowed money is the most common reference obligation category. Bond or loan is generally, but not necessarily, chosen as the deliverable obligation category.[64] Most of these details are based upon the evolving and differing market conventions for trades in credit default swaps.

Credit linked notes

[3.410] The terms of the credit linked notes largely resemble those of the credit default swap. The credit events, for example, are typically defined by reference to those in the credit default swap. After the occurrence of a credit event, a cash settlement amount has been determined and this amount will be applied to reduce the principal of the classes of notes in reverse order of seniority. The SPV will be obliged to pay out to the originator (or other, interposed credit default swap party, if any) the same amount.

The proceeds of the notes are used to purchase collateral for the obligations of the SPV under the credit default swap with the swap counterparty as well as its obligations under the notes. Typically, a security trustee will hold the collateral primarily for itself to pay for fees and costs and expenses, secondly, to cover any obligations owed to the swap counterparty (most importantly, the contingent obligation to make the credit event payment) and only thirdly to repay the noteholders' principal on the notes and any interest accrued thereon. As a result, the originator ranks prior to the noteholders.[65]

As the SPV only has a contractual relationship with the originating bank, it (and by reference the noteholders) has no rights or recourse towards the reference entities in the portfolio. Hence, the SPV and the noteholders do not benefit from any collateral posted by the reference entity in favour of the originator, nor from remedies that would normally be available to a holder of such information.

As mentioned at **[3.200]**, the write-down of the credit linked notes after the issuance of the credit event notice may vary. The write-down could be instant and in full. Upon the calculation of the actual loss, the notes may be partially reinstated. Alternatively, the notes may be written down only after the loss amount has been established. Obviously, the first scenario would be preferable from the point of view of the originator, given the "financing" of the loss. A compromise solution that has recently found favour in several transactions would be to write down based on an estimate of the loss, eg based upon historical data for the reference obligations.

In general, the documentation of synthetic transactions builds upon the 2003 Definitions. These are very complex. In addition, they have been drafted for trading in single-name credit derivatives, such as credit default swaps, rather than portfolio transactions, such as synthetic securitisations. As a result of this "translation", amendments in the documentation of synthetic structures are inevitable. Fortunately, these definitions have been stress tested in recent years and the recent publication of the 2003 Definitions has further enhanced the maturity of the definitions. However, understanding the definitions is still required for a proper assessment of synthetic securitisations.

LEGAL ISSUES

Synthetic securitisation: legal issues
[3.420] The analysis of legal issues in synthetic securitisation builds upon the analysis of credit default swaps. For a complete overview, readers are advised to refer to that analysis as well (see **[2.40]** – **[2.370]**). This chapter focuses on legal aspects that are particular to a synthetic

transaction in comparison to a true sales transaction. Some overlap may exist with regard to the issues in structured transactions generally, such as, for instance, the requirement for an SPV to be bankruptcy remote.

The main topics include recharacterisation (see **[3.430]**), confidentiality (see **[3.460]**), liability for retail issues (see **[3.500]**) and several capita selecta (see **[3.520]**).[66]

Recharacterisation

Insurance

[3.430] Traditional and synthetic securitisations each have a recharacterisation aspect. A traditional securitisation could be argued to resemble a secured loan.[67] A synthetic securitisation bears similarities to an insurance contract.[68]

To the core, any synthetic transaction is prone to the allegation that substance should prevail over form. In economic terms, a credit default swap used in a synthetic securitisation resembles an insurance contract. Such a recharacterisation could affect the enforceability of the credit default swap. It might even be considered null and void. In addition, the seller of protection might be deemed to have carried out an insurance business without the appropriate permits and may be subject to insurance tax and/or fines.[69]

In synthetic securitisations, further analysis of this issue is required. The main argument to distinguish synthetic securitisations from insurance contracts is that the buyer of protection need not have incurred loss as a precondition to claim payment of a settlement amount. Indemnity is not an issue, as it is in an insurance contract. In the context of trading credit default swaps the fact that the buyer of protection need not have incurred a loss is particularly true, as the buyer of protection need not necessarily own the reference obligation. In (balance sheet) synthetic securitisations the originating bank continues to hold the reference obligation. The manner in which the valuation process of the defaulted assets is documented then becomes the focal point. Careful drafting is required; for instance, if the settlement amount is based upon the diminution in market value of the reference obligations, rather than on a pre-agreed lump sum, as the former more closely resembles a compensation of loss incurred. The credit default swap could specifically provide that the obligations of the seller of protection exist irrespective of whether the buyer of protection suffers a loss or is exposed to the risk of loss following the occurrence of a credit event and regardless of whether the buyer of protection has any legal or beneficial interest in the reference entity or any economic interest in respect thereof.[70]

Legal opinions

Rating agencies require a legal opinion that the synthetic transaction does not contravene insurance laws.[71] The theoretical aspects of this issue have been debated,[72] but so far no relevant case law specific to synthetic securitisation has been published.[73] Nevertheless, legal opinions under English law tend to be relatively clean on recharacterisation. In cross-border transactions care should be taken to assess this issue in all relevant jurisdictions, including, for example, the jurisdiction of the incorporation of the SPV. Insurance laws tend to be of public order and therefore a simple choice of a particular law as the governing law in the documentation will not side-step this issue.

So far, the lack of detailed guidelines by either regulators or courts in relevant jurisdictions has not affected the volume and further evolution of this market. On the contrary, the synthetic market has shown itself to be resilient.

Transfer of beneficial ownership

[3.440] It could be argued that the transfer of credit risk in a synthetic securitisation largely resembles the transfer of the entire beneficial ownership of the reference portfolio. This is also a form of, albeit different, recharacterisation.[74] This is not commonly seen as a valid argument, as the entire beneficial ownership comprises more than the simple credit risk transfer. Most importantly, the transfer of credit risk does not involve market risk.[75] This issue too can be addressed by performing a (partial) due diligence on the reference portfolio. In that due diligence, it is verified that the terms and conditions of the underlying assets do not prohibit the transfer of the beneficial ownership. On a side issue, the transfer of economic interest might have tax effects as well.

Bond or loan

[3.450] In the recent US *Caiola case*[76] the question was discussed whether equity derivatives would qualify as securities under US securities laws. While the matter specifically related to equity, rather than credit, derivatives, the court focused its analysis on "synthetic transactions". It defined a synthetic transaction as "a contractual agreement between two counterparties, usually an investor and a bank, that seeks to economically replicate the ownership and physical trading of shares and options". Credit derivatives and synthetic securitisations intend to mimic the ownership and trading of (mostly) bonds and loans. If the court were to find that equity derivatives constituted securities, then this might have a bearing on the recharacterisation of credit derivatives as well.

The district court found that equity derivatives did not constitute securities. On appeal this judgment was overturned. However, the appeal court arrived at that conclusion by distinguishing between and analysing separately the two distinct tools used in Caiola's synthetic options (cash-settled OTC options and equity swaps). The judgment does not seem to affect credit derivatives or synthetic securitisations.[77]

Confidentiality

Portfolio disclosure
[3.460] A third legal consideration relates to the duty of confidentiality that a banker has towards his borrowers. The originating bank will usually be prohibited from divulging the names of the underlying portfolio being securitised, while on the other hand investors are looking for in-depth information on the reference portfolio in order to make a proper assessment of the risk involved.

In some cases, this issue may be overcome by simply discussing with the relevant borrower and obtaining the required consent. For instance, one of the first major synthetic structures, Bistro, originated by JP Morgan, contained a complete list of the pool of underlying reference assets. This option, however, will not always be available to the originator, either because of the feared effect on the business relationship or because the local jurisdiction does not allow the parties to contract out of this duty of confidentiality.

The disclosure not only relates to the name of the reference entities, but also to facts and circumstances that constitute a credit event. Solely relying on the concept of publicly available information would put the buyer in a delicate position to prove a credit event has occurred. The buyer would be prohibited from disclosing material facts known only to it and its client (the reference entity). In addition, it could take a long time before such facts would come out into the public domain (if at all). That would raise the prospect that the protection under the credit default swap has elapsed, while circumstances constituting a credit event have occurred.[78]

To accommodate the seller's concerns, reliance on publicly available information is usually combined with confirmation of the occurrence of the credit event by an independent third party, such as an accountant (obviously a different accountant to the originator's). Any relevant information would be disclosed to that party only for the purposes of determining whether a credit event has occurred. In a number of European transactions originators have taken the step to disclose the trust agreement almost entirely.

Blind pools
[3.470] To overcome concerns by investors in blind pools, the originator typically provides substantial information about the portfolio as a whole

(portfolio characteristics). This information includes the country of origination, as well as industry classification and information on the rating of the reference obligations and their respective maturity. This information allows investors to properly assess the risk involved in the purchase of the notes.

Disclosure of reference entities
[3.480] Given the strict nature of the banker's duty of confidentiality, the noteholders are usually bound in the documentation that they will not be entitled to receive or require information as to the identity of the reference entities or the reference obligations concerned. The list of reference entities is only disclosed to the rating agencies, the trustee and the SPV.

Levels of disclosure
[3.490] An interesting issue is whether an originator is allowed to divulge different levels of information to prospective noteholders. As a general rule, the originator as well as its managers would have to treat each noteholder equally. In practice, however, things may be different. A prospective client who is willing to invest in a large portion of the AAA notes may be demanding more information, while, on the other hand, an originator may be inclined to disclose more information to a party which is interested in a share in the equity note (as the retention of the equity note would be a significant burden on the originator from a regulatory capital point of view).

It is difficult to ascertain whether the obligation to treat each noteholder equally is actually completely met. In the course of road shows, including one-on-one presentations, it will not always be easy to maintain that same level of information. From a legal point of view, such an issue might be prevented by entering into different credit linked notes with respect to separate classes of the notes for that matter, with regard to separate investors. That might also allow the terms of the note to be amended to accommodate investors' requests. It is emphasised that this analysis is likely to be different in different jurisdictions.

There may be not be as strong an incentive for the originating bank, where it continues to hold the underlying asset, rather than transferring it to an SPV, to continue to use its best efforts and its client relationship to prevent a credit event from occurring. After all, upon a credit event occurring, it will receive a credit protection payment under the credit default swap. This "moral hazard" can be alleviated by requiring the bank to retain (a portion of) the equity note (and possibly mezzanine notes as well) and trap cash flow, such as excess spread within the structure.[79]

Issuance to retail investors

Retail investors: disclosure
[3.500] Recently several synthetic transactions have targeted retail investors, either in a full retail offering or in combination with an offering to sophisticated investors. Two examples are the Nexus Bonds and Hy-Fi (in Australia and New Zealand) and Robeco VII (in Europe). While these transactions highlight a potential extra market for CDOs, they do raise various legal concerns. In particular, the sponsors need to carefully address any increased disclosure obligations to avoid prospectus liability. A related matter is that the offering of very sophisticated notes to retail investors entails a potential reputation risk.

Across jurisdictions, lead managers of a securities offering are obliged to provide investors with all information they would reasonably come to expect in order to make an informed assessment of the rights and liabilities and other particulars of the securities being offered, as well as of the financial position of the issuer (although the latter seems less relevant if the issuer is an SPV). If the securities are to be listed, this information is usually contained in a prospectus memorandum. If a prospectus does not contain such information, or is otherwise deemed misleading, that could expose the lead manager to civil liability.[80] This is obviously a concern that applies to any offering of complex products. Current transactions tend to go an extra mile to make investors understand the underlying risks in synthetic transactions, eg by including an analysis and table of how many credit events a structure can withstand before the first loss is consumed and debt investors are hit.[81]

Retail investors: risks
[3.510] In applying this analysis to synthetic securitisations, the sponsor and lead managers must ensure that retail investors fully understand the risks of investing in credit linked notes and thus the nature of the credit derivative used. Or, as one prospectus puts it: investment in the (credit linked) notes is only suitable for investors who are highly sophisticated, willing to take considerable risks and able to determine for themselves the risk of an investment linked, in part, to the credit performance of the reference entities and who can absorb a partial or complete loss of principal and interest.[82] Explaining the details of synthetics to retail investors simply put seems quite a challenge.

In addition, an assessment should be made of the way a court would interpret the relevant law if a retail investor cried foul. Generally, a court would most likely be sympathetic to any claims of individuals put up against the sophistication of the originators. Relevant statutes might even be interpreted contra preferentem.

Furthermore, issuing a complicated structure such as a synthetic transaction to retail investors carries reputation risk. In this respect, a comparison may be drawn to the issuance of share leases to retail investors in the Netherlands.

> **Legio Lease**
>
> In Legio Lease retail investors were encouraged to borrow funds, which were subsequently invested in the share market. It was a successful product, aggressively marketed in a booming market. When the market went sour investors incurred significant losses as well as a debt. This led to class actions, in which investors alleged they were not properly informed of the underlying risks.
>
> Although so far no wrongdoing has been confirmed in court, the matter has been in the public eye since April 2002, prompting the local financial market supervisor to launch an investigation and the matter to be discussed in parliament.[83]

Share leases (and the share lease securitisations built on it) are not synthetic securitisations. However, this case does emphasise the reputation risk that, in a nightmare scenario, may be attached to offering complex products to retail investors. It underscores that if notes in, for instance, a synthetic CDO are offered to retail investors, careful scrutiny of the relevant consumer legislation is essential. Disclosure requirements must be balanced against the marketing potential of an increased investor base. That is probably why only few banks so far have cast this die.

Capita selecta

Other legal issues: overview

[3.520] From a legal point of view, several other issues merit attention. These include the diminished relevance of set-off in synthetic securitisations (see **[3.530]**), redemption of the notes (see **[3.540]**), profit roaming (see **[3.550]**) and security (see **[3.560]**).

The Schedule to the ISDA Master Agreement is different in a structured finance transaction than in a regular inter-bank deal. This is further discussed in Ch 4, which covers arbitrage synthetics.

Set off

[3.530] In true sale securitisation set off is usually a matter of consideration. In general terms, the true sale may affect the rights of the borrower of the originating bank to set off any claim on that originating bank against its debt to the SPV. The risk of set off is particularly relevant in true sale securitisation after the bankruptcy of the originator.[84] However, a synthetic transaction will provide for the redemption of the notes upon the originator's insolvency. This element is an advantage in synthetic structure, as it is generally difficult to obtain a clean legal opinion on the enforceability of the waiver by the borrowers of their rights in respect of set off after the bankruptcy of the originator.[85]

Set off in traditional securitisation is built upon the premise that the underlying borrower has a legal relationship with the originator. The originator sells to an SPV the assets arising out of that relationship. In a synthetic securitisation, however, there is not necessarily such an underlying legal relationship. The assets are not sold to an SPV, but solely the credit risk thereof.

Termination of the synthetic deal after the insolvency of the originator also eliminates the issue of proceeds from the securitised assets being trapped in the originator's estate. In that scenario, the SPV may not be able to service the interest on the notes on time, exposing investors to liquidity risk.

Redemption events

[3.540] The redemption events of the credit linked notes usually are not all the same as those used in true sale securitisations. Mandatory redemption events common to both transactions include:
- failure by the SPV to make a payment when due under the notes;
- failure to comply with a material obligation under the trust deed;
- the trustee's interest in the security failing to be valid and enforceable; and
- the SPV being subject to bankruptcy or a similar proceeding.

Apart from termination risk, the conditions of the notes commonly provide for early redemption events, which are not common in true sale transactions. This implies that specific risks of the originating bank are passed through to the investors. Regulatory and tax changes are common. This allows the bank to redeem the notes if, for example, the costs of the transaction would be adversely affected as a result of the introduction of new capital adequacy rules under the proposed Basel II accord. In a true sale transaction, however, early termination is usually limited to a call by the issuer. Not calling the option to redeem the notes would expose the originator to increased interest rates ("step up").

In addition, documentation usually provides for a "clean sweep". Under a clean sweep, the swap counterparty is entitled to redeem the notes in full once the aggregate principal balance of the outstanding notes is less than, for example, 10% (or recently, 15%) of the initial principal balance. And, as in traditional securitisations, the documentation may provide that the notes can be redeemed in full after a specific non-call period.

Profits

[3.550] In true sale transactions particular attention must be paid to how profits, if any, are roamed from the SPV, but this is much less of an issue from a legal perspective in synthetic transactions. In a true sale transaction, this is usually done by including a deferred purchase price for the notes. The drafting should address any concerns over fraudulent conveyance. Another method is to increase the servicing fees. In a synthetic transaction there is neither a sale contract nor a servicing agreement. Within the framework of a synthetic CDO it is not easily conceivable that a creditor of the originator would allege the credit default swap between such originator and the SPV should be a case of fraudulent conveyance. And even if it did, it would require particular sophistication to prove that this was the case.

Insolvency considerations

[3.560] A discussion of the legal issues in synthetic securitisation is not complete without briefly mentioning the effect of the *Enterprise Act 2002* (Cth) on securitisation generally. This Act limits the ability of an originator to call upon an administrator to manage the affairs of the SPV on its behalf. Instead, it is now more likely that receivers will play a part in the structured transactions. Fortunately, this prospect seems limited to during the life of the transaction itself, due to an exemption for securitisation transactions. It has been argued that there is an effect, however, on the warehousing of assets for the purpose of securitisation.[86]

REGULATORY ASPECTS

Limited current guidance

[3.570] In balance sheet deals the main objective is the reduction of regulatory capital. Some regulators are more advanced than others in terms of providing guidance to the market by issuing regulations on capital relief for synthetic securitisations. Generally, the capital adequacy treatment of synthetic securitisation is based upon that of credit derivatives.[87] With the advent of Basel II, a number of regulators have embarked upon a consultation to put in place regulations specifically aimed at synthetic securitisations or at updating existing regimes.[88]

In several jurisdictions, regulators have recently put forward guidelines or prospective regulations for consultation with the finance industry. These include the relevant regulators in Australia, the UK and the US.[89]

Capital adequacy rules applied

[3.580] This part of the chapter addresses how the current regime under Basel I is applied to synthetic securitisation. It distinguishes between the capital relief that is sought by means of entering into a credit default swap with the SPV, on the one hand, and a credit default swap with a super senior investor, on the other.

The originator can obtain substantial, if not complete, capital relief in respect of the credit risk that is transferred to the SPV (and then from the SPV to investors by the issue of credit linked notes). This capital relief is not granted on the basis of the fact that the credit linked notes are cash collateralised (as that only applies to the SPV). It is granted because the obligations of the SPV to the originator under the credit default swap (ie the contingent obligation of the SPV to pay the settlement amount to the originator) have been fully collateralised by means of AAA collateral. If this is eligible AAA collateral, this amounts to zero risk weighting, for instance, in the case of several government bonds. Alternatively, other types of AAA collateral may be and are used, such as AAA structured finance securities. The regulator may require an additional haircut as a pre-condition for granting capital relief.

It is important to note that these same obligations of the SPV to the originator are (almost) at the very top of the priority of payment throughout the life of the transaction.[90] If the proceeds of the notes are (partially) used to deposit with a deposit bank, then the risk weight will be increased to reflect the increased credit risk that the originator bears on the deposit bank, ie if that deposit bank is another bank. When the deposit bank is in fact the originator, then the obligations of the SPV are fully collateralised and a zero risk weighting can apply.

Capital relief by risk transfer to super senior investor

[3.590] The investor in a super senior piece is usually a reinsurance company or a monoline insurer. From a practical point of view, the super senior investor is often, but not necessarily, a single entity. This facilitates the negotiation process. If the credit default swap were entered into by the originating bank and the insurer directly, the obligation of that insurer under the swap would carry the full 100% risk weight for corporates. This full risk weighting can be substantially reduced with additional structuring. The originating bank may then enter into a mirror credit default swap with another OECD bank, which acts as go-between. This enables the originating bank to reduce its regulatory risk charge to 20% instead. The intermediary OECD bank could reduce its applicable risk weight by marking to market the obligation of the super senior investor. This could substantially reduce the capital charge.[91] Of course, the originating bank could mark its exposure to market as well to sidestep this issue.

The objective to obtain regulatory capital relief can be explained as follows.[92] Under current BIS rules all corporate debt carries an identical risk weight of 100%.[93] Higher-rated but lower-yielding corporate loans require the same amount of capital to be held as lower-rated but higher-yielding loans. By entering into a true sale securitisation, a bank can remove these highly rated assets from its balance sheet and obtain full regulatory capital relief and use the funds to increase its return on equity. In a synthetic securitisation, the credit risk of such assets is transferred to investors.

On the other hand, it is more expensive for an originating bank to buy credit protection in unfunded form than in funded form. If a bank purchases protection in unfunded form, it will not obtain funds up front. For that reason it will need to retain capital against its counterparty's obligation to make the contingent payment in its capacity of seller of protection. If the protection is purchased in funded form, this obligation is collateralised and carries a zero percent solvency risk weight. The cost of retaining capital for the unfunded piece will be reflected in a lower spread being offered to the investor in that unfunded tranche.

The pricing of the super senior tranche may contain a "premium" to account for the fact that the super senior counterparty, if it is an OECD bank, is more or less "lending" its capability to get capital relief to the originator. The super senior counterparty (if a bank) may be interested for arbitrage reasons. It may be able to buy credit protection in the market at a rate more favourable than it has sold to the originator. One opportunity would be for the OECD bank to repackage the super senior risk in a new CDO and tranche it.

Equity note

Any equity note (also referred to as *first loss piece* retained by the originator, whether or not issued in funded form) will have to be deducted from capital in its entirety.[94]

Basel II and synthetic securitisations

[3.600] The blueprint for the revised Basel Accord[95] contains specific operational requirements for synthetic securitisations, which apply on top of the requirements for credit derivatives discussed in Ch 2. The use of credit derivatives for hedging the underlying exposure may be recognised for capital purposes only if these requirements are met.

Operational requirements

The requirements relate to the collateral, the transfer of credit risk and certain prohibited provisions. The collateral must be "eligible financial collateral", which includes cash and investment grade securities issued by banks as well as other high rated securities (eg structured finance securities). In addition, the bank must transfer "significant" credit risk associated with the underlying exposure to third parties. The blueprint does not provide specific guidance as to what "significant" credit risk transfer is, apart from the requirements for credit derivatives, such as the necessary credit events.

The blueprint does specify certain provisions that are not acceptable for capital relief purposes. Specifically mentioned are:
- clauses that materially limit the credit protection or credit risk transference (eg significant materiality thresholds below which credit protection is deemed not to be triggered even if a credit event occurs or those that would allow for the termination of the protection due to deterioration in the credit quality of the underlying exposures);
- clauses that require the originating bank to alter the underlying exposures such that it can result in improvements to the pool's weighted average credit quality;
- clauses that increase the bankers' cost of credit protection in response to deterioration in the pool's quality;
- clauses that increase the yield payable to parties other than the originating banks, such as investors or third party providers of credit enhancement in response to a deterioration in the credit quality of the underlying pool; and
- clauses that provide for increases in a retained first loss position or credit enhancement provided by the originating bank after the transaction's inception.

Also, it is a requirement that an opinion be obtained from a qualified legal counsel that confirms the enforceability of the contracts in all relevant jurisdictions. Notwithstanding the above, the ultimate decision on what constitutes "significant" credit risk transfer is in the hands of the local supervisor.

Attractive as they may seem, hard and fast rules are not always easy to apply. In particular, the type of underlying asset, the credit risk of which is hedged through a synthetic transaction, may necessitate a more lenient regulatory approach. For instance, credit events may require modification in respect of specific assets, such as highly volatile loans as opposed to mortgage receivables, or simply be unfit, in the case of structured finance securities. In the former, significant credit risk transfer may be achieved even if the grace period is substantially longer (and perhaps longer than in the underlying documentation). In the latter case, the time involved in cash settlement may need to be stretched in order to obtain a reliable market value.

Risk weights
[3.610] The proposed revised Basel Accord will have a significant impact on the risk weights for investing in securitisation tranches. As a matter of fact, a bank would be worse off in terms of risk weights if it held all the notes in a securitisation it originated itself. Securitisation treatment is

not neutral under the revised rules. As a result, the gap for regulatory capital arbitrage has tightened. Alternatively, the finetuning of risk weights to the actual level of risk involved creates arbitrage opportunity to involve parties other than banks.[96]

External credit assessment	AAA to AA-	A+ to AA-	BBB+ to BBB-	BB+ to BB-	B+ and below and unrated
Risk weight	20%	50%	100%	350%	Deduction

Super senior swaps

[3.620] Investing in a super senior swap carries a 20% risk weight under the proposed regime, which does not distinguish between senior and super senior tranches.[97] As a result, this proposal is controversial. Recently, a global coalition of industry organisations has criticised it as discriminating synthetic securitisations against cash transactions. The coalition argues that the proposals for risk weighting for super senior tranches do not reflect the superior quality of such tranches as compared with senior tranches below the super senior tranches.[98]

Interestingly, one effect of the implementation of the Basel II Accord might be that super senior tranches lose their appeal in securitisations generally. In the US, regulators have come to recognise that the risk profile of super senior swaps is at last equal to that of a AAA tranche, which is subordinated to that super senior swap. Under the current regime an originator purchasing protection on a reference portfolio from a super senior investor, typically a monoline insurer, would have to go to great lengths to lower the 100% risk weighting applied to non-OECD banks. In effect, it would have to mark to market the value of the credit default portfolio swap, posing a considerable burden on its operations. Instead, once regulators recognise that the risk profile of a super senior tranche is akin to that of a AAA note, originators can obtain that 20% risk weighting instantly, without the need to enter into a super senior credit default swap.[99]

However, it should be emphasised that the relevant US regulations contain several preconditions to granting the full capital relief.[100] In fact, these regulations go even further, as they would render super senior swaps obsolete. The regulators recognise that since the risk involved is so small, it does not require a 20% risk weighting. This would relieve the originator from having to pay the protection premium to the (typically) monoline insurer. Although this premium is relatively small in terms of basis points, it adds up to a substantial amount of money given the large percentage of the portfolio it reflects (between 70 and 90%).

A related issue is that, over the last few years, synthetic securitisation has effectively transferred substantial parts of credit risk away from the banking industry to the insurance industry. Although this may have been a positive thing for the banking industry in general, regulators have expressed concern about this transfer of credit risk to an industry they perceived as being less regulated than the banking industry.[101]

Implementation "avant la lettre"
[3.630] Recently an increasing number of regulators have updated or have started the process of consulting with the industry in order to update the regulatory requirements for synthetic securitisation. While recognising the importance of providing guidance for an innovative and new product, care should be taken to maintain a global level playing field as much as possible.[102]

SYNTHETICS: DEVELOPMENTS AND CONCLUSION

Evolution of synthetic market
[3.640] The synthetic market continues to evolve. In documentation, the recent publication of the 2003 Definitions has eliminated a number of uncertainties in the market for credit default swaps and, by reference, in the market for synthetic securitisations. It is expected that market participants will in the near future work towards further standardisation of documentation for portfolio transactions, such as synthetic securitisations. Such standardisation would be a major accomplishment and further boost investor confidence in this relatively new market.

Trend towards managed synthetics
[3.650] A major development in the market is the continuing trend from static structures towards more managed synthetic securitisations. In managed structures a separate collateral manager is engaged, which may have varying degrees of freedom in managing the collateral. It may only be entitled to replenish (part of) the portfolio upon amortisation or prepayment during a predefined replenishment period. Alternatively, its management rights may be limited to a small "bucket" or it may be entitled to actively transfer assets in and out of the portfolio during the full life of the transaction. The latter form of managed structure raises additional concerns about the qualifications of the collateral manager. Nevertheless, this structure is proving more popular. The specific issues associated with this particular kind of synthetic securitisation are addressed in Ch 4.

Referenced assets
[3.660] Another important development is the trend to include or diversify the referenced assets in synthetic securitisations.[103] Increasingly, balance sheet synthetic deals reference other assets, eg mortgage receivables. This growth is particularly fostered by the German market, where synthetic

securitisation is very popular.[104] Furthermore, the market has evolved to include the repackaging of structured finance assets, such as ABS, RMBS, CMBS and CDOs, revolving credit facilities and letters of credit, offering increased diversification.

A related theme is the growing number of hybrid deals.[105] In such a deal, cash flow and synthetic elements are combined. To some extent the cash flow generated by underlying assets does help to pay for the interest on the notes (Jazz, Robeco VII). These deals are discussed in more detail in Ch 4.

Synthetic market: future developments
[3.670] Further evolution of the balance sheet synthetic market depends to a significant degree upon the final outcome of the Basel II negotiations. The current Basel Accord contains very little guidance on the treatment of securitisations. The latest proposals[106] make good that omission in two respects. First, they stipulate risk weights for securitisation exposure which is much more tailored to the credit risk ratings of the underlying asset. Secondly, the proposals detail a number of operational requirements for synthetic (as well as traditional) securitisation. Further monitoring of the negotiations is required, to ensure that regulators guide, rather than obstruct, market growth and development.

Finally, the emergence of the covered bond market as an alternative to (synthetic) securitisation is also noteworthy. These structures do not achieve capital relief, however, so at this stage this development appears more a complement than a threat to the (synthetic) securitisation market.[107]

Synthetics benefits: a summary
[3.680] Synthetic securitisations offer substantial benefit over traditional structures: there is more choice in securitisable assets, as well as an increased inherent flexibility. Among the attractions to originators and investors alike is the capacity to tailor the risk to be transferred. This market has the potential to boom. Key to the further development of this market is the understanding of credit derivatives technology and, in particular, the credit derivatives definitions.

In this chapter some of the most significant issues in the structuring and documentation of synthetic securitisation have been addressed. It is intended that by familiarising market participants with synthetic securitisations, the growth of this market can be enhanced.

CASE STUDIES

Case studies: overview

[3.690] To facilitate the synthetic securitisation of various asset classes, several case studies are included. Three questions are addressed in each study:

- Which credit events are used and how are they defined?
- What are the conditions to settlement; and?
- What kind of settlement method is used and how is it detailed?

The asset classes described are:

- corporate loans (see **[3.700]**);
- industry-specific corporate loans (see **[3.710]**);
- personal loans (see **[3.720]**);
- residential mortgage loans (see **[3.730]**).

Corporate loans

[3.700] As the 2003 Definitions are most suited for loans as reference obligations, the synthetic securitisation of corporate loans usually does not require amending. However, modifications may be required depending on the type of loan. Is it secured, unsecured, term or revolving?

The credit events found in synthetic securitisations of corporate loans are primarily bankruptcy and failure to pay. The definition of "failure to pay" is usually modified as a failure to pay by the reference entity of the reference obligation for an amount not less than the lower/the higher of either a lump sum, usually US$1,000,000 (or its equivalent in any other eligible currency), or a percentage (usually 2) of the total size of the reference obligation.

The conditions to settlement typically include the delivery of a credit event notice, as well as a notice of publicly available information. In most transactions, an independent expert, eg an accountant, would be expected to confirm that the reference obligation (with respect to which the credit event occurred) satisfied all eligibility criteria and servicing guidelines at the time of its inclusion in the reference portfolio. As additional comfort, the auditor will usually also verify on an annual basis that the reference portfolio meets the portfolio requirements. If the reference obligation is inserted after the last annual audit, then the auditor would be expected to verify that the inclusion of that reference obligation also met the relevant criteria.

The settlement method in balance sheet synthetic securitisations referencing corporate loans is typically cash settlement, based on market valuation. The details of the market valuation process are usually modified from the standard procedure outlined in the 2003 Definitions. Some transactions have sought to alleviate investor concern regarding the amount of the cash settlement amount by combining market valuation by a bidding process and valuation by independent appraisers or accountants. Other transactions preset the cash settlement amount at an estimated loss, which figure is subsequently corrected depending on the amount of actual recovery. This may be attractive for originators as this mechanism avoids waiting periods. It does, however, complicate calculations down the line.

Particular issues for investors to verify include the start of the first valuation period (usually more than 30 business days after the occurrence of a credit event), the number of eligible dealers and any re-runs of the valuation process. In addition, some transactions may include as extra protection for investors a minimum value that a bid must have in order for it to be taken into account in the valuation process. This may be particularly relevant if a minimum number of bids within a round must be obtained in order for the market value to be established. Typical back-up methods of valuation include a reference to one of the standard valuation processes referenced in the 2003 Definitions or, alternatively, the valuation of the reference obligation by an independent appraiser.

Corporate loans: industry-specific

[3.710] Over the last few years several synthetic collateralised loan obligations (CLOs) that reference industry specific corporate loans, particularly in the shipping and aircraft industry, have been closed. Generally, the transport sector is characterised as substantially more volatile than other industries. This is usually reflected in a tighter definition of the credit events. Though typically the credit events still are bankruptcy and failure to pay, the latter is substantially modified from its standard definition in the 2003 Definitions. Usually, failure to pay is defined in the same way as in comparable synthetic CLOs. However, the increased volatility may be, but is not necessarily, reflected in the timing associated with a failure to pay. To accommodate for the increased volatility, a reference obligation may be required to be in arrears for as long as 180 days on top of the underlying grace period in the relevant contract.

As with other corporate loans synthetically securitised, the settlement method is cash settlement. The cash settlement amount is usually based upon realised losses calculated through a recovery procedure. Obviously, the work-out of a reference obligation of this kind would involve selling a relevant vessel or aircraft. Though the originator may have experience with that procedure, it tends to be a protracted procedure, which could take more than a year. In addition, the international context could give rise to insolvency and other legal issues.

In order to alleviate any investor concern, these transactions may incorporate a cut-off date. If the recovery process is not completed by that specific time, then a valuation process is relied on. This valuation process may be started at the time of the occurrence of a credit event so that it could be finalised by the cut-off date (eg 12 months after the occurrence of a credit event). In that case, loss is calculated as the outstanding debt minus the appraisal value.

If unsecured, rather than secured, loans are included in the portfolio, then the loss calculation may be preset, based upon standard loss assumptions.

Residential mortgages

[3.720] The common credit events used in balance sheet synthetic securitisations of residential mortgages are bankruptcy and failure to pay. Typically, the credit event failure to pay is amended from the standard definition in the 2003 Definitions, as a failure by a reference entity to make a payment of interest or principal on a reference claim within a specific number of days (eg 90) after the due date for a specified threshold amount (eg not less than US$ 5,000 or its equivalent in any other currency).

The conditions to settlement are modified for this asset class. They typically include the following conditions: finalising the foreclosure process in accordance with the foreclosure guidelines of the originator, notification of an independent auditor of the occurrence of the credit event and the performance of a loss audit, which includes a review of the relevant reference obligation and its compliance with eligibility criteria and servicing principles.

The common settlement method is cash settlement, based upon the actual recovery method. In terms of residential mortgages this concept is usually translated into the calculation of realised losses. This is calculated as the notional of the initial mortgage loan minus (principal payments plus recoveries). Transactions may differentiate whether the investor's risk is limited to the principal only or to interest and penalties as well. For example, some transactions may define "realised losses" as the principal foregone and unpaid at the end of the collection period. Whenever interest and penalties may be part of the cash settlement amount, further analysis of the underlying standard mortgage documentation is advised.

Generally, the work-out of residential mortgages is linked to established servicing and recovery procedures, which the originator may have outsourced to a specialist third party. However, the time involved in the recovery period may result in some reference obligations not being settled by final redemption. In that case, the loss on the reference obligation is usually determined in a valuation process based upon independent valuation experts. Alternatively, transactions may defer repayment of the relevant classes of notes (eg by 12 months) to be able to rely entirely on the recovery period. This additional comfort for investors must be balanced against a potential deferral in the repayment of any of the notes.

Personal loans

[3.730] A relatively recent trend is the synthetics securitisation of personal loans, such as consumer loans, leasing contracts and unsecured home loans.

The analysis is largely similar to that of mortgage receivables. The common credit events are bankruptcy and failure to pay. The latter is defined as the failure by a reference entity to make any payments due under the reference obligation, eg 90 consecutive days. Alternative definitions have been used referencing the number of unpaid instalments (not necessarily consecutive) instead of the number of days.

The conditions to settlement typically include the delivery of a credit event notice and the verification by an independent accountant that a credit event has occurred. Also, the rule of an independent auditor may be similar to that with respect to mortgage receivables.

The applicable settlement method is cash settlement, based upon actual recovery. The analysis is mostly similar to that of mortgage receivables. However, some transactions include interest and penalties payable by reference entities into account in the calculation of loss. In that case, a detailed analysis of the underlying standard documentation would be required to make a full assessment of the potential loss.

1. Basel Committee on Banking Supervision, *Consultative Document, The New Basel Capital Accord* (Bank of International Settlement, April 2003) No 503.
2. "Glossary of Securitisation Terms" (Standard & Poor's, June 2003).
3. London's market share was reported to be 53% of the global market by the end of 2002: "European CDO Transactions Embrace Synthetic Technology" (Standard & Poor's, 3 October 2002).
4. "2002 Review and 2003 Outlook: Collateralised Debt Obligations in Europe" (Special Report, Moody's, 21 January 2003). Standard & Poor's estimates are a bit more conservative, stating that 60% of public issuance in the CDO market was completed in synthetic form: see "European CDO Transactions Embrace Synthetic Technology" (3 October 2002) and "Credit Derivatives Find Favor in Explosive European CDO Market" (21 October 2002). Fitch's estimates are in between; they suggested at a recent conference that 75% of CDO transactions in Europe were effected in synthetic form.
5. "2002 US CDO Review/2003 Preview" (Special Report, Moody's, 7 February 2003). For example, Bank of America structured Residential Finance, a jumbo $17.2 billion USD Synthetic RMBS deal. See also O'Connor CM, "Synthetic CDOs Gain Market Share in the US", *Asset Securitization Report*, 28 July 2003, 2003 WL 7469592, which references estimates from JP Morgan Securities.
6. Refer, for instance, to Mizuho Corporate Bank's US $10.3 billion synthetic CDO and ALCO 1, a SGD 2.8 billion balance sheet synthetic structure undertaken by the Development Bank of Singapore, ASIA IG CDO and United Global Investment Grade CDO I and II.
7. "Asia's Securitisation Market Seen Shifting More Toward Synthetic CDOs" (Standard & Poor's, 23 July 2003), discussing Merilion CDO 1 as a classic synthetic CDO.
8. "Japanese Structured Finance Market: Master Trust Transactions a Highlight of 2Q" (Standard & Poor's, 7 August 2003).
9. Medallion 1999-1, Nexus Bonds (corporate loans), SMART 2002-1 (auto and equipment loans), PRISE (commercial property loans). See also Hall K and Stuart E, "Credit Risk Transfer Markets: An Australian Perspective", *Reserve Bank of Australia Bulletin* (May 2003) pp 55-62.
10. For instance, the Nexus transaction, allegedly one of the first synthetic securitisations to do so.
11. "Credit-linked Notes – A World of Opportunities for Australian Investors" (Standard & Poor's, July 2003) and "RMBS, CDO Activity Lead Australian Securitization Issuance Growth in 2003" (Standard & Poor's, 16 July 2003).
12. In Australia, assignments of bank loans are typically effected via "Clayton's contracts" in equity, to avoid the imposition of ad valorem stamp duty. A "Clayton's contract" is a contract effected by written offer (the bank offers to sell specified loans to the issuer) and acceptance by conduct (the offer may only be accepted by the issuer paying the consideration for the transfer). Loans are not dutiable property under s 11 of the *Duties Act 1997* (NSW). Further, s 284(1) exempts "loan-backed securities" from stamp duty and gives the Commissioner the discretion to exempt the underlying transactions leading to the establishment of a loan-backed securitisation program. However, the other States and Territories do not all have an equivalent to s 284(1), nor do all those jurisdictions exclude transfers of loans from duty. In addition, it is unlikely (but not entirely free from doubt) whether Clayton's contracts are consistent with statutory provisions such as s 23C(1)(c) of the *Conveyancing Act 1919* (NSW), which require dispositions of equitable interests subsisting at the time of disposition to be made in writing by the assignor. It is arguable that since the assignment effects a division of the equitable estate in the loan from the legal title to the loan, there is at the time of assignment no subsisting equitable interest in the loan and, accordingly, s 23C(1)(c) and the corresponding provisions in other States do not apply.
13. An assignment in breach of an anti-assignment prohibition or a provision requiring the prior consent of the underlying borrower may be void: *Linden Gardens Trust Ltd v Lenesta Sludge Disposals Ltd* [1994] 1 AC 85; *Don King Productions Inc v Warren* [1999] 3 WLR 276. The result depends upon the construction of the provision; if it is a warranty, the sole remedy for the breach will be damages: *Anning v Anning* (1907) 4 CLR 1049. See further McCormack G, "Debts and Non-Assignment Clauses" [1999] JBL 422.
14. "Synthetic CDOs: European Credit Risk Transfer 'à la Carte'" (Moody's, 27 July 2000).
15. Refer, for instance, to ABN Amro's Amstel program (Amstel 2001-1 and 2), jumbo synthetic offerings of corporate loans originated in a number of different jurisdictions.

[16] The obvious exception is in managed synthetic transactions, although in those particular transactions a separate collateral manager is engaged.

[17] "Credit Considerations of Synthetic Mortgage-backed Securitisations in Europe" (Special Report, Moody's, 20 November 2002).

[18] For a succinct overview see Lyons JD, "AFMA Issues Paper on Credit Derivatives" p 20, http://www.afma.com.au viewed June 2003.

[19] This is particularly true if the mechanism of a credit default swap is used, as that only transfers credit risk. Alternatively, total return swaps can be employed to transfer the full economic effect of an underlying asset. In the latter case, synthetic securitisations may be employed to manage the balance sheet.

[20] APRA AGN 112.1, item 23; Financial Services Authority, *Interim Prudential Source Book for Banks,* Ch CD, para 5.2, sub 5.

[21] While the focus of this chapter is on the potential of synthetic securitisation for banks and financial institutions, the credit risk management aspects may offer substantial opportunity to corporates as well, by investing in this product or "reverse engineering" a synthetic transaction.

[22] "Global Rating Criteria for Synthetic CDOs" (Fitch Ratings, 5 September 2002); "Global Rating Criteria for Collateralised Debt Obligations" (Fitch Ratings, 14 July 2003); "Global Cash Flow and Synthetic CDO Criteria" (Standard and Poor's, 21 March 2002), "Criteria for Rating Synthetic CDO Transactions" (Standard & Poor's, September 2003); and "Moody's Approach to Rating Synthetic CDOs" (Moody's, 29 July 2003). See also Homer E, "Summer Reading: CDOs the Name, Rating's the Game", *Asset Securitization Report,* 21 July 2003, 2003 WL 7469572.

[23] "Criteria for Rating Synthetic CDO Transactions" (Standard & Poor's, September 2003), section 1, p 7.

[24] A third type of synthetic securitisation is the market value transaction. As that structure is not prevalent, it will not be further discussed in this publication.

[25] Or, as Moody's puts it: in a typical balance sheet synthetic structure, there is a sponsoring financial institution (the buyer of credit protection) that uses a credit default swap to remove credit exposure from its balance sheet while retaining ownership of the assets: "Moody's Approach to Rating Synthetic CDOs" (Moody's, 29 July 2003) p 2.

[26] The dividing line may not always be clear cut. Usually the assets to be securitised in an arbitrage transaction are, or recently have been, purchased in the open market, rather than taken from the originator's balance sheet. Standard & Poor's for instance treats a transaction as an arbitrage CDO where the assets are purchased directly by the securitisation vehicle from third-party market participants, or purchased from a financial institution that has itself purchased them from a third-party market participant in the previous three months and where the assets were always booked in that institution's trading book. See "Criteria Regarding Legal Opinions in the Context of CDOs" (Standard & Poor's, 12 May 2003).

[27] Financial Services Authority, *Interim Prudential Source Book for Banks,* Ch CD, para 5.7, no 20.

[28] Alternatively, a first to default or -*nth* to default structure could be used. In such a structure, when the *n*th reference entity experiences a credit event, the transaction will be settled and then terminated. Investing in this structure entails a leveraged position, with increased risks, but also increased yields. Refer to "Moody's Approach to Rating *n*th-to-default Basket Credit-linked Notes" (Special Report, Moody's, 17 April 2002). As to the regulatory regime, see Financial Services Authority, *Interim Prudential Source Book for Banks,* Ch CD, para 5.7, sub 19; see also AGN 112.4, no 27-28.

[29] For a more detailed discussion of credit derivatives, refer to the Chapter 2

[30] Henderson SK, "Synthetic Securitisation, Part 1: The Elements" (2001) 16 *Journal of International Banking and Financial Law* 404.

[31] For example, an adverse change in (tax) law.

[32] For a rating agency point of view, refer to "Synthetic Collateralised Debt Obligations and Credit-Linked Notes, A Ratings Perspective" (Standard & Poor's, 27 September 2001).

[33] Uwaifo E, "Key Issues in Structuring a Synthetic Securitisation, A European Perspective" (2001) 16 *Journal of International Banking and Financial Law* 30.

[34] Hyder I, "Collateralised Debt Obligations and the Role of Monoline Insurers", *Euromoney*

Handbook 2003, http://www.xlca.com/pdf/euromoneyhandbook2003/pdf viewed June 2003, p 38.

[35] See Henderson SK, "Mahonia: Purchase Contract or Loan, and Does it Matter?" (2003) 18 *Journal of International Banking and Financial Law* 47-51 and the public letter from Robert M Morgenthau to Alan Greenspan, dated 28 July 2003, outlining the structure of the Mahonia transactions.

[36] The topic of the (future) regulatory capital treatment of super senior swaps is further explored at **[3.620]**.

[37] The SPV will be a bankruptcy-remote vehicle and the transaction documentation will provide for the customary non-petition and limited purpose clause.

[38] This issue is further explored in Ch 4, which covers synthetic arbitrage transactions.

[39] This ceiling may be pierced, however, if the bank purchases separate collateral that is rated higher than itself and has that collateral pledged to a trustee in favour of the investors to protect their claims under the issued note.

[40] The effectiveness of a downgrade clause depends on the then current rating of the counterparty, the conditions that must be met on a threshold event and the time required to satisfy such conditions: see "Moody's Approach to Assessing Secondary Risks in Synthetic CDOs" (Special Report, Moody's) p 4.

[41] "Global Rating Criteria for Synthetic CDOs" (Fitch Ratings, 5 September 2002) p 9.

[42] See "Global Cash Flow and Synthetic CDO Criteria" (Standard & Poor's, 21 March 2002), Appendix D: Swap Agreement Criteria for CBO/CLO Transactions; see also Henderson SK, "Synthetic Securitisation, Part 3: Credit Risk of the Issuer and the ISDA Master Agreement" (2001) 16 *Journal of International Banking and Financial Law* 505-513.

[43] "Moody's Approach to Assessing Secondary Risks in Synthetic CDOs" (Moody's, 17 March 2003).

[44] "Global Rating Criteria for Synthetic CDOs" (Fitch Ratings, 5 September 2002) p 10.

[45] Standard & Poor's requires all of any repo counterparties, put option providers and liquidity providers to have a rating of at least A-1+. See "Criteria for Rating Synthetic CDO Transactions" (Standard & Poor's, September 2003), section 5, p 12.

[46] If the settlement currency is nonetheless different from the liability currency, then a regulator may reduce the amount of protection recognised for capital relief purposes. Refer to Financial Services Authority, *Interim Prudential Source Book for Banks*, Ch CD, para 5.5 (reduction by 8%); see also AGN 112.4, no. 36.

[47] Regulators tend not to be specific about the credit events that are required in order to have credit risk transfer recognised for regulatory capital relief purposes. Refer to Firth S, *Derivatives Law and Practice* (Sweet & Maxwell, 2003) at 16-234 and 16-235, submitting that the FSA's regulatory objectives would be achieved if the only credit events required were bankruptcy and failure to pay. This view is supported in practice. The vast majority of synthetic balance sheet securitisations in 2003 had only these two credit events.

[48] APRA letter dated September 4, 2003, regarding the revision to ADI Guidance Note: AGN 112.4 – Treatment of Credit Derivatives in the Banking Book, posted at http://www.apra.gov.au. The letter further specifies that APRA plans to review its position on restructuring as a required credit event.

[49] Section 4.8(d) of the 2003 Definitions.

[50] Section 3.7 of the 2003 Definitions.

[51] However, some basic risks remain as reporters tend to protect their sources.

[52] Refer to discussion of disclosure in the legal analysis at **[3.480]**.

[53] See ss 7.3 and 7.4 of the 2003 Definitions. If the cash settlement amount is not specified in the confirmation, then its calculation is based upon the difference between the reference price and the final price (expressed as a percentage of the notional amount).

[54] "Synthetic CDOs and Investment Grade Assets: Analytical and Structural Issues" (Special Report, Fitch Ratings, 13 December 2001) p 4.

[55] "Synthetic CDOs; European Credit Risk Transfer 'à la Carte'" (Special report, Moody's, 27 July 2000).

[56] Section 7.5 of the 2003 Definitions. In Verdi Synthetic, for instance, the standard ISDA procedures for obtaining quotes were amended to carve out bids below 30% to accommodate investors.

[57] This accountant would obviously not be the accountant of the originator, to avoid conflicts or interest arising.

[58] See "Credit Events in Global Synthetic CDOs 2002-2003" (Special Report, Fitch Ratings, 12 May 2003) p 7. Fitch identifies the following factors that contribute to higher recoveries: total number of bids, the length of the valuation process, the type of valuation method used, the type of valuation obligation and the origination location.

[59] "Moody's Approach to Rating Synthetic CDOs" (Moody's, 29 July 2003) p 16. Standard & Poor's ratings criteria also specify terms in cash settlement that transactions have to abide by. Examples include the quotation amount (between US$1 and 15 million) and the number of bids (at least five requested of which three should be obtained): see "Criteria for Rating Synthetic CDO Transactions" (Standard & Poor's, September 2003), section 2, p 8.

[60] For the sake of simplicity, the role of excess spread is not discussed here.

[61] See the discussion of managed arbitrage synthetic structures in Ch 4.

[62] The calculation agent has a number of additional obligations. See s 1.14 of the 2003 Definitions.

[63] Section 14 of the 2002 ISDA Master Agreement (definition of "close-out amount").

[64] The category "payment" is usually not accepted by rating agencies as a reference obligation category. This is because it includes all commercial contracts, including, for instance, trade receivables, which probably are not covered in the historical data of the rating agencies. Standard & Poor's, for example, does not accept "payment" or "borrowed money" as deliverable obligation categories, as it is difficult to establish a recovery value for anything else than bonds or loans.

[65] Depending on the insolvency law of the originator, this first pledge may cease or continue to exist (Germany). In the latter case, the enforcement proceeds from selling the collateral will be used to first pay the originator, which potentially could cause a loss for investors: "Credit Considerations of Synthetic Mortgage-backed Securitisations in Europe" (Special Report, Moody's, 20 November 2002) p 7.

[66] Of course SPVs used in any securitisation need to comply with the rating agencies' requirements for bankruptcy remoteness. See, for example, "Global Cash Flow and Synthetic CDO Criteria" (Standard & Poor's, 21 March 2002) pp 89-92. Other general issues involve (under US laws) substantive consolidation.

[67] For further information on the recharacterisation of traditional securitisations as disguised loans, refer to Schwarz SL, "Securitisation Post-Enron" 25 *Cardozo Law Review*; 2003 Symposium Issue on Threats to Secured Lending and Asset securitisation; and Henderson SK, "Mahonia: Purchase Contract or Loan, and Does it Matter?" (2003) 18 *Journal of International Banking and Financial Law* 47-51. It emerges from these articles that the collapse of Enron, and its use and abuse of special purpose vehicles to manipulate its balance sheet, has made it more likely that judges will use the "substance over form" approach over structured finances, particularly if the transaction is perceived to be manipulative in nature.

[68] Refer to the discussion of recharacterisation as an insurance contract at **[2.270]** – **[2.330]**. More generally, the recharacterisation approach in England is usually based upon *Welsh Development Agency v Export Finance Co Ltd* [1992] BCLC 148 and in Australia on *Sharrment Pty Ltd v Official Trustee in Bankruptcy* (1998) 18 FCR 449.

[69] In Australia, a person who conducts an "insurance business" without being authorised to do so by the Australian Prudential Regulation Authority will be subject to criminal penalties: *Insurance Act 1973* (Cth), ss 10(1) and 11.

[70] See Firth S, *Derivatives Law and Practice* (Sweet & Maxwell, 2003) at 16-031. Firth alerts to the fact that if the reference obligation will inevitably be held by the buyer (originator, for example, because it is not transferable) throughout the life of the transaction, an insurable interest may be found to exist.

[71] "Credit Considerations of Synthetic Mortgage-backed Securitisations in Europe" (Special Report, Moody's, 20 November 2002).

[72] Ali PU, "Unbundling Credit Risk: the Nature and Regulation of Credit Derivatives" (2000) 11 (No 2) *Journal of Banking and Finance Law and Practice* 73.

[73] Some comfort may be drawn from a US decision, *Caiola v Citibank NA* Second District NY 2002, 137 F Supp 2d 362, in which the court recognised that an equity swap replicated a secured loan to buy shares, but saw no grounds to requalify the equity swaps as securities.

74 Recharacterisation under English and Australian law typically concerns the recharacterisation of a sale (eg an assignment of loans from the bank to the securitisation vehicle) as an equitable mortgage or charge. If an assignment is recharacterised by a court as a mortgage or charge, the assignor will be taken to retain an equity of redemption in the securitised assets (as opposed to the entire equitable estate in those assets having been vested in the assignee via the assignment), with the result that the securitised assets will form part of the pool of assets available in an insolvency to the creditors of the assignor. See further Ali PU, *The Law of Secured Finance An International Survey of Security Interests over Personal Property* (Oxford University Press, 2002) pp 26-27; Schroeder JL, "A Repo Opera: How Criimi Mae got Repos Backwards" (2002) 76 Am Bankr LJ 565.

75 See Firth S, *Derivatives Law and Practice* (Sweet & Maxwell, 2003) at 16-071.

76 *Caiola v Citibank NA*, Court of Appeals, Second Circuit 2002, 295 F.3d312, appeal from 137 F Supp 2d 362 (SDNY). For a more general discussion on securities and swap agreements under US securities laws, see Gooch AC and Klein LB, *Documentation for Derivatives* (Vol 1, 4th ed, Euromoney Books, 2002) pp 135-176.

77 Along different lines: Henderson SK, "Mahonia: Purchase Contract or Loan, and Does it Matter?" (2003) 18 *Journal of International Banking and Financial Law* 47-48.

78 Firth S, *Derivatives Law and Practice* (Sweet & Maxwell, 2003) at 16-037.

79 Another moral hazard is in the selection of the portfolio. An originator might be tempted to cherry-pick assets for the transaction which do not reflect the general average quality of the loan book.

80 A full discussion of prospectus liability is beyond the scope of this publication. Refer to ss 710 and 728(i) of the *Corporations Act 2001* (Cth) under Australian law.

81 HY-FI Securities Ltd Series 3 (Structured Finance Presale Report, Standard & Poor's, 1 September 2003, posted at http://www.hyfis.com.au, along with the prospectus) p 8.

82 ESAF Navigator CDO I prospectus, p 31.

83 The sponsoring institution is working on an out-of-court settlement. Refer to http://www.forbes.com and http://www.overheid.nl, search for "Legio Lease".

84 See s 553C of the *Corporations Act 2001* (Cth).

85 Standard & Poor's, for instance, requires full and enforceable waiver of set-off by the relevant borrowers. This may be particularly cumbersome in RMBS transactions. See also "Global Cash Flow and Synthetic CDO Criteria" (Standard & Poor's, 21 March 2002). However, insolvency set-off, as opposed to pre-insolvency equitable or contractual set-off, is in many jurisdictions (such as Australia) mandatory and any purported contracting out of insolvency set-off will be viewed as contrary to public policy and consequently void. See further Wormell M, "Securitisation and Set-off" (1998) 9 JBFLP 181.

86 Ambery R, "How the UK Enterprise Act Makes Warehousing Difficult" (2003) XX117 IFLR 54.

87 Discussed in Ch 2.

88 For instance, the Financial Services Authority (Consultation Paper 189, Report and First Consultation on the Implementation of the New Basel and EU Capital Adequacy Standards, dated July 2003). The German and Dutch regulators have embarked on a similar exercise.

89 *Australia: APRA Guidelines for New Basel Capital Accord*, discussed in *Australian Banking and Financial Law Bulletin*, Vol 19, No 1, p 1.

90 In fact only costs incurred by the SPV are senior to the obligation to the originator.

91 Off-balance sheet items, such as swaps, need special capital treatment as banks are not exposed to credit risk for the full face value of the their contracts, but only to the cost of replacing the cash flow if a counterparty defaults, implying that the swap should be marked to market. The actual exposure is calculated using either the current exposure (or in some countries the original exposure) method: APRA AGN 112.3, item 21.

92 Choudhry M, *An Introduction to Collateralised Debt Obligations,* published at http://www.yieldcurve.com (viewed February 2003), p 6.

93 Basel 1988 Accord, p 11; APRA AGN 112.1, item 29.

94 Financial Services Authority, *Interim Prudential Source Book for Banks,* Ch SE, para. 9.5.2 sub 9 through 13.

95 Basel Committee on Banking Supervision, *(Third) Consultative Document, The New Basel Accord* (Bank of International Settlements, April 2003). This document is posted at http://www.bis.org.

[96] The Bank for International Settlements has published the non-confidential comments on the proposed New Basel Accord on its website (http://www.bis.org). The proposed treatment of securitisations is among the issues under criticism. See, for instance, Standard & Poor's Response, 22 August 2003, which highlights two concerns about the treatment of securitisation: first, the effective discouragement of securitisation on bank funding and, secondly, the coherence of treatment on an unsecuritised basis relative to those on a securitised basis.

[97] Basel Committee on Banking Supervision, *(Third) Consultative Document, The New Basel Accord* (Bank of International Settlements, April 2003) no 528.

[98] Global Coalition of Industry Organisations, "Comments on Securitisation Issues in the New Basel Capital Accord" (letter to the Basel Committee on Banking Supervision, 1 August 2003) p 9.

[99] On the US regulatory approach generally, refer to Nolan ARG, *Synthetic CLOs and Traditional Asset Securitizations: Legal and Regulatory Issues for Banks* (Client Publication, Shearman & Sterling, 2002).

[100] Letter from the Board of Governors of the Federal Reserve System, "Capital Treatment for Synthetic Collateralized Loan Obligations" (Supervision and Regulation (SR) Letter 99-32, 17 November 1999), reiterated in 2001.

[101] Recently, some insurers have retreated from the synthetic market. Some may argue that this is part of a more general reassessment of the risks involved.

[102] Apart from the cooperation efforts required between regulators to achieve cross-border implementation of the new rules, see *High-level Principles for the Cross-border Implementation of the New Accord* (Bank for International Settlements, August 2003).

[103] "Underlying Assets in European CDO Transactions Widen to Meet Specific Investor Needs" (Standard & Poor's, 8 October 2002).

[104] Recent tax changes may allow the true sale market to develop further. On the other hand, established German synthetic programs, such as Provide, referencing mortgage receivables, are moving abroad to Austria and the UK. See Colomer N, "Euro Market: KfW Moves in on UK Terrain" *Asset Securitization Report*, 14 July 2003, 2003 WL 7469561.

[105] "European Balance Sheet CDOs", in *Global CDO Quarterly* (Fitch Ratings, February 2003).

[106] Basel Committee on Banking Supervision, *Second Working Paper on Securitisation* (October 2002).

[107] Colomer N, "HBOS Initiates UK Covered Bond Market" *Asset Securitization Report*, 7 July 2003, 2003 WL 7469545.

Chapter 4

SYNTHETIC ARBITRAGE: MERGER OF CREDIT DERIVATIVES, SECURITISATION AND ASSET MANAGEMENT

SYNTHETIC ARBITRAGE: INTRODUCTION, DEFINITION AND EVOLUTION

Synthetic arbitrage: an introduction

[4.10] Synthetic collateralised debt obligations (CDOs) have been described as the "most toxic element of the financial markets today".[1] In Chs 2 and 3, credit derivatives and balance sheet synthetic securitisations are discussed. In this chapter the focus is on arbitrage synthetics, in particular, on managed transactions. It explores the potential of these deals, as well as the risks for investors. This chapter also seeks to familiarise market participants with the documentation and legal issues that are relevant to this type of transaction. Where relevant, references to recent transactions are included. Also, recent developments in this market are addressed, such as the trend to include structured finance securities in managed transactions.[2]

The development of managed synthetic securitisation is comparable to that of balance sheet synthetics. Again, it is particularly in Europe where this type of transaction first gained significant market share. This is illustrated by the fact that Fitch recently published a "Synthetic Index", which serves as a window to view the performance of this type of transaction in Europe.[3] The index incorporates a number of risks particular to this deal type. In the US the market has built upon the experience in managing true sale CDOs. A number of promising transactions have been closed and account for a significant market share. The Australasian markets, though not as far developed yet as their European and North American counterparts, are steadily gaining ground. Significant transactions have closed in Asia, including Golden Jade, Ruby Finance and Artemus, adding to a growing trend to use managed synthetics.[4] In Australia, the publicly rated managed synthetic deal used to be a rarity. Latest industry estimates indicate that this is about to change.[5] On the other hand, this growth is hampered by a climate of tight spreads.

What are arbitrage transactions?

[4.20] Arbitrage transactions seek to exploit the difference in yields between the underlying assets and the interest due on the notes. Unlike in a balance sheet transaction, these underlying assets are not part of the balance sheet of an originator. Rather, these assets are purchased in the open market by a special purpose vehicle (SPV), which is funded by the issuance of notes. Generally, the spreads that are offered in the credit default swap market are higher than those offered in the cash bond market. In particular, these spreads payable are higher than expected given historical default data available from rating agencies. This is the arbitrage gap, the positive basis, which (synthetic) arbitrage transactions seek to capture.

Credit default swap market v cash bond market

[4.30] So why do the spreads payable in the credit default swap market and the cash bond market diverge? There are a number of, sometimes opposing, forces at work.[6] Several factors drive the credit spreads down and closer to those of the cash market, including the launch of synthetic arbitrage CDOs, as well as the inherent flexibility that synthetic CDOs offer to investors over their true sale equivalents. As to the first, in order to launch a synthetic arbitrage CDO, the sponsoring institution has to source and sell protection on a substantial number of names in the market to build a representative portfolio. This process can continue after the transaction is closed (see **[4.170]**). If the portfolio were not complete at closing, it would have to be "ramped up" afterwards. The supply from protection sellers drives spreads down.

The second significant factor is the investment flexibility that the credit default swap market provides in comparison to the cash bond market, eg a broader range of maturities[7] is available than in the cash market. In addition, the number of names that can be accessed in the credit default swap market is significantly larger than those in the cash bond market. These factors attract additional protection sellers, increasing supply, driving spreads down.

A third factor is that buying protection does not eliminate credit risk, but rather replaces the credit risk on the reference obligations or entities by that of the protection seller. This residual risk may impact on buyers' willingness to pay large spreads.

Risks for protection buyers

[4.40] The factors driving the credit spreads down are usually offset by others, the most important of which relate to additional risks for protection buyers in the credit derivatives market for which the seller will want to be compensated by higher credit spreads. These additional risks include the "cheapest-to-deliver" risk and the inclusion of "soft" credit events. Also, credit default swaps do not offer the same liquidity as their cash equivalents, so the seller will want to receive a higher spread to be compensated for that risk.

The cheapest-to-deliver risk refers to the possibility that, once settlement is triggered of a transaction to which physical settlement applies, the buyer will be able to deliver any deliverable obligation.[8] The protection seller is concerned that this deliverable obligation may have a smaller value than the reference obligation in respect of which protection was purchased. The inclusion of restructuring as a credit event may give rise to the transaction being triggered as a result of so-called "soft" credit events. These are credit events that are perceived to cover a risk beyond that of strict default (as defined by the rating agencies[9]). As a result, the premium payable by the buyer to obtain protection in respect to this additional risk will be higher.

For various reasons, the Australian credit default swap market more often than not trades on a negative, rather than a positive, basis.[10] This may be partly due to the increased appetite of financial institutions in building a portfolio for the issue of CDOs. The latest rating agencies data seems to mirror this increased appetite.[11]

Static and managed deals
[4.50] Synthetic transactions can be divided into static and managed deals. In a managed synthetic transaction, a collateral manager (or simply "manager") is engaged by the SPV to manage the "synthetic" portfolio. This manager may have different degrees of freedom. In a static transaction, the portfolio is typically identified before closing and is not traded during the life of the transaction. Balance sheet synthetic transactions are usually static in nature or allow only a limited number of substitutions. In late 2002 and early 2003 the number of actively managed deals increased globally.[12]

In the Australian market, synthetic transactions have been primarily static, rather than managed, deals.[13] The main reason managed deals have not yet developed appears to be that no managers with the required experience have come forward. Rating agencies assess the manager's experience as pivotal in the rating process of any managed transaction. Nevertheless, the prospect for development is there. Parallels may be drawn to the development of managed CDOs in Europe, where initially few managers had the required experience. In that case, overseas management experience could be used. Alternatively, the managing task for the different markets was split between managers experienced in their home region. Given this precedent, the Asia-Pacific market could overcome this issue in the same way. There are promising signs, such as the Silk Road deal in Taiwan.

Managed synthetic transactions: evolution

[4.60] So why has the managed synthetic transaction developed? A number of factors have contributed to the increased use of this particular structure over static synthetic transactions.[14] First, the substantial number of corporate defaults in recent times has left some investors in static transactions more or less "locked" in a portfolio with deteriorating credits and little or no flexibility to trade assets out of the portfolio to either mitigate or prevent losses. This risk has been particularly hard to swallow for investors, given the high number of so-called "fallen angels".[15] Secondly, managed synthetic transactions ensure stable fee income for originators, at least as long as the notes are not callable. A third factor is that arrangers are able to target a broader investment base. Managed transactions can also appeal to investors who have limited experience and want to rely on the expertise of the manager to make (re)investment decisions for them.

Another contributing factor to the emergence of synthetic managed transactions has been the further maturation of the credit derivatives market. Its increased liquidity and number of names traded have bolstered global investor confidence in a relatively new product. It is a market that continues to attract new market participants, because of its (at least in relative terms) strong performance in recent troubled times.

STRUCTURE

Arbitrage v balance sheet

[4.70] In this chapter the structural differences between a synthetic arbitrage structure and a synthetic balance sheet deal are addressed. The main topics discussed are:
- the position of the collateral manager;
- the use (or non-use) of SPVs; and
- the use of synthetic reference obligations.

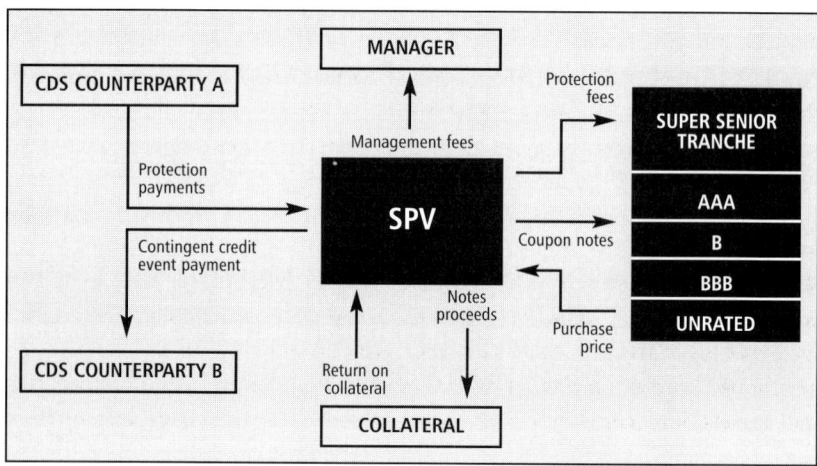

A managed synthetic structure substantially resembles a balance sheet synthetic structure. An SPV issues credit linked notes to investors referencing a portfolio of reference entities. A super senior tranche may be sold in unfunded form to a super senior investor. Separate collateral agreements are entered into.

In comparing a managed synthetic structure with its static counterpart, two distinguishing features are noted. First, a manager is engaged to manage the portfolio. Secondly, the portfolio itself is tailored to maximise the managing opportunity (usually by including credit default swaps, but other assets, such as structured finance securities, have surfaced too). These features have an impact on specific risks (counterparty, liquidity) and on structural protection in the transaction. Other distinguishing features exist with regard to trading and credit event settlement.

In static synthetic CDOs, the collateral is identified prior to the closing. Managed deals introduce flexibility in trading in the collateral. An experienced manager is engaged by the SPV for that purpose. The manager is usually assisted by a portfolio administrator and sometimes by a separate investment adviser. The collateral management agreement is a key document. It addresses the duties and responsibilities of the manager, the control over the manager, the fees and expenses payable, the replacement and resignation of the manager and, in particular, the extent of trading discretion.

Collateral manager
[4.80] The manager is authorised to manage and administer, supervise and effect the investment, disposal or reinvestment of the collateral. The manager covenants to perform these obligations in good faith and to exercise an appropriate standard of care. Rating agencies hold (justifiably so) the manager's expertise of paramount importance in rating a managed transaction. For that reason, the manager will be reviewed by the rating agencies to assess its expertise in credit derivatives and managing the relevant kind of asset types. Separate manager reports are published by rating agencies to familiarise investors with the particular capabilities and experience of a manager.[16]

Fee structure
[4.90] The collateral management agreement will detail the fees and expenses payable. Usually at least part of the fees payable depends on the performance of the pool, so as to provide an incentive to the manager. This is achieved by dividing the fee into separate components: a senior, a junior and sometimes even a mezzanine fee. Each of these will be allocated a

different priority in the interest priority of payments. Separate "incentive" fees may also be included, which are only payable if the subordinated noteholders have received a specified "hurdle rate" on a given payment date.

In recent transactions this fee structure has been slightly amended. Instead of being payable on any payment date, a single incentive fee is payable at maturity of the transaction, provided the subordinated noteholders have received their hurdle rate of return over the entire life of the transaction. The fee may be tweaked to be payable either if the hurdle rate test is satisfied on each payment date or on average over all payment dates. Alternatively, subordinate fees may be used to reinstate principal of the notes written off due to poor pool performance.

The management fee may include compensation for expenses incurred in the performance by the manager of its obligations. Otherwise, they will be separately payable. In the latter case, issuers will generally try to make these expenses as transparent as possible. That way, investor concerns on profit roaming by equity investors can be alleviated. The management fee payable is usually calculated over the aggregate balance of the portfolio, rather than its market value. This ensures the originator of stable fee income during the transaction.

Obviously, the amount of fees payable to the manager depends on the kind of management obligations in the structure. In comparison with cash structures, synthetic CDOs allow for substantially smaller management fees. In addition, these management fees tend to be payable over the life of the transaction, rather than up front.[17]

Manager change

[4.100] The choice of the collateral manager is one of the primary considerations for investors in managed (synthetic) transactions. This concern is underscored by the fact that debt investors generally have very limited capabilities to replace the manager.

Removal without cause

The manager can be removed with or without cause. Removal without cause is only possible in very limited circumstances; it usually requires a 66⅔% majority of each class of noteholders. As the sponsoring institution will retain a stake in the equity note of the transaction, such a removal is sometimes dependent on its consent. When the sponsoring institution is affiliated with the manager, debt investors should ensure that the equity stake is not taken into account in the calculation of the specified majority.

Removal with cause

The manager may also be removed with cause. The market has evolved to include a number of standard events that constitute such cause. These include:

- wilful violation by the manager of any of its material obligations;
- violation of any material provision of the management agreement and failure to remedy;
- any representation or warranty by the manager proving to be materially incorrect;
- certain bankruptcy or insolvency events with respect to the manager;
- the occurrence of an event of default by the issuer;
- fraud or criminal activity on the part of the manager; and
- the manager ceasing to be authorised as such under a relevant jurisdiction.

The qualified majority and the notice to be observed required for this removal are a little more lenient.

Rating agencies' consent

Whether the manager's appointment is terminated with or without cause, the rating agencies' consent is required. Such consent will only be forthcoming if an appropriately qualified replacement manager is appointed on substantially the same terms as the original manager. In line with this, usually the manager is not allowed to assign its rights and obligations to a third party. A resignation by the manager would also be subject to the appointment of a suitable replacement manager. In exceptional circumstances, eg where a continuation of its position would constitute an illegality under applicable law, the manager would be allowed to resign immediately.

Portfolio administrator

[4.110] A separate portfolio administrator may be engaged to perform certain administrative functions with respect to the collateral, such as the calculation of certain tests and the determination whether the eligibility criteria have been met. The administrator may also be charged with providing market participants with regular reports on performance containing these details. The portfolio administration agreement will specify which details should be included in the reports.

Investment adviser

[4.120] Sometimes a separate investment adviser is engaged to advise and present investment proposals to the SPV. The SPV establishes an investment committee to assess and approve these proposals, usually at very short notice so as not to limit the capacity of the investment adviser to take swift action. The investment adviser may also counsel the SPV on how to use the proceeds of the notes if the structure allows for alternative eligible investment possibilities, or propose additional credit default swap counterparties.

Special purpose vehicle?

[4.130] In most synthetic arbitrage transactions, a separate SPV is used because it allows the investors in the notes to be insulated from the credit risk on the originator. As a result, in an SPV structure, the notes can obtain a AAA rating.

However, recently a number of synthetic deals have been structured without an SPV, eg Imperial II. In this particular transaction, the highest rating of the notes was AA-, equal to the originator's credit rating. Note that a drawback of this structure is that a downgrade of the originator directly affects the rating of the highest tranche of notes. This is because the ratings on the credit linked notes reflect the investors' risk that the originator will fail to comply with its obligations for full repayment of principal and interest under the notes. In such a situation, it might be preferable to transfer the credit risk in unfunded form, through a credit default swap instead. In that case, the investor, in the capacity of protection seller, would not make any up-front payment and, as a result, would not bear any credit risk on the originator for full repayment. This would allow the protection premium payable by the originator to reflect a lower risk, possibly even equal to or higher than that of a AAA rating.

Enron

The move towards non-SPV structures may be partly "inspired" by Enron's demise. As one of the major corporate defaults in US corporate history, it has led to intense debate among US law-makers about the proper procedure to prevent such events from happening in the future. A particular spin-off appears to be that any structure involving an SPV, and in particular the use of securitisation and derivatives, has been "contaminated".[18] Although the structures that were prevalent in Enron were basically tailored to manipulate the balance sheet, its effect has been significant upon structured finance in general.

Super senior investor

[4.140] Similar to a balance sheet synthetic CDO, arbitrage transactions typically incorporate a super senior credit default swap. By virtue of its strong negotiation position, the super senior investor typically requires specific issues in the credit default swap regarding the super senior tranching, which may have an impact on the eligibility criteria. In static synthetics, such an investor, often a monoline insurer, will want consent over changes in the transaction structure and important benchmarks. It may require that the liquidity risk in the portfolio is borne by the third parties.[19] In managed synthetics, the investor may require additional control over asset selection in case the portfolio performs unsatisfactorily. And it may negotiate the right to replace the manager if certain performance triggers are breached.[20]

Synthetic reference obligations

[4.150] In a static CDO, the proceeds of the notes would be used to purchase a variety of pre-agreed assets, most probably bonds and/or loans found on the balance sheet of the originating bank or in a warehousing arrangement. These assets would then generate the cash flow needed to service the interest on the notes. As a result, the cash flow would have to be more or less predictable. The synthetic structure enables originators to eliminate the cash flow constraint typically by having the SPV enter into a single credit default swap with the originating bank. The protection payments of the bank then provide the funds needed to service the notes. In a *managed* synthetic structure, things are taken a step further. The SPV enters into a variety of credit default swaps with selected dealers and the manager can trade positions in these swaps in order to enhance the portfolio performance.

The use of credit default swaps is appropriate as that market has become mature and very liquid over recent years. Managers are thus able to quickly react to market developments and limit any losses by using their expertise. In addition, credit default swaps allow managers to take positions that would not, or only at prohibitive time and cost, be possible, such as entering into off-setting and/or open positions. A number of managed synthetic deals referencing a portfolio of credit defaults have recently closed (eg the Robeco series, allegedly the first in Europe, Cheyne, ESAF Navigator, Brookland and Bernstein). Other asset classes have started to follow suit (loans, Cibeles 1, ABS, other bonds and loans, Euro Multi-Credit).

Managed Synthetic CDO Structure

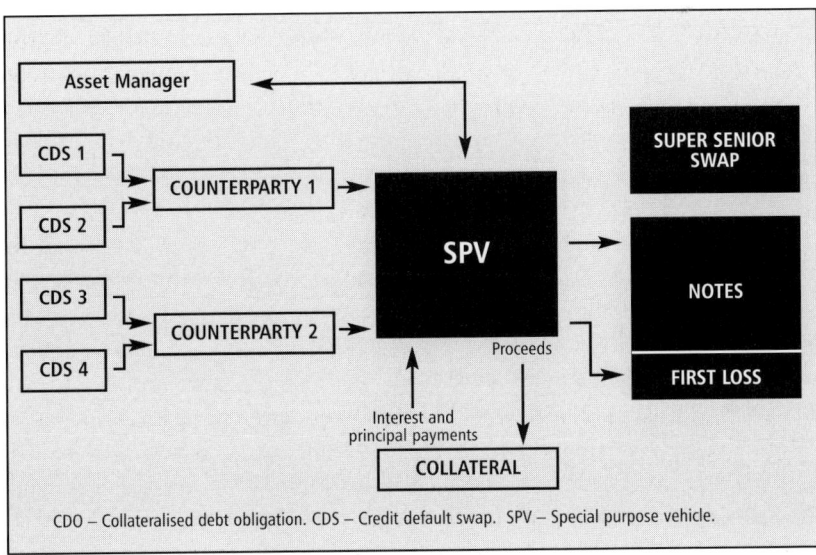

CDO – Collateralised debt obligation. CDS – Credit default swap. SPV – Special purpose vehicle.

Bullet structure

[4.160] A further advantage of credit derivatives as the means to gain exposure is that their maturity can be tailored. In a true sale CDO the maturity of the loans is linked to the amortisation of the assets. In a synthetic structure the underlying credits are only referenced, not purchased. As a consequence, the liquidity of the credit default swap market allows the exposure to be negotiated or set by the sponsoring financial institution. This entitles the credit default swaps in the portfolio to be structured into a simultaneous maturity date. This may be advantageous from an investor's point of view, as it facilitates a bullet structure, in which the notes are paid down fully upon maturity, rather than the protracted timing associated with amortisation of assets. No step-up mechanism is needed.[21]

In some cases the exposure to the reference portfolio may be created both in synthetic form (with credit default swaps and total return swaps) and through the purchase of a portfolio of bonds (including ABS) and loans. These transactions are referred to as "hybrid" deals (Jazz I and II and Symphony II).[22] As the transaction referencing a portfolio of credit default swaps is most prevalent, that is the focus here. However, most issues described apply to other assets as well.

MANAGEMENT PROCESS

From ramp-up to post-investment

Managed synthetic portfolio: milestones

[4.170] This part of the chapter analyses in some detail specific risks that are associated with managing synthetic transactions, highlighting the opportunities that credit derivatives provide for that management and the means to control the extent of freedom that the manager has in a particular transaction. For that reason, the managed synthetic transaction is first analysed chronologically.

The workings of a managed synthetic portfolio are easiest explained by reference to a chronological order of events. The following "milestones" can be distinguished:
- the ramp-up of the portfolio (see **[4.180]**);
- the effective date (see **[4.190]**);
- the reinvestment period (see **[4.200]**); and
- the post-reinvestment period (see **[4.210]**).

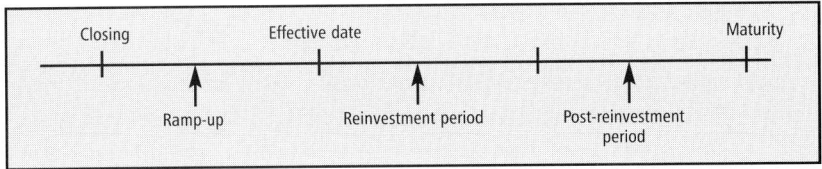

Ramp-up

[4.180] In most managed securitisations only part of the collateral is identified at closing. Such deals involve an initial period of time post-transaction closing, during which the manager purchases the assets (in *cash* terms, or rather acquires exposure, in *synthetic* terms) to complete the portfolio pool, usually in the open market. This period is referred to as the "ramp-up" period. Its duration depends on the (liquidity of) the assets in the pool, but usually lasts around 90 or 120 days.[23] The intended advantage of a ramp-up period is to increase the manager's flexibility to identify assets that will add diversity and solid credit standing to the portfolio. The manager is able to choose from a larger range of assets as new issuance is brought to the market. The use of a ramp-up period also reduces the need to warehouse assets before closing.

Investors' risks

Although investors may appreciate the increased flexibility of their manager to ramp up the portfolio during the ramp-up period, its inclusion has certain risks for the investors as well. For instance, as the portfolio is not yet complete during the ramp-up period, it will not yield the full return needed to service the interest on the credit linked notes. In other words, a ramp-up period adds negative carry. There may also be a liquidity risk due to payment date differences in the accrued interest flows. A further matter of concern is that investors must rely on the manager actually being able to originate the required portfolio. If market conditions, such as prices or spreads, are adverse, the manager may not be able to complete the ramp-up. Finally, while the portfolio as a whole is subject to constraints, such as portfolio guidelines (eg as to diversity), prior to completion the portfolio may not meet such requirements.

Solutions

Various solutions are available to mitigate these risks for investors. A target portfolio may be identified in the collateral management agreement. This outlines the composition and any particular characteristics or tests to be met by the portfolio.[24] In respect of a portfolio of credit default swaps, these could include target notional amounts for each reference entity to be included in the portfolio, a weighted average rating and a weighted average spread. To reduce risks during the ramp-up, recent deals have incorporated a "phased" ramp-up. For example, a nine-month ramp-up period could be divided into three three-month components and the portfolio would have to meet increasingly stringent characteristics at the end of each period. Ultimately, if the intermediary targets have not been met at the end of a phase, the notes may be redeemed. But usually there is some kind of grace period. During that time, the manager has a short period (eg five business days) to submit to the rating agencies a plan containing proposals to ensure satisfaction of the infringed guidelines, with the purpose of obtaining a confirmation of the ratings. If such confirmation is not obtained, then, depending on the structure of the transaction, either the notes may be redeemed or the transaction may become static. The latter would in most circumstances seriously affect the fees the manager might earn and therefore serves as an incentive to the manager to avoid such a situation.

Effective date

[4.190] The effective date marks the end of the ramp-up period. It may be the last date of the ramp-up period scheduled or earlier if the required exposure has been acquired at such earlier date. At such time, the portfolio administrator verifies whether the conditions set for the target portfolio have been met. If not, the portfolio administrator informs the rating agencies, which can then decide whether to re-affirm the credit ratings of the notes or reduce or withdraw them, causing the redemption of the notes.

Reinvestment period

[4.200] After the ramp-up, the "revolving" or "reinvestment" period begins. This may last around three to five years from the closing date. During the reinvestment period the manager may not only actively sell assets (including exposure), but also reinvest the proceeds in new assets.

The extent of trading allowed may vary significantly. In a more defensively managed transaction, the manager is typically confined to substituting defaulted assets (such as credit default swaps or securities). In a less defensive structure, the manager may be allowed to trade specifically defined assets and "credit-improved" securities as well. Even further along the spectrum of managed deals, the manager is allowed to trade at its discretion. This is mostly subject to a bucket limitation (eg capping the aggregate principal amount purchased in a calendar year or during the life of the transaction).

From the perspective of the investors, it is important to protect the portfolio from churning, high turnover and undue exposure due to price erosion by precise designation and application of proceeds rules. A clear definition of what exactly constitutes a credit risk or credit-improved security can control how often a trade is allowed to occur.[25] The application of proceeds controls the release of sales proceeds out of the structure towards equity or subordinated noteholders.[26]

Post-reinvestment
[4.210] Typically, some trading is allowed after the reinvestment period. This is usually restricted to trades in credit-improved securities. However, in some transactions the reinvestment period pretty much covers the entire life of the notes. The noteholders thus benefit (or are exposed, whichever way you look at it) to the fullest extent from the managerial trading experience.

Opportunities in managed synthetics

Styles of management
[4.220] The essence of the managed synthetic CDO is in the management of the portfolio. This management may range from "light" to "full". In lightly managed transactions, the activities of the collateral managers may be limited to exiting positions of credit risk, such as terminating an existing contract to limit losses. As mentioned at **[4.240]** and **[4.340]**, each style carries with it different trading requirements. Investors will need to balance the cost for the larger role of a collateral manager against the flexibility and the comfort that they may derive therefrom. In addition, different trading conditions will apply depending on whether the trade is done during the ramp-up period, the revolving period or the post-revolving period.

Focusing on synthetic CDOs referencing credit default swaps, a division may be made depending on the positions that the SPV is allowed to take in such transactions. In particular, an SPV may be limited to enter into
- offsetting trades with either the same party or third parties (see **[4.230]**);
- offsetting trades with open ("naked") positions (see **[4.240]**).

Further down the line, the SPV could enter securities lending transactions or other derivatives, such as total return swaps and equity swaps. Each of these tools has additional benefits and risks.

Ultimately, an SPV may be entitled to invest in several types of derivatives, but also in cash securities, turning the managed synthetic CDO into a hybrid transaction.

Offsetting credit default swaps
[4.230] Some transactions enable the SPV not just to substitute credit default swaps in the portfolio, but also to enter into offsetting credit default swaps. The intention of such trades is to hedge the exposure of the SPV as seller of protection under an existing credit default swap. This reduces the aggregate exposure of the portfolio, opening up new trading opportunities. It also enables the manager to use available reserves to limit losses by paying additional protection, rather than paying out to equity investors. The ability to enter into offsetting trades adds flexibility to the managed synthetic CDO. However, it carries additional risk as well.

Special requirements

To ensure a true hedge of the exposure, offsetting credit default swaps must meet specific requirements. Most notably, the terms and conditions of the offsetting swap should be identical in all material respects to the swap it is designed to hedge (eg, having the same scheduled termination date, credit events, obligations and deliverable obligations, with the obvious exception that the SPV will be a buyer of protection instead). To be truly offsetting, the offsetting swap should be entered into with the same counterparty as the original swap. Earlier transactions stressed this requirement, eg by allowing only a small bucket of offsetting swaps with other counterparties. Later deals have evolved to be less strict in this respect, although most require the SPV at least to use commercially reasonable efforts to enter into the offsetting swap with the same counterparty first.[27]

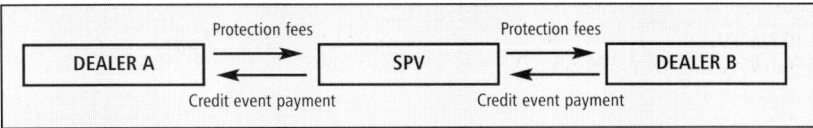

Additional risks

If the offsetting trade is not done with the same counterparty, this obviously introduces additional credit risk. The concept of offsetting trades carries a few extra risks, which can be properly addressed in the structure. For instance, although the conditions may be the same, the actual physical settlement date may be different (due to the time of fulfilment of the conditions to settlement). To bridge any gap, the SPV should be able to temporarily invest or divest part of the eligible investments. To minimise that use, rights and obligations arising out of the offsetting and hedged swap should be netted (if the counterparties are the same) or executed (if not) first. To mitigate the additional risk, caps on the notional amount of offsetting trades allowed and specifically with respect to a single counterparty may be imposed.

Furthermore, the SPV must be able to perform its payment obligations under the offsetting credit default swap. To establish whether it has sufficient funds, an analysis of the future spreads to be received is required. Obviously the SPV should also be able to source deliverable obligations if the transaction is physically settled.

Open positions

[4.240] The manager may be entitled to enter into open credit default swaps during a predefined period. The SPV then buys credit protection in respect of a specified reference entity without having any exposure to that reference entity. Any open credit default swap should satisfy the eligibility criteria. And to minimise credit risk, the counterparty would be required to take customary measures (posting collateral etc) in the event of a downgrade below the agreed threshold.

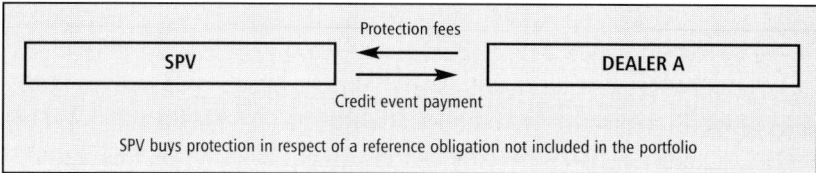

As the open credit default swap does not intend to hedge any exposure, it is a slightly more speculative investment. For that reason, rating agencies may curtail the volume of these transactions. The documentation is materially based upon the standard terms of the credit default swap confirmation (see Ch 2). However, the manager may be granted additional flexibility in respect of particular terms, such as the selection and definition of the credit events, the range of reference obligations and deliverable obligations.

Entering into open credit default swaps allows managers and, by reference, investors to capitalise on a negative outlook on a particular reference entity. It will also allow the manager to differentiate between different credit risks within the same industry, while maintaining a neutral stand on that industry.[28]

Securities lending
[4.250] An alternative tool to generate income from the securities in the portfolio is by engaging in securities lending. So far few transactions have used this option.[29] This activity too is subject to certain volume limits and conformity to market practice. Credit risk on the securities lending counterparty can be limited by requiring it to post collateral in cash in accordance with market value of the securities lent, plus a haircut.

Other assets/hybrids
[4.260] In some transactions the underlying assets have evolved to be both synthetic (including, for example, total return swaps) and cash (with a variety of assets available). The increased diversity may benefit investors, eg in allowing the manager to reinvest proceeds in other asset categories. However, each asset has its own risk profile and investors will have to take that into account as well.

Management control

Management issues: an introduction
[4.270] Management control has two aspects. The first is the legal one. What opportunities does the SPV have to guide or curtail the manager's

decisions? This aspect is discussed at **[4.580]**. The second aspect relates to the "rules" of the trading game. Which are the variables a manager should abide by when it sells or purchases (reinvests) assets? Another important question is how the verification process is organised.

Managed portfolios are governed at two levels: the asset level (by eligibility criteria) and the portfolio level (by portfolio guidelines). In addition, defining the different types of securities is an important tool in understanding the trading game.

Eligibility criteria
[4.280] The asset eligibility criteria apply at the outset of the transaction, when the portfolio is ramped up, but also if individual assets are either removed or added to the portfolio during the trading period. Obviously the criteria depend on the type of asset. In this chapter the focus is on credit default swaps, as they are most prevalent in managed synthetic CDOs.

An asset included in a portfolio typically could be required to meet the following eligibility criteria:
- a specific credit rating floor of the reference entity (eg BBB-);
- a specific type of reference entity (eg corporation, financial institution, sovereign);
- a specific country or region of reference entity (eg North America, Europe, Asia, Australia, New Zealand);
- a specific credit rating floor for the country of incorporation of the reference entity (eg AA-);
- standards for documentation, such as the confirmation (eg settlement, maturity, valuation, (deliverable) obligations categories and characteristics, denomination, payment dates).

In hybrid transactions eligibility criteria for cash assets may include:
- the assignability of the asset;
- the asset being non-convertible;
- not prepayable at less than par;
- no deferral of interest allowed.

As to "removals" (offsetting credit default swaps) of credit default swaps from the portfolio, the eligibility criteria are likely to focus on the concern that the removal is a true hedge. It is thus of the essence that terms such as maturity are the same in the offsetting credit default swap as in the original credit default swap.

Portfolio tests
[4.290] On the portfolio level the requirements are portfolio "guidelines" or tests. These are developed by the various rating agencies and are sometimes

incorporated in their proprietary models. These tests can be divided into three subcategories: portfolio profile tests, quality tests or coverage tests.

Portfolio profile tests

Portfolio profile tests include requirements as to the size of a specific part of the portfolio. For instance, the test may specify a limit on the aggregate notional amount of any offsetting or open credit default swaps in the portfolio, or maximise the aggregate notional amounts of credit default swaps referencing a single entity, a single country of incorporation of the reference entity or a specific credit rating of the reference entities. Alternatively, limits may be imposed on the aggregate amount of assets added or removed in a given time period to avoid churning.

Quality tests

Quality tests address issues like the credit quality, diversity, total spread and expected recovery rate of the assets in the portfolio. They are measured by:
- a minimum weighted average spread (WAS) on the credit default swaps (to ensure sufficient cash flow is available to the SPV from the credit default swaps in which protection is sold to pay coupon on the notes);
- a weighted average recovery rate (WAR or portfolio recovery rate);
- a maximum portfolio rating test (to assess the average rating quality of the portfolio on a measurement date);
- a minimum diversity score (which reflects the allocation of assets between different industry categories, whether correlated or not);
- a default expectation test (such as Standard & Poor's CDO Monitor); and
- the ISDA Stress Factor test (which translates the differing risk profiles associated with the divergence in customary credit events between the various regional markets, particularly in terms of their susceptibility to the occurrence of "soft" credit events).[30] This may result in an increase of assumed level of defaults, a decreased recovery rate or an additional haircut in the case of non-US obligors.[31]

Coverage tests

Coverage tests include the over-collateralisation coverage test (OC) and interest coverage (IC) tests. These are not necessarily included in a managed synthetic CDO. The OC test ensures that the aggregate market value of the portfolio divided by the aggregate value of the super senior swap notional amount plus the respective level of notes outstanding meets a minimum level. The required minimum level increases with the rating of the notes. Earlier synthetic CDOs did not have any OC tests.[32] The incorporation of this test is a protective feature as it uses excess spread to reduce leverage or build up reserve accounts. Even if an OC test is included, it is important to note that the calculation of the OC ratio may differ between transactions, depending upon whether or not the notional value of the super senior tranche is included.

The IC test ensures that the total amount of interest proceeds from the portfolio for a given period divided by the super senior swaps premiums plus interest payments due on the various tranches of notes outstanding during the same period meets a minimum level (eg 110%).[33]

By requiring both these tests to be met each time a new asset is added to the portfolio, the notes can retain their credit rating. The specifics of these tests will depend on the underlying assets of a particular transaction.[34]

Verification

The manager or the portfolio administrator is usually charged with carrying out these tests at regular intervals, eg on each payment date. The results of the tests are incorporated in detailed reports to be delivered to relevant transaction parties. These reports usually also include the balances of the various accounts used in the transaction, as well as liquidity facilities, if any.

From tests to models

[4.300] Transactions are increasingly complex in terms of the variety of underlying assets and the conditions the (portfolios of) assets should meet. To help this rapidly growing market, rating agencies have developed (or are developing) proprietary models to assist in the packaging of assets and the required collateral and tranching of the classes of notes. Standard and Poor's has developed its CDO Evaluator,[35] Fitch has recently launched its Vector model,[36] and Moody's is said to be working on its own model. These models facilitate the structuring of true sale, as well as synthetic, transactions and rely on simple input. They may be used for hypothetical portfolios and for ramping up. Their advantage is that they incorporate a range of different elements, such as the industry concentration and credit rating of the underlying. Allegedly, their use allows a rating agency to be more flexible on individual eligibility criteria. These models will by necessity be based upon assumptions, such as recovery rates. Market participants will find ways to arbitrage these models, resulting in a continuous spiral of upgraded models and new innovative tricks.

Capturing the performance of the managed transaction is a related matter. Rating agencies have their own performance indicators.[37]

As is apparent from (not just) this paragraph, the role of the rating agencies is more pronounced in a managed synthetic CDO. A full analysis of the ratings process is beyond the focus of this book.[38]

Defining categories of securities

[4.310] An element of trading control is the definitions of "credit risk" securities and "credit-improved" securities. These are categories within which trading may differentiate.

A "credit-impaired" security (or credit default swap) is usually defined as a security that in the reasonable judgment of the manager has a significant risk of declining in credit quality (which is unrelated to general market conditions).[39] In other words, it is the manager who calls the shots. This definition underscores that investors rely on the manager's decisions. The focus on the subjective element of the manager's judgment is also said to be relevant from a liability perspective. It is not the rating agency which decides what a credit-impaired security is, but rather the manager. However, not all rating agencies follow this analysis.[40]

The manager's flexibility is usually substantially reduced if the senior or mezzanine notes are downgraded by a single or a couple of notches. This may be achieved by redefining a credit risk security on the basis of the change in the bid spread on the credit default swap instead of when it was entered into.[41] To illustrate the relevance of the definition, its security is at issue when a manager intends to purchase assets at a discount to par, but still be awarded to full par treatment for the purposes of the coverage and quality tests. According to one rating agency, entering into these purchases violates at least the spirit of the definition.[42]

The definition of a "credit-improved" security is modelled along the same lines. The manager judges whether a credit default swap has significantly improved in credit quality. The decision is either "reasonable" or based upon a specific occurrence, such as improved financial results or a significant decrease in the bid spread (eg 10%). In the event of a downgrade, trading may be limited by redefining a credit-improved security as one the reference entity of which has been upgraded or put on the watch list for possible upgrade.[43]

Surveillance issues

[4.320] Surveillance is key. As is apparent from the definition of "credit risk" security (see **[4.310]**), a ratings downgrade of the credit linked notes may have a substantial impact on the manager. In particular, its ability to trade might be infringed. Add to this the reputation risk of the sponsoring institution and it is clear that if something can be done to avoid a downgrade, it will be done.

One option has been not to deliver a credit event notice after the occurrence of a credit event. Apparently the reasoning behind this was to (for the time being) avoid having to run a rating agency test.[44] In a recent note, Standard & Poor's has outlined that 50 (cumulative) credit events have occurred in European synthetic CDOs in the past year. For 30% of these credit events a credit event notice is yet to be issued. And even if the notices were issued, the time lag mostly amounted to one to three months.[45]

Liquidity facility

[4.330] Some synthetic CDOs incorporate a liquidity facility for the SPV. This is predominantly a factor in transactions in which the referenced asset has the capacity to defer interest payments (so-called "payment-in-kind" or "PIK-able" assets), such as CDOs. Such deferment would create a funding gap for the SPV (as it relies on the continued payment of interest on the CDOs to pay the interest on the notes[46]). It is not per se necessary to incorporate a liquidity facility in a transaction simply because offsetting credit default swaps are used.[47]

STRUCTURAL RISKS AND ENHANCEMENTS

Relevant risks

[4.340] The focus of this part of the chapter is on the risks that are particular to managed synthetic CDOs and the ways these risks are mitigated. These issues to some extent overlap with the discussion of risks in the balance sheet equivalents.[48] The relevant risks are:

- credit risk (see **[4.350]**);
- collateral risk (see **[4.360]**);
- portfolio risk (see **[4.370]**);
- cash flow risk (see **[4.380]**);
- interest divergence (see **[4.420]**); and
- currency risk (see **[4.430]**).

Credit risk

[4.350] Just as in a synthetic balance sheet transaction, the SPV bears credit risk on its credit default swap counterparty ("dealer").[49] The credit risk implications may be different if not a single but multiple dealers are involved. This issue is further discussed at **[4.470]**.

Collateral risk

[4.360] The analysis of collateral risk in managed synthetic CDOs is not materially different from the approach in other synthetic structures. The methods used (GICs, deposit accounts, repo agreements) are the same. Different is that the SPV needs to be able to pay out credit event payments under multiple credit default swaps, possibly to multiple dealers, rather than under a single credit default swap.

Portfolio risk

[4.370] An obvious concern for investors is the risk of the (referenced) portfolio. A distinction may be made between referencing corporate credits, which is customary in the credit default swap market, and the use of structured finance securities.[50]

Structured finance securities (AAA) have also increasingly been used as collateral in synthetic CDOs. While the credit rating of this type of collateral is the same as of the types of government bonds that are more regularly used, its liquidity is substantially less. For that reason, rating agencies require overcollateralisation to compensate for this defect.

Cash flow
[4.380] In a managed synthetic CDO, an SPV has two sources of income: protection payments under the credit default swaps in which it sells protection and trading gains. If the SPV has entered into any offsetting credit default swaps, then it may also have certain income from credit event payments. This cash flow may be "leaked" to equity investors through the priority of payments. An elementary way to verify whether a synthetic structure protects the interests of the (mezzanine and senior) noteholders (as well as the super senior investor, if any) is to find out how the SPV allocates its proceeds.

Excess spread
[4.390] A distinguishing feature in (managed) synthetic CDOs is the use, if any, of excess spread to protect investors. Excess spread is the difference between the spreads received on the credit default swaps entered into with counterparties and the coupon payable under the credit linked notes less losses incurred on the portfolio, during any payment period.[51] In earlier deals, excess spread was usually paid out to the equity investor at the next payment date. As a result, this structure was prone to reduced subordination: if the portfolio incurred losses in any given payment period, then that would directly result in a reduction on the principal of the notes in reverse order of seniority.

More recent deals tend to protect investors by trapping excess spread in a reserve account to cover losses until the scheduled termination date. This reserve account would have a "target level". Only funds in the account exceeding the target level amount would be available for distribution to the equity investors. The target level can be, but is not necessarily, a set amount. In a recent transaction, for instance, excess spread was trapped to provision against losses of at least 8% of the notional balance of defaulted reference obligations following a credit event.

Trading gains
[4.400] Depending on market conditions, the manager may be able to generate gains in trading with the portfolio. For example, it may be that the spread on a name with respect to which the SPV has sold protection has tightened and the transaction has subsequently been unwound. The counterparty would then have paid the mark to market value of the credit default swap to the SPV. Again, this income flow may be leaked to equity

investors or trapped within the structure for the benefit of the other noteholders, either by reserving such funds in a separate account or by allowing the manager to reinvest these proceeds.

Rating agencies typically require any trading gains first to be netted against incurred trading losses and, secondly, to trap these in a reserve account to serve as a buffer against later trading losses. Trading gains will also be trapped if the transaction is failing any quality or coverage tests, until they are once again satisfied.[52]

If the proceeds are reinvested, then a related concern is that the reinvestment of proceeds should not adversely impact on the pool quality profile. A reinvestment is usually treated as any other addition of an asset to the portfolio. As a result, eligibility criteria, but also asset specific and portfolio tests, must be satisfied. The reinvestment criteria balance the noteholders' desire to maintain (or improve) portfolio quality with the manager's need for some flexibility to invest in the credit default swaps it views as underrated. This flexibility may be achieved by trapping gains in a selected account that the manager may tap to finance the next purchase.

Trading losses
[4.410] If trading is not as profitable as hoped, consideration should be given to how to cover such losses or mitigate them using excess spread. Several types of loss triggers have been used for this purpose.

Some loss triggers are linked to excess spread. If credit losses increase above the loss trigger threshold, the excess spread is diverted. It is no longer available for distribution to the equity investors. Rather, the SPV may either use the excess spread to pay down the notes sequentially (thus increasing the subordination) or put the funds at the disposal of the manager to purchase additional assets (or pay down the notes sequentially).

Alternatively, the loss triggers may have an impact on the ability to trade altogether.

Interest divergence
[4.420] The underlying concern in managed transactions is the divergence of interest between the mezzanine and senior noteholders (including the super senior investor, if any), on the one hand, and the equity investors and (if different) the manager, on the other. There are different ways[53] to align the interests of the managers and noteholders, for example:
- structuring the management fees in such a way as to reward the manager for long-term, rather than short-term, success (see **[4.90]**). The challenge is to trap excess spread within the structure, not distribute it on day one to equity investors;

- participation by the manager not just in the equity note, but also in the other notes (having a "skin in the game"); and
- a similar alignment of interest between the sponsoring institution and the noteholders can be achieved if the former has (at least) the same exposure to the reference obligation as the SPV has.[54]

Currency risk
[4.430] Presuming physical settlement of the managed synthetic CDO,[55] currency risk is an issue. It relates to the risk that the SPV has delivered to it by a credit default swap counterparty deliverable obligations denominated in another currency than the notes issued. Recovering these obligations would expose the SPV to currency rate fluctuations. This risk can be mitigated in various ways. Moody's suggests adjusting the recovery rate or, alternatively, cash settling only where foreign currency securities are delivered or using a fixed exchange rate to transfer the currency risk to the credit default swap counterparty.[56]

Obviously, if the transaction is static, rather than managed, and the assets of the portfolio are preset in advance, currency risk may be avoided as well.

Depth of the market
[4.440] A final consideration in managed synthetic transactions backed by credit default swaps is the depth of the market. Though the number of names available is increasing, critics will argue that only a limited number of names is actively traded. As a result, the occurrence of a credit event with respect to an actively traded name is bound to affect a number of synthetic CDOs in the market, as WorldCom and Enron have proven. This "dependency" is underlined by a recent study by Fitch on credit events.[57] Interestingly, despite the substantial numbers of corporate defaults in recent times, synthetic CDOs have proven to be relatively resilient.[58] This is remarkable, given that the number of available names in the credit default swap market is still growing.

DOCUMENTATION

Managed synthetics: documentation
[4.450] This part of the chapter outlines the issues that are particular to a managed synthetic transaction from a documentation point of view. These include:
- documenting the credit default swap or credit linked note between the SPV and the investors (see **[4.460]**);
- detailing the various ways in which dealers can be involved in a managed synthetic structure (see **[4.470]**);
- the format of the underlying documentation for the credit default swaps that are part of the synthetic pool of assets (see **[4.480]**); and

- specific issues in credit linked notes (see **[4.520]**).

Documenting credit default swaps

[4.460] The documentation of the credit default swap and credit linked notes in an arbitrage structure closely resembles that in a balance sheet structure. However, there are significant differences, especially considering that most of the arbitrage structures build upon physical, rather than cash, settlement.[59]

The credit events are usually selected from the six that are standard for corporate reference entities, as discussed at **[1.50]**. If other assets are referenced, particularly structured finance securities, specific credit events are used.[60]

In terms of the choice of credit events, obviously this choice is not constrained by the originator's requirement to have regulatory approval in order to get full capital relief. As a result of that, some arbitrage transactions include other "soft" credit events.

The choice for physical settlement (as discussed further at **[4.500]**) – more common in arbitrage structures – has inherent risks. First, the buyer of protection is, upon the occurrence of a credit event, under the obligation to deliver specified deliverable obligations. Depending on the definition of these deliverable obligations in the confirmation, the buyer of protection has the opportunity to buy and then deliver the cheapest in the market. This is also referred to as the "cheapest-to-deliver" option. The second risk associated with physical settlement is that investors, as the sellers of protection, have no assurance as to the value of the deliverable obligations as realising a market value will depend on the liquidity of the delivered obligations and the market conditions.

Dealers

[4.470] Initially, managed synthetic CDOs involved a single dealer with which the SPV was allowed to trade credit default swaps. This prompted concerns on pricing dependency and concentrated credit risk. The market has since evolved to involve a number of dealers. Most deals now disclose the list of approved dealers that may be traded with. The increase in dealers in turn raised concerns as investors run credit risk on multiple parties. These concerns have been addressed in different ways.

Basically, there are two approaches: "gatekeeper" and a structure which involves a preset list of credit default swap dealers.

Gatekeeper approach

In the first, the ability to manage the credit default swaps revolves around a single dealer. This approach has been used in several transactions.[61] In this structure, other dealers are only invited into the structure provided that the first dealer (the "primus inter pares") does not veto. Obviously, this type of transaction is crucially dependant upon the experience of the dealer. Also, it is a money-maker for that specific dealer, particularly if the synthetic portfolio is actively managed.

Intermediary swaps

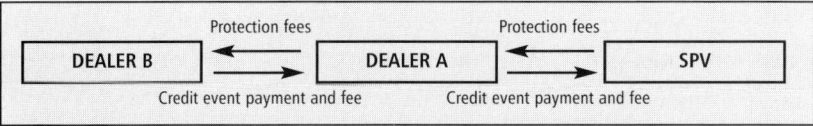

Noteholders can also benefit from this type of structure, eg by using "intermediary" swaps. In this structure the SPV first enters into a swap with the first dealer. The first dealer in turn then enters into a swap with another dealer. The advantage of such a structure is that the dealers down the line do not realise they are actually dealing with a back-to-back arrangement with the SPV. The noteholders are effectively profiting from the supposed marketing strength of the first dealer. However, this profiting comes at a price, as the documentation may provide that if a credit default swap is entered into with another dealer instead of with the first dealer, then the first dealer will receive a form of compensation. Essentially, this is a method to drive costs down for the SPV and inherently for the noteholders.

Pre-agreed list of dealers

The gatekeeper structure can be contrasted with a more transparent structure in which the dealers with which the SPV can enter into credit default swaps are actually on a pre-agreed list. The Robeco VII transaction provides an example, listing ten major market players with which the SPV could trade. From the perspective of a noteholder, the competition between these various dealers should guarantee the lowest possible cost. It also reduces the dependency upon a single major market player. This is substantially different from the gatekeeper structure, in which the first dealer may actually withhold or give its consent in its absolute and sole discretion.

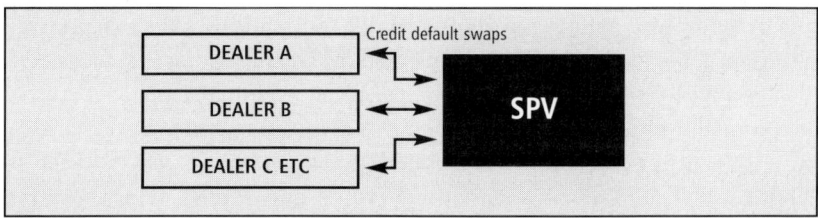

Rating agencies typically set specific requirements, including ratings for dealers that are eligible to be included in the pre-agreed list (typically the required ratings are at least A1 and A-1+/P-1 respectively). If the SPV intended to trade with additional dealers, they too would have to meet these requirements.

Should a dealer be downgraded below this threshold, the SPV would not be allowed to enter into further trades with that dealer unless specific measures were taken to isolate the noteholders from the increased credit risk on the dealer. These measures could include any of posting collateral with the SPV equal to the exposure of the SPV, transferring all rights and obligations to an entity that has the required ratings, providing a guarantee or indemnity reasonably satisfactory to the rating agencies or any other action acceptable to the rating agencies.

The size of synthetic CDOs enables a higher level of diversification. However, this advantage is to a certain extent offset because of the concentration in the credit default swap market, particularly in the US.

ISDA documentation for credit default swaps
[4.480] In order for the SPV and the collateral manager to efficiently trade in credit default swaps, the documentation of these credit default swaps needs to match market practice. This implies substantial differences in the documenting of the schedule to the ISDA Master Agreement in comparison to the format used in the inter-bank market.

It is prudent custom only to trade in credit derivatives if an ISDA Master Agreement and Schedule have been entered into by the trading parties. The selections and further conditions of the schedule impact on the credit risk on the counterparty. When, as in most managed synthetic CDOs, a number of dealers are engaged, it is essential to control that credit risk by stipulating standard conditions the schedule must meet. Most transactions now disclose the material conditions of this standard schedule in the offering circular, enabling investors to properly assess the associated credit risk.

The terms of the standard schedule tend to deviate from market practice. Foremost, the credit risk borne by investors should be minimised. In addition, the SPV is a structured finance vehicle, no ordinary bank. This, too, may prompt changes in the schedule. All in all, this is not materially different from static synthetic transactions. The exception is that a single dealer's wishes to include events of default or termination events may be accommodated in a static balance sheet transaction. The credit risk for investors in a managed synthetic CDO is for the most part reduced by limiting the number of termination events and events of default. The major risk for investors lies in termination of an underlying derivative transaction in respect of which the SPV would be out of the money when marked to market.

This could affect the SPV's ability to service the interest due on the notes in several ways. First, as opposed to the static synthetic CDO, more than one credit default swap counterparty or dealer may be engaged to trade with. Secondly, the ISDA Master Agreement and Schedule should reflect this ability to trade whilst minimising credit risk for the investors. Thirdly, the credit default swap documentation should facilitate trading by adhering to market standards.

The documentation of the credit default swaps in managed synthetic CDOs differs from the static and balance sheet synthetic CDOs. In the latter case the SPV enters into a single credit default swap with the originating bank and this swap is tailor-made to accommodate both the intentions of the originating bank and the underlying assets. In the former case, the credit default swaps are tradeable commodities and should therefore conform to the prevailing market standard to ensure liquidity.

In either case, the documentation is based on the 1999 Definitions and the customary supplements.[62] The recently published 2003 Definitions entail a thorough review of their predecessors and contain significant improvements.[63] Though this will benefit the market in the long term, it raises some risk for investors in the short term. If the new definitions are adopted as market practice, additional costs may be incurred in trying to effect old trades on terms other than the then prevailing market conditions.

Selecting credit events

[4.490] In static and balance sheet deals, the credit events are often tailored to reflect the underlying assets, eg by modifying the threshold amount in the failure to pay credit event or by omitting restructuring altogether. In managed synthetic CDOs, however, market convention specifies that bankruptcy, failure to pay (with a threshold of US$1 million, no grace period applying) and restructuring (either old or modified depending on the market of the reference entity, with a threshold of US$10 million) should be included.

In selecting the credit events the structuring institution should be aware that rating agencies still have concerns over restructuring. It should come as no surprise that some kind of penalty is applied if restructuring under the 1999 Definitions (Old R) is used as a credit event, given the open window for a cheapest-to-deliver option. However, even if restructuring under the 2003 Definitions (Mod R or Mod Mod R) is used, a rating agency may apply additional stress to the default probability.[64] In addition, haircuts may be applied on the modelled recovery rate to account for the fact that even under 2003 Definitions restructuring (whether Mod R or Mod Mod R), the cheapest-to-deliver option entails a risk for the protection seller.[65]

Settlement issues

[4.500] A further difference between synthetic balance sheet transactions and arbitrage synthetic deals is the settlement method. Static synthetic deals tend to rely on cash settlement and intricate valuation processes, whereas managed synthetic deals build on physical settlement instead, containing the timeframe within which the trade is executed. Nevertheless, this settlement method carries other risks for investors as a trade-off for the increased liquidity.

First, the SPV as seller of protection is open to the cheapest-to-deliver risk. Upon the occurrence of a credit event, the relevant dealer as buyer of protection may choose the deliverable obligations from the category specified (usually bond or loan). Although this risk has been substantially reduced by the introduction of the Restructuring Supplement, this has not been accepted in the European market. It remains to be seen whether the modified restructuring option introduced in the 2003 Definitions will change this for the better.

Secondly, there can be no assurance that the deliverable obligations will have any realisable or market value or that any payment due will be made by the relevant reference entity. It may be difficult for the SPV to realise any deliverable obligations it may hold as there may be no, or only a limited, market for such deliverable obligation (eg convertible or zero coupon bonds). It may be difficult to dispose of these or other illiquid deliverable obligations in a timely fashion and for a fair price. This issue is addressed in the documentation by allowing the SPV sufficient time to sell the delivered obligation, usually one year from delivery. Consequently, the scheduled termination date of the credit default swap is generally required to be no later than one year before the legal maturity date of the notes. This extended sale effort may, however, carry additional costs in view of the increased services of the manager.[66]

The further conditions of the credit default swap confirmation (obligations category and characteristics, for instance) will conform to market practice. Some specifics, such as payment dates and denomination, may be specified in the eligibility criteria to avoid additional liquidity or currency risk.

Credit risk

[4.510] The involvement of multiple dealers may give rise to higher credit risk exposure than if only a single credit default swap counterparty were involved. This is because in the latter case all outstanding transactions would be netted. In a multiple dealer structure it would theoretically be possible to be in the money towards a single dealer, and out of the money towards all others. In addition, the dealers could be creditors both in respect of settlement amounts due under separate credit default swaps and in respect of termination payments as a result of marking the terminated swaps to market. In order to alleviate any investor concern, multiple dealer transactions are likely to include additional risk-reducing measures, such as pre-agreed collateral agreements, eg ISDA Credit Support Annexes (CSAs).

Rating agencies have published extensively on the terms and conditions they require in the ISDA Schedule of structured transactions, providing transparency (or at least reliance) to investors in the process. Some arbitrage deals have started to include the ISDA Schedule in their prospectus.

Recently, this transparency has started to envelop collateral agreements. As the terms of CSAs may substantially differ, the impact of the use of these documents on credit risk reduction is not necessarily clear. In order to assess to what extent credit risk has actually been reduced, investors may require further detailed analysis of collateral agreements, either in offering circulars or otherwise. In a recent publication a rating agency has outlined the elements it typically checks in a CSA in the context of a (managed) synthetic CDO. The purpose of this exercise is to ensure that the noteholders do not suffer a loss if the SPV receives less collateral than it had counted on.[67]

Credit linked notes: overview
[4.520] In general, the analysis of credit linked notes in a managed synthetic CDO is similar to that in balance sheet synthetic securitisations.[68] The differences relate primarily to the calculation of principal to be repaid (see **[4.530]**), the waterfall (see **[4.540]**), the security package (see **[4.550]**) and the redemption of the notes (see **[4.560]**).

Principal reductions
[4.530] In a balance sheet synthetic CDO, the calculation of principal to be repaid is a fairly straightforward exercise. The calculation of the payment is based upon the applicable method.[69] The SPV will set off its claim for the cash settlement amount against its obligation to repay principal at maturity.[70]

In an arbitrage transaction referencing credit default swaps, this calculation is a bit more complex. These transactions are usually physically settled and the documentation should thus set out how the difference between the delivered obligations and the physical settlement amount is calculated. This calculation may need more detailing if the structure provides for offsetting credit default swaps. For example, the shortfall could be calculated as the difference between the aggregate amount of collateral liquidated for the purpose of settling the credit default swap (and any related offsetting credit default swap) and the aggregate proceeds of such swap(s). If there were no offsetting credit default swap, the delivered obligations would be sold and the proceeds available for collateral investment.

The liquidation of any delivered obligations will be in the hands of the managers. From an investor's point of view, it is important to verify the manager's commitment to maximising the proceeds of such a sale. Obviously, the manager may not have as much of an incentive to maximise the proceeds.[71]

Waterfall
[4.540] In a balance sheet synthetic CDO the noteholders' claims on the SPV are subordinated to those of the originator in its capacity as credit default swap counterparty. In a synthetic arbitrage transaction, similarly, the rights of the various dealers as credit default swap counterparties are senior to the rights of the noteholders. Furthermore, the management fees need to be reflected in the interest priorities of payments (or "waterfall"). A typical and simplified waterfall in a managed synthetic arbitrage transaction would be as follows:
- payment of administrative expenses (trustee, tax, rating agencies);
- payment on a pro rata basis of each swap counterparty;
- payment of the senior management fees;[72]
- payment of the senior noteholders;
- payment of the mezzanine noteholders;
- payment of the junior management fees; and
- payment of the equity investors.

The waterfall in a balance sheet synthetic CDO tends to be easier to document than in a cash CDO. For instance, in a balance sheet synthetic CDO, the originator will be the sole party providing the income cash flow for the SPV. There is no need, as in cash CDOs, to incorporate both principal and interest payments generated on the securitised assets into the waterfall. This difference is less apparent in managed synthetic CDOs, in which multiple dealers may be involved (and payers to the SPV).

Security package
[4.550] The prevalent choice for physical settlement in managed synthetic structures results in a slightly different security package. As in any other securitisation, the collateral (both eligible investments in highly rated securities and cash deposits) would secure the obligations of the SPV. In addition, the rights of the SPV to any obligations delivered (including, for instance, dividends) to it in a physically settled credit default swap serve as security.

Given the dynamic structure of a managed transaction, these securities do not sit idle. In order to meet ongoing obligations arising out of settled credit default swaps, the manager is most likely empowered to sell collateral and delivered obligations to pay settlement amounts.

The rights of the SPV under ISDA Master Agreements, the supporting collateral agreements such as CSAs, with the various dealers would be included in the security package as well.[73]

Redemption of notes

[4.560] Managed synthetic CDOs referencing corporate credits usually have a maturity of five years. If structured finance securities are referenced, this may be significantly longer. Just as in a synthetic balance sheet transaction, the notes of an arbitrage deal may be redeemed at the option of (a specified majority of) the equity investors if the raison d'être of the transaction falls away. This option may be available to the SPV upon the occurrence of:

- a (qualified) failure to ramp up the target portfolio. Subject to a grace period during which the manager must obtain confirmation of the ratings of the notes from the relevant rating agencies, the notes may be redeemed immediately after the effective date;
- a tax event (eg payments due from credit default swap counterparties would become subject to a withholding tax or the imposition of a tax change which adversely affect payments to the SPV of investments in eligible collateral); or
- any payment date after the non-call period (of typically three years; presumably this would allow the sponsoring institution through its equity stake to terminate the transaction if it would no longer be profitable, eg if the spreads in the credit default swap market would substantially tighten).

In a managed transaction, the manager may have a similar option to have the notes redeemed after the non-call period.

Apart from optional redemption, the structure of the transaction may require mandatory redemption. For example, if certain coverage tests are breached, notes may be partially redeemed until such tests are again satisfied. At any rate, the precise conditions to redemption may vary between transactions and thus merit careful scrutiny by investors.

LEGAL AND REGULATORY ISSUES

Manager: legal issues

[4.570] The legal issues that arise in managed synthetic CDOs are largely the same as in more traditional synthetic structures. Therefore, recharacterisation, due diligence, set-off and confidentiality issues also apply. Those issues are not reiterated here. Instead, the focus of this part of the chapter is on legal issues pertaining to the role of the manager and disclosure issues in arbitrage deals.

From a legal point of view, several issues relating to the manager in a managed synthetic arbitrage deal merit attention, including:
- the relationship between the SPV and the manager (see **[4.580]**);
- the way in which any conflicts of interest between the manager and the noteholders is addressed in the documentation (see **[4.590]**);
- confidentiality (see **[4.600]**);
- conditions imposed (if any) by managed investments regulations (see **[4.610]**);
- any regulatory requirements imposed on the manager (see **[4.620]**); and last but not least
- netting considerations.

SPV/manager relationship
[4.580] The collateral management agreement contains procedures upon which the manager may exercise discretion and make recommendations to the SPV in relation to the composition and management of the portfolio. Although in the end the relationship between the manager and the SPV is one of the experienced adviser and the decision-maker, this relationship may be drafted in different ways. Usually the recommendations from the manager are subject to review and approval by the board of directors or a specific investment committee of the SPV. The SPV may delegate authority to the manager to enable it to carry out its trading activities on a day-to-day basis efficiently without specific approval by the SPV. This does not derogate from the fact that the board of directors is ultimately responsible for the management and control of the portfolio.

Alternatively, the manager may be required to request consent and confirmation for each trade from an investment committee of the SPV. Though this more clearly separates the different responsibilities, this may limit the manager somewhat in its trading opportunities as it must await this consent before acting upon it. To mitigate this disadvantage, clear-cut guidelines for swift procedures, eg within a business day, are essential.

Manager/noteholder conflict
[4.590] As discussed at **[4.420]**, there is potential conflict of interest between the manager and the mezzanine and senior debt holders in a managed synthetic deal, particularly if the manager has an equity stake in the notes issued. For example, the manager may be inclined to buy protection in respect of reference entities or obligations with which the manager itself or the originator with which it is usually affiliated has a strong client relationship. To a certain extent, these interests may be similar; it is obvious that the long-term interests of the noteholders are

not per se served by the manager pursuing its own client relationship priorities, as that will not necessarily lead to the highest long-term returns on the portfolio.

Confidentialty

[4.600] Due to the (potentially) continuously changing profile of the portfolio, confidentiality merits extra attention. In a static synthetic CDO the originating bank will typically hold the obligations of the reference entities in respect of which the credit risk is transferred to the issuer by means of a credit default swap. As the bank owes a duty of confidentiality towards the obligor, it is not entitled to disclose any information on the obligor or the obligation itself to investors. In a managed synthetic CDO, chances are, the originating bank or investment advisers hold few (if any) of the underlying obligations. However, given the bankers' confidentiality, such information still cannot be disclosed. As a result, the documentation will not contain representation whether or not a possible credit event exists. To alleviate this lack of information, the issuer and by reference the noteholders are informed on a regular (monthly and/or quarterly) basis on the composition and quality of the portfolio as a whole through the distribution of portfolio reports.

Managed investments regulations

[4.610] Across jurisdictions, particular attention should be given to whether relevant managed investments regulations contain restrictions that impact on a managed CDO, whether synthetic or true sale.[74]

The manager's liability is usually limited to acts or omissions constituting bad faith, negligence, wilful misconduct or a material breach of a fiduciary duty in the performance of its obligations or any representations and warranties made by it proving to have been incorrect in a material respect when made. In an investment advisory structure the responsibilities are more clearly divided. All ultimate decisions rest with the SPV. This adds strength to the exclusion of liability clause towards the issuer and noteholders alike.

In Australia, all pooled investment vehicles are potentially subject to regulation as "managed investment schemes" under Chapter 5C of the *Corporations Act 2001* (Cth).[75] A "managed investment scheme" is broadly defined as a "scheme" where:[76]

- investors contribute money or equivalent consideration (eg securities) to acquire rights to benefits generated by the scheme;
- these contributions are pooled, or used in a common enterprise, to produce financial benefits for investors in the scheme; and
- the investors do not have day-to-day control over the operation of the scheme.

A managed synthetic CDO possesses these features. However, the vast majority of managed synthetic CDOs and other securitisations should fall outside the scope of Chapter 5C, for the key reason that that Chapter does not apply to institutional-offer or wholesale securitisations (eg where the CDO debt securities have a minimum subscription price of $500,000 or more or are only offered to institutional investors and other professional investors).[77]

For completeness, it is worth noting that the Corporations Act also provides two alternative heads of relief for securitisations. First, the Corporations Act excludes from the definition of "managed investment scheme" the issue of "debentures" by bodies corporate.[78] Thus, if the SPV is a body corporate, rather than a trust, and the CDO securities are "debentures" for the purposes of the Corporations Act, then the CDO will not be subject to Chapter 5C. Secondly, even if the "debenture" exception is not available or not considered viable,[79] the Corporations Act provides a broad exception for bodies corporate.[80] This has the effect of limiting the application of Chapter 5C to non-corporate pooled investment vehicles, such as SPVs that have been structured as trusts. (The presence of this exception naturally raises the question of why a specific exception for debentures issued by bodies corporate is necessary.)

Accordingly, in Australia, the managed investment regulations contained in Chapter 5C of the Corporations Act should not be an issue for managed synthetic CDOs, apart from such CDOs where the SPV is not a body corporate and the CDO debt securities are being offered to retail investors.

Whenever the transaction encompasses the possibility for the SPV to enter into offsetting credit default swaps, netting is a concern as well. Essentially, the SPV should be legally allowed under the relevant jurisdictions to net the contrasting positions.[81]

Regulatory perspective

[4.620] In setting up a managed synthetic CDO, obviously a major consideration is who will actually fill the spot of the manager. Not only do the rating agencies stress the importance of experience in managing the relevant type of assets, but also regulatory provisions may prevent a financial institution from undertaking non-core activities, such as management activities.

Disclosure

On the regulatory front, the managed synthetic transactions have the edge. In these arbitrage deals, regulatory capital is not the primary goal. The ramifications of Basel II therefore seem to be far less of a concern. The originator will typically intend to obtain regulatory capital relief by means of the super senior swap. However, as the risk in that tranche is after all super senior and the proposed Basel II changes particularly target lower rated tranches of issuance, arbitrage transactions seem relatively unaffected.

SYNTHETIC CDOS: DEVELOPMENTS AND CONCLUSION

Recent market developments
[4.630] The market for synthetic CDOs has seen several recent developments, including:
- evolution of asset classes;
- development of rating quality and the related trend towards more defensively managed structures (see **[4.640]**);
- emergence of tranche-only CDOs (see **[4.650]**); and
- the trend towards more transparency (see **[4.660]**).

In general, CDOs have come to reference an increasing variety of assets, from ABS, CDO, index linked securities, private equity and hedge funds.

Ratings quality
[4.640] In recent times the market has developed in terms of rating quality. During the earlier years of the CDO market, the weighted average rating of portfolios referenced ranged between BBB and BBB-. The reference obligations were usually corporate debt. Following the recent economic downturn and rise in corporate default levels, returns in synthetic CDOs have been affected (although still faring better than corporate bonds). It appears that investors are looking for safer investments as well. The result has been a shift in the asset class referenced, from corporate debt to re-packaged securitisations, with an increasing share of RMBS, CMBS and ABS. In addition, the weighted average rating has increased to AA and even AAA in a number of recent deals.[82]

The same concern for safer CDO harbours has also boosted the case for "defensively managed CDOs", which only allow trading in credit impaired securities. However, the appetite for less defensive structures does not seem to have abated, prompting a growing market with a further growing investor base.

Tranche-only CDOs
[4.650] A further market development has been the growth of "tranche-only" CDOs. These transactions may be viewed as bilateral CDOs. Only one tranche of securities is issued, to a single investor. This investor has selected the characteristics of the portfolio, the exposure and any equity position, "reverse engineering" the transaction. Tranche-only CDOs are tailored to the wishes of individual investors, something which is much more difficult to accomplish in a full-fledged synthetic CDO, which must

balance the interests of the various noteholders. Aligning interests between debt and equity investors is not an issue.

An added advantage is in the shortened documentation process. However, cautions have been issued in respect of these deals, in particular for new investors who may be guided into particular investments.[83]

Increased disclosure
[4.660] A further development, possibly related to tranche-only CDOs, has been increasing disclosure. It seems originators have responded to investors' concerns about transparency. Earlier transactions tended to include a blind pool of dealers and provided relatively scarce information on the standard documentation. The more recent deals provide more transparency by including the standard credit default swap confirmation and master confirmation in their entirety (Robeco, for example). Building on the publication by ISDA of Master Credit Derivatives Confirmation Agreements for the various regional markets, it is expected that this trend will continue, supported by the rating agencies, and will perhaps include collateral documentation and, if successful, securities lending documentation in the future.

Managed synthetic CDOs: a summary
[4.670] Managed synthetic CDOs offer a new tool to the palette of structured finance transactions. Although it might appear otherwise at first sight, it is a structure that can appeal to investors across the risk spectrum, not just the high-yield risk-eager investors. The variety in managing opportunities from defensively managed to rather aggressive and the relevant experience of the managers themselves ensure that all risk investment appetite and managers' flexibility can be catered for. And even in the less defensively managed transactions, investors can take comfort in the tests that the rating agencies have developed to carry out effective surveillance of the portfolio. In addition, the flexibility of the market is enhanced by the development of hybrids and structures referencing other credit derivatives.

Managed synthetic CDOs successfully merge credit derivatives, securitisation and asset management technology. As arbitrage transactions they are less prone to changes in the regulatory environment. It is therefore anticipated that this structure has a promising future in structured finance.

1 "Credit Default Swaps, High Risks, Few Rules" (Bloomberg Markets, August 2003) p 56.
2 These so-called CDO squares are the focus of a new Chapter.
3 "Synthetic Index, Benchmarking Portfolio Performance" (Special Report, Fitch Ratings, 4 June 2003).
4 In the Golden Jade CDO the Agricultural Bank of China acts as collateral manager. These transactions indicate that the use of managed synthetic arbitrage represents a growing trend in non-Japan Asia. Refer to Murra F, "Asian Synthetic Arbitrage CDO Market Becomes Active", *Asset Securitization Report*, 30 June 2003, Westlaw 7469496.
5 "Australian Securitisation Term Market Quarterly Issuance Round-up, First Quarter 2003" (Standard & Poor's, 17 April 2003).
6 For a further and detailed analysis, refer to *Credit Derivatives Handbook 2003* (Merrill Lynch, 2003) Ch 6.
7 Bakalar N and Prince JT, "Synthetic CDOs Come of Age; an Investors Guide" (Wachovia Securities, Structured Products Research, CDOs, 18 July 2003) posted at http://www.securitization.net, viewed September 2003.
8 Refer to Ch 2 on credit derivatives generally for a further analysis.
9 "Moody's Approach to Rating Synthetic CDOs" (Moody's, 29 July 2003) p 14.
10 "Aussie Credit Volumes Plummet as Spreads Grind Tighter" (Derivativesweek.com, 27 July 2003).
11 In the Golden Jade CDO the Agricultural Bank of China acts as collateral manager. These transactions indicate that the use of managed synthetic arbitrage represents a growing trend in non-Japan Asia. Refer to Murra F, "Asian Synthetic Arbitrage CDO Market Becomes Active", *Asset Securitization Report*, 30 June 2003, Westlaw 7469496.
12 "Managed Synthetic CDOs" (Criteria Report, Fitch Ratings, 22 January 2003), which states that as of the date of this report it had approximately 20% managed synthetic deals in the pipeline and 80% static compared with the same period in 2002, when it had less than 5% managed and approximately 95% static. A prime example is Cheyne CDO I, referencing a synthetic portfolio of US$4.4 billion.
13 For instance, Nexus and Prise.
14 "Managed Synthetics CDOs" (Criteria Report, Fitch Ratings, 22 January 2003) p 2.
15 "Fallen angels" are companies which were rated investment grade one year prior to default.
16 "Rating CDO Asset Managers" (Criteria Report, Fitch Ratings, 24 September 2002). See also "Criteria for Rating Synthetic CDO Transactions" (Standard & Poor's, September 2003) Section 6, p 5, where the operation review process of the manager is further detailed. In the same report, Section 6, p 7, specific structural requirements are discussed that may be used in a managed synthetic CDO to capture the performance of the transaction in the light of the manager's actions.
17 Bakalar N and Prince JT, "Synthetic CDOs Come of Age; an Investors Guide" (Wachovia Securities, Structured Product Research, CDOs, 18 July 2003) p 20, posted at http://www.securitization.net, viewed September 2003.
18 Refer to discussion in Ch 2.
19 This risk may be caused by payment-in-kind assets. These assets have the ability to defer and capitalise current interest without triggering an event of default under their terms of issuance.
20 Hyder I, "Collateralised Debt Obligations and the Role of Monoline Insurers" in *Euromoney Handbook 2003*, www.xlca.com/pdf/euromoneyhandbook2003/pdf, viewed June 2003, p 38.
21 However, this is different if the underlying assets include structured finance securities, which are drawn from prior securitisations.
22 This type of transaction remains the execution of choice, according to "CDO Spotlight" (BancOne Capital Markets, 25 August 2003).
23 If the referenced assets include (less liquid) structured finance securities, then the ramp-up period is typically longer.
24 In order to induce the collateral manager to arrive at the target portfolio, the transaction may provide that the fees payable are significantly reduced (in case of the senior fee) and or even wiped out (in the case of the subordinated fee). See ESAF Navigator transaction.

25 See **[4.310]**.
26 "Global Cash Flow and Synthetic CDO Criteria" (Standard & Poor's) p 28. See **[4.340]**.
27 Some deals have included the possibility to enter into offsetting swaps in which the protection payments are all paid in advance, thus reducing credit risk for the counterparty. These transactions are referred to as "up-front offsetting swaps", as opposed to the common "ongoing" credit default swaps. In an up-front offsetting credit default swap, only one fixed amount is payable by the SPV.
28 Bakalar N and Prince JT, "Synthetic CDOs Come of Age; an Investors Guide" (Wachovia Securities, Structured Products Research, CDOs, 18 July 2003) p 12, posted at http://www.securitization.net, viewed September 2003
29 Jazz CDO is an exception.
30 See **[4.50]**.
31 Bakalar N and Prince JT, "Synthetic CDOs Come of Age; an Investors Guide" (Wachovia Securities, Structured Products Research, CDOs, 18 July 2003) p 22, posted at http://www.securitization.net, viewed September 2003
32 "Moody's Approach to Rating Synthetic CDOs" (Moody's, 29 July 2003) p 8.
33 "Managed Synthetics CDOs" (Criteria Report, Fitch Ratings, 22 January 2003) p 3.
34 According to "Criteria for Rating Synthetic CDO Transactions" (Standard & Poor's, September 2003) Section 6, p 6, there has been much discussion about eliminating the IC test from synthetic CDOs as the total spread income coming into the portfolio, due to leverage, usually dwarfs the interest that needs to be paid. Standard & Poor's does not require an IC test if enough comfort can be drawn from a minimum spread test and if the loss of a couple of the highest spread obligations does not lead to non-payment of any of the rated tranches.
35 "CDO Evaluator Applies Monte Carlo Simulation to Determine Portfolio Quality" (Standard & Poor's, 13 November 2001).
36 The model is posted at http://www.fitchratings.com.
37 See **[4.10]**. Standard & Poor's refer to their Rated Overcollateralisation indicator. See "Rated Overcollateralisation Benchmark: A New Tool for Primary and Secondary Market CDOs" (Standard & Poor's, 2 October 2002).
38 Reference may be made, however, to "Criteria for Rating Synthetic CDO Transactions" (Standard & Poor's, September 2003) Section III: Sizing of Defaults and Recoveries and Calculating the Credit Enhancement. It provides a thorough overview of the ratings process and particular attention is drawn to the explanation of the six standard haircuts that Standard & Poor's will consider for a synthetic CDO. These include: the general cheapest-to-deliver haircut (the broad ability of the calculation agent to find the worst-priced eligible obligation to be bid upon during the valuation process following a credit event), the specified currencies haircut (relating to the pricing discrepancy that arises when the obligations of a reference entity are priced differently in different markets, the convertibility haircut (with lower possible valuation), the consent-required loan haircut (which kind of loan may be more difficult to sell downstream), the insufficient period before bidding haircut (minimum time after credit event) and the old restructuring haircut (increased likelihood of credit event compared to standard probability).
39 In a recent transaction it was specified that the manager's judgment could not be called into question (by investors) as a result of subsequent events.
40 Standard & Poor's is arguably more flexible on the definition of what, for instance, a credit risk security is.
41 "Moody's Approach to Rating Synthetic CDOs" (Moody's, 29 July 2003) p 12. Moody's suggests that the definition of a "credit risk trade" may require pre-specified objective measures from the beginning of the transaction in addition to the manager's judgment that with the passage of time the reference entity will experience a credit event. A loss- or ratings-based trigger to shut off credit risk trading, with the ability of the investors to turn the trading back on if they feel that is warranted, is also recommended.
42 "CDO Spotlight: Par-Building Trades Merit Scrutiny" (Standard & Poor's, 15 July 2002). This memo also highlights that such a purchase could also lead to leakage of uninvested proceeds to the equity investor on the first payment date, unless the managing fee structure has been adapted for that purpose.
43 Several rating agencies' approaches to reinvestment are that it must "maintain or

improve" the quality. The manager would, for example, be able to sell a BBB asset and reinvest it in a AA asset or shorten the term of the asset. Refer to "Beyond Defaults and Recoveries: Structural Provisions in CDOs" (Standard & Poor's, 13 November 2002). All reinvestments other than credit risk sales must maintain or improve the CDO Monitor test. This reduces the likelihood that the manager will be able to arbitrage certain tests. For example, the manager would not be able to buy pairs of securities with high and low ratings (so-called "bar bell distribution of the portfolio") to achieve a stated average rating, without the likelihood of deteriorating the CDO Monitor tests. See also "Moody's Approach to Rating Synthetic CDOs" (Moody's, 29 July 2003) p 13.

[44] Refer to "An Insight into CDO Surveillance: Collateral Pools and the Risks that Govern Them" (Standard & Poor's, 30 April 2002). The "removal" of the defaulted asset appeared to be linked to the delivery of the credit event notice.

[45] "Surveillance Policy Clarified for Events of Default in Synthetic CDO Transactions" (Standard & Poor's, 18 August 2003). Standard & Poor's stipulates that immediately upon an identification of an asset in default, the collateral pool is run through the CDO Evaluator. After receipt of final recovery, this process is repeated.

[46] "Rating Criteria for Cash Flow ABS/MBS CDOs" (Fitch Ratings, 9 November 2000) p 10.

[47] Refer to the ESAF Navigator transaction, p 34.

[48] Refer to Ch 2.

[49] Refer to **[3.250]**.

[50] Synthetic CDOs referencing structured finance securities are the focus of a follow-up contribution.

[51] Banking Committee on Banking Supervision, *(Third) Consultative Document, The New Basel Capital Accord* (Bank for International Settlement) no 512, posted at http://www.bis.org, viewed September 2003, for a more detailed definition.

[52] See "Moody's Approach to Rating Synthetic CDOs" (Moody's, 29 July 2003) p 13.

[53] For a more detailed overview, see "Balancing Debtholder and Equityholder Interests in CDOs" (Standard & Poor's, 13 November 2002).

[54] Refer to Imperial II CDO presale report.

[55] Currency risk in cash settled transactions are discussed in Ch 3.

[56] "Moody's Approach to Rating Synthetic CDOs" (Moody's, 29 July 2003) p 18.

[57] O'Connor CM, "Who Generated Top Credit Events?", *Asset Securitization Report*, 19 May 2003, 2003 Westlaw 7469350. See also "Credit Events in Global Synthetic CDOs: 2002-2003" (Special Report, Fitch Ratings, 12 May 2003) pp 1 and 4.

[58] "Corporate Defaults Drive European Synthetic CDO Rating Actions" (Standard & Poor's, 26 June 2003).

[59] This is a rule of thumb rather than a must. There are several managed synthetic CDOs which incorporate cash settlement instead. For these kinds of transactions reference should be made to the discussion in Ch 3 on cash settlement.

[60] A discussion of synthetic securitisation referencing structured finance securities is to be published as a follow-up to this publication.

[61] Such as Cheyne and Jazz.

[62] The *Supplement Relating to Successor and Credit Events* (28 November 2001), the *Supplement Relating to Convertible, Exchangeable and Accreting Obligations* (9 November 2001) and, in the case of North American reference entities only, the *Restructuring Supplement* (11 May 2001).

[63] Refer to discussion of the changes brought about by the 2003 Definitions in Ch 2.

[64] "Moody's Approach to Rating Synthetic CDOs" (Moody's, 29 July 2003) p 15. Moody's will add a 12.5% stress to the modelled default probability if Old R is used, and 5% if Mod R is used. If any other soft credit event (obligation acceleration without mitigation, bankruptcy without the Successor and Credit Event Supplement) is included, an additional 12.5% stress will be applied. Moody's notes that if physical settlement is an option in the CDO, the soft credit events may not be as problematic.

[65] "Moody's Approach to Rating Synthetic CDOs" (Moody's, 29 July 2003) p 17. Moody's notes that it will publish several reports shortly detailing these findings.

[66] Alternatively, a distinction could be made between those credit default swaps that are

settled on maturity and those that are not. As to the latter, the "unsettled" credit default swaps, the maturity date could be extended. All protection payments made to the SPV regarding the unsettled credit default swap could then be held as a reserved amount. See ESAF Navigator, terms and conditions of the notes, s 8(a)(i).

[67] "Criteria for Rating Synthetic CDO Transactions" (Standard & Poor's, September 2003) Section 7, p 1. The list includes amongst others: the base currency of the collateral (if different than the currency of the notes, there could be currency risk), the independent amount (should be zero) and the threshold amount (should be infinite in respect of the SPV, to prevent the SPV from becoming obligated to post collateral) and the minimum transfer amount should be as low as possible to minimise any remaining credit risk.

[68] Refer to **[3.200]**.

[69] Refer to **[3.370]**.

[70] This is, of course, a simplification. Most synthetic transactions will provide for some kind of cushion to protect noteholders, whether by means of excess spread or otherwise: see **[4.390]**.

[71] To a certain extent, this moral hazard may be offset by structuring the management fees and aligning its interests with the noteholders.

[72] In a structure incorporating a super senior swap between the SPV and a super senior investor, the protection fees payable to such investor would rank prior to the coupon payable on the senior notes.

[73] In order to manage the synthetic portfolio, eg to substitute or transfer a credit default swap (CDS), that CDS must be released first. To that end the issuer must issue an Issuer Order to the Trustee, specifying the substitution, transfer or whatever. The trustee then countersigns to release the security. The same approach applies with respect to rights in eligible investments and/or deliverable obligations/delivered obligations. That order is subsequently passed on to the custodian (in the case of eligible investments, delivered obligations) or the portfolio administrator (in the case of (offsetting and other CDS).

[74] In Australia, for instance, particular attention should be paid to the *Managed Investments Act 1998* (Cth) and subsequent legislation. Refer to von Nessen, P and Robertson S, *A Practical Guide to Managed Investments* (Lawbook Co, 2002).

[75] As regards the regulation of managed investment schemes, see generally Ali PU, Stapledon G and Gold M, *Corporate Governance and Investment Fiduciaries* (Thomson Legal & Regulatory, 2003) at [5.37]-[5.45].

[76] *Corporations Act 2001* (Cth), s 9. The term "scheme" is not defined in the Corporations Act. It is arguable that a mere plan of action will be sufficient to give rise to a "scheme": *Clowes v FCT* (1954) 91 CLR 209; *Australian Softwood Forests Pty Ltd v A-G (NSW)* (1981) 148 CLR 121.

[77] *Corporations Act 2001* (Cth), s 601ED(2).

[78] *Corporations Act 2001* (Cth), s 9, para (j) of the definition of "managed investment scheme".

[79] The complicating factor here is that the definition of "debenture" excludes "bills of exchange" and certain "promissory notes" (those with a face value of $50,000 or more). It remains unclear whether either of those carve-outs to the definition would apply to the limited recourse debt securities issued in managed synthetic CDOs and other securitisations: *Corporations Act 2001* (Cth), s 9, paras (c)(iii) and (d) of the definition of "debenture".

[80] *Corporations Act 2001* (Cth), s 9, para (d) of the definition of "managed investment scheme".

[81] Although some general comfort may be drawn from the ISDA netting opinion, caution is advised. The opinions focus on the effect of automatic early termination and may not cover related set-off issues that are relevant in the transaction at hand.

[82] "High Grade Structured Finance CDOs" (Special Report, Fitch Ratings, 31 March 2003).

[83] O'Connor CM, "Single-tranche CDOs: Fitch Cautions ... Sellers Retort", *Asset Securitization Report*, 7 July 2003, 2003 WestLaw 7469535; "Innovations in the Synthetic CDO Market: Tranche-Only CDOs" (JP Morgan Global Structured Finance Research, 22 January 2003).

Chapter 5

INSURANCE SECURITISATION: CONVERGENCE OF THE INSURANCE AND CAPITAL MARKETS

INSURANCE SECURITISATION: INTRODUCTION

Insurance and reinsurance

[5.10] Insurance companies generally resort to reinsurance to manage capacity issues. An insurance company can, by transferring or ceding risk to a reinsurance company, enhance its ability to absorb high-value losses on individual insurance policies (large line capacity) or write a substantial volume of policies in respect of a particular event or in a specific geographic region (premium capacity).[1] The reinsurance company, however, faces the same problem as the ceding insurer; too much of any one risk and the occurrence of the reinsured event may lead to a substantial erosion of the reinsurance company's capital or insolvency. Again, reinsurance companies have traditionally addressed the issue of risk accumulation by laying off or retroceding reinsured risks to other reinsurance companies (retrocessionaires).

Securitisation offers insurance and reinsurance companies a powerful alternative to traditional methods of risk transfer. Insurance securitisation involves the issue of debt securities backed by the cash flow from underwriting particular risks and so enables insurance and reinsurance companies to transfer those risks to investors in the capital markets.[2]

To date, the vast majority of insurance securitisations have involved the securitisation of "peak peril" or catastrophic risk, in particular the risk of the occurrence of relatively infrequent, but financially devastating, natural disasters, such as earthquakes, hurricanes and tornados. More recently, it has been suggested that securitisation can be employed to provide coverage in respect of other catastrophic risks, such as the risk of terrorism.[3]

Another emerging class of insurance securitisation is the securitisation of life insurance policies.

CATASTROPHIC RISK SECURITISATION

Market for catastrophe-linked securities

Development of CAT bond market

[5.20] The first securitisations of catastrophic risk were executed in 1994-1995.[4] The market for catastrophe-linked securities (the so-called "CAT bonds") remains, however, relatively small: in 2002, there was a total of nine transactions involving the issuance of approximately US$1.2 billion CAT bonds.[5]

To date, the principal cedents of catastrophic risk in CAT bond transactions have been US, Japanese and European insurance and reinsurance companies.[6] (As of 30 December 2002, only two companies outside the insurance and reinsurance sectors had executed catastrophic risk securitisations: Tokyo Disneyland and Vivendi.[7]) The principal classes of catastrophic risk that have been transferred to investors are:[8]
- California earthquake risk;
- European windstorm risk;
- Florida hurricane risk; and
- Japan earthquake risk.

The development of the CAT bond market has been driven by the heavy losses suffered by insurance and reinsurance companies in the early to mid-1990s in relation to a series of "mega-catastrophes":[9]
- 1990: winter storms (Europe) – estimated US$10 billion of insured losses;
- 1991: Typhoon Mireille (Japan) – estimated US$5.2 billion of insured losses;
- 1992: Hurricane Andrew (US) – estimated US$14 billion of insured losses;
- 1994: Northbridge earthquake (US) – estimated US$12 billion of insured losses; and
- 1995: Kobe earthquake (Japan) – estimated US$4.1 billion of insured losses.

Insurance securitisation: advantages

[5.30] The most significant advantage of insurance securitisation over traditional methods of risk transfer is the far greater capacity of the global capital markets, compared to the global reinsurance markets, to absorb the losses flowing from natural disasters and other catastrophes. It is considered that a series of natural disasters in the order of the magnitude of Hurricane Andrew or the Northbridge earthquake would be likely to lead to the insolvency of a substantial number of insurance and reinsurance companies, consequently imposing severe stress on the ability of industry survivors and public insurance funds to cover the insured losses.[10] The greater depth of the global capital markets should also mean more stable and cheaper pricing for the transfer of catastrophic risks (compared to pricing in the global reinsurance markets).[11]

CAT bonds and other insurance-linked securities are also attractive to institutional investors. The occurrence of natural disasters does not follow any discernible pattern and consequently is not correlated to the price performance of conventional investment assets, such as equity securities and government and corporate debt securities.[12] The combination of relatively high rates of return (to compensate investors from assuming the particular catastrophic risk) and zero correlation to conventional investment assets means that the inclusion of CAT bonds in an investment portfolio should not only increase the portfolio's return, but also reduce the collective risk of the portfolio.[13]

Structure

Generic CAT bond transaction structure

[5.40] CAT bonds are created by synthetically securitising catastrophic risk.[14] The structure of a generic CAT bond transaction is similar to the structures employed in fully funded synthetic collateralised debt obligations.

A bankruptcy-remote, off-balance sheet special purpose vehicle (SPV) is established by the ceding sponsor (generally, an insurance or reinsurance company) for the purpose of assuming particular catastrophic risks and issuing debt securities to investors in the capital markets backed by the cash flow from the assumption of such risks. Most CAT bond transactions involve the securitisation of "single perils" (ie a specific class of catastrophic risk), rather than "multiple perils".[15]

Risk transfer agreement

[5.50] The transfer of risk from the ceding sponsor to the SPV is effected via a risk transfer agreement. Under the risk transfer agreement, the sponsor agrees to make periodic premium payments to the SPV in exchange for the SPV making certain payments (the different payment mechanisms are discussed at **[5.70]**) to the sponsor on the occurrence of the stipulated catastrophe.[16] The premiums paid to the SPV and the cash flows generated by the investment by the SPV of the subscription proceeds for the debt securities issued by it are used to service those debt securities.

In common with other securitisations, the debt securities are limited recourse secured instruments (ie the recourse of the investors and the SPV's other creditors is limited to the proceeds from the enforcement of the security interest granted by the SPV to support its obligations to such parties). The proceeds of subscription will generally be invested in highly rated, short-term debt securities.

The structure of a generic CAT bond transaction is set out below.

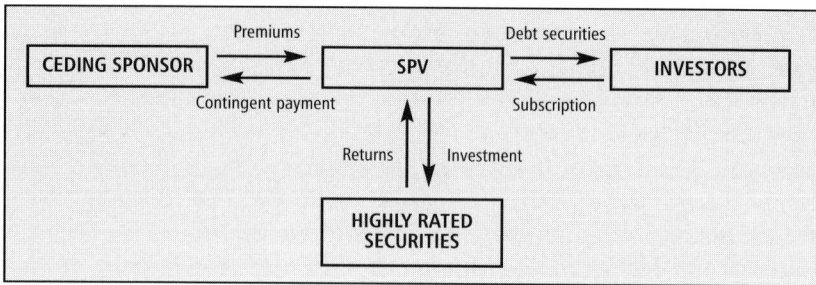

Occurrence of catastrophe
[5.60] The SPV's obligation to repay the principal amount of the debt securities issued by it (and, in the case of principal-protected tranches, its obligation to make interest payments on the debt securities) is contingent upon the occurrence of the stipulated catastrophe.[17]

If the maturity date for the debt securities arrives without the stipulated catastrophe having occurred, the principal amount of the debt securities will be repaid in full to the investors by the SPV. If, however, the stipulated catastrophe occurs during the term of the debt securities, the SPV will generally be entitled to redeem the debt securities immediately with its obligation to repay the principal amount of those securities being reduced by the amount necessary to discharge the SPV's payment obligations to the ceding sponsor under the risk transfer agreement.

Payment triggers
[5.70] The SPV's payment obligations to the ceding sponsor under the risk transfer agreement will usually be subject to a parametric or other non-indemnity trigger.[18] These triggers are preferred to indemnity triggers as they overcome the problems of the moral hazard of the ceding sponsor over-reporting its losses from the catastrophe or the ceding sponsor not taking sufficient steps to mitigate its losses.[19]

There are two classes of payment triggers: indemnity and non-indemnity payment triggers.[20]

Indemnity trigger (or "book of business" trigger)
The SPV agrees to indemnify the ceding sponsor in respect of all insured losses incurred by the sponsor due to the occurrence of the catastrophe.

Non-indemnity triggers

There are three types of non-indemnity triggers (of which the most common is the parametric trigger):[21]

1. *Parametric trigger*: the SPV agrees to make a payment to the ceding sponsor calculated by reference to the magnitude of the catastrophe in a specific geographic location.
2. *Index trigger*: the SPV agrees to make a payment to the ceding sponsor calculated by reference to the change in the level of an industry loss index (such as the Guy Carpenter Catastrophe Catastrophe Index, RMS CAT Index or US Property Claims Services Index) following the occurrence of the catastrophe.
3. *Modelled loss trigger*: the SPV agrees to make a payment to the ceding sponsor calculated by reference to the estimated impact of the catastrophe on a portfolio of hypothetical insurance or reinsurance policies.

Tranching

[5.80] In general, the investors' principal will be at risk on the occurrence of the stipulated catastrophe. However, the CAT bonds issued to investors may include a principal-protected tranche.[22] In the case of principal-protected CAT bonds, the occurrence of the stipulated catastrophe during the term of the securities will not lead to the loss of principal, but will instead result in the extension of the maturity date for the securities and the cessation of all further interest payments on the securities. Accordingly, the investors' rights to receive interest and the return of the principal on the original maturity date, but not the principal amount of the securities itself, will be at risk on the occurrence of the stipulated catastrophe.

Also, the CAT bonds may be part of a partially defeased structure, in that the CAT bonds are issued by the SPV in conjunction with conventional debt securities.[23] The latter securities are not exposed to catastrophic risk.

In common with synthetic and cash securitisations, the CAT bonds may be tranched; certain debt securities will be more exposed to catastrophic risk than other debt securities.[24] Tranching is generally effected through the combination of a security interest and a priority agreement. The SPV grants a security interest over its assets (comprising the debt securities in which the subscription proceeds have been invested and the chose in action constituted by the SPV's right to receive periodic payments of premium under the risk transfer agreement) to an independent trustee for the benefit of the investors. However, the different tranches of debt securities do not share equally in the benefit of the security interest; the junior tranche's entitlement is limited to the residue remaining after principal and arrears of interest on the mezzanine and senior tranches have been paid in full, and the mezzanine tranche's entitlement is likewise limited to the residue remaining after principal and arrears of interest on the senior tranche have been paid in full.

Upon the occurrence of the stipulated catastrophe, the payment obligations of the SPV under the risk transfer agreement will be met out of the assets of the SPV with any residue being applied to redeem the debt securities in order of their ranking. The junior tranche therefore protects the other tranches against loss and, consequently, investors holding the junior tranche of debt securities will receive, along with a greater risk of loss, a higher interest rate than the senior and mezzanine tranche investors (and investors holding the mezzanine tranche of debt securities will receive a higher interest rate than the senior tranche investors).

Insurance

Insurance risks

[5.90] CAT bonds are subject to recharacterisation risk. This is the risk that they will, as a matter of law, be characterised by a court as constituting contracts of insurance with the result that the SPV, and arguably also the investors in the CAT bonds, will be considered to be carrying on an insurance business. A party that carries on an "insurance business" in Australia must be formally authorised to do so by the Australian Prudential Regulation Authority.[25] Non-compliance will subject the contravening party to criminal liability.[26] In addition, there is a real risk that, under Australian law, the risk transfer agreement and the CAT bonds themselves, as insurance contracts written by an unauthorised insurer, may be void.[27]

SPV and insurance business

[5.100] "Insurance business" is defined by the *Insurance Act 1973* (Cth) as "the business of undertaking liability, by way of insurance (including reinsurance), in respect of any loss or damage, including liability to pay damages or compensation, contingent upon the happening of a specified event".[28] The Insurance Act does not provide further guidance as to what constitutes "insurance" (or "reinsurance") beyond excluding certain classes of business from the statutory definition of "insurance business". Thus, the issue of whether a particular contract or instrument is an insurance contract is a matter for the general law.

Under general law, an insurance contract is a contract that possesses the following attributes:[29]
- one party has provided consideration to the other party and the latter has, in exchange, agreed to pay money or confer an equivalent benefit on the former on the occurrence of a stipulated event, and there is uncertainty as to whether or when that event will occur; and

- the recipient of the contingent payment has an "insurable interest" in the subject matter of the contract.[30]

The requirement for an insurable interest has been substantially modified by the Australian *Insurance Contracts Act 1984* (Cth).[31] It is not necessary, in the case of contracts of non-marine insurance, for the recipient of the contingent payment to have an insurable interest in the subject matter of the contract. This does not, however, mean that a mere promise, supported by valuable consideration, to pay an amount contingent upon an uncertain event will constitute an insurance contract. The payee must, as a result of the occurrence of the stipulated event, suffer loss through damage to or a diminution in the value of the subject matter of the contract.[32]

Accordingly, with regard to contracts of non-marine insurance, the requirement for an insurable interest at general law must be read as follows. First, the payee is to have a pecuniary interest in the subject matter of the contract and, secondly, the contingent payment to be made under the contract must be by way of indemnification for the loss suffered by the payee on the occurrence of the stipulated event.[33]

This requirement for indemnification of the loss suffered by the payee means that it is unlikely that a risk transfer agreement where the SPV's payment obligations to the ceding sponsor are subject to a non-indemnity trigger (ie a parametric, index or modelled loss trigger: see **[5.70]**) will constitute an insurance contract. A risk transfer agreement that incorporates an indemnity trigger is, in contrast, at risk of constituting a contract of insurance: the SPV is liable, on the occurrence of the stipulated event, to make the ceding sponsor whole in respect of the insured losses incurred by it due to that event.

Investors in CAT bonds and insurance business

[5.110] It is arguable that CAT bonds cannot constitute insurance contracts (irrespective of the type of payment trigger in the underlying risk transfer agreement). The investors will, on the occurrence of the stipulated event, be releasing the SPV from liability to repay the principal amount of the CAT bonds (or repay the principal on the original maturity date and make future interest payments, in the case of principal-protected tranches of CAT bonds), as opposed to undertaking liability to indemnify the SPV in respect of the losses incurred due to the occurrence of the stipulated event.[34]

This issue has not, to date, been the subject of judicial scrutiny. It may, from the perspective of investors, be preferable, ex abundante cautela, to take heed of a possible counter-argument. By agreeing to place their principal at risk on the occurrence of the stipulated event and, consequently, to release the SPV from liability should that event occur, the investors in the CAT bonds are effectively increasing the SPV's capital and thereby allowing it to discharge the liability (to the ceding sponsor under the risk transfer agreement) imposed on it as a result of the stipulated event occurring. This arrangement, pursuant to which the SPV is made whole in respect of the liability incurred by it to the ceding sponsor, constitutes an insurance contract, thus rendering the investors in the CAT bonds subject, among other things, to the licensing requirements of the *Insurance Act 1973* (Cth).[35]

Having said this, it is again arguable that the risk of the investors in the CAT bonds being considered to be carrying on the business of insurance is minimal where the SPV's payment obligations under the risk transfer agreement are subject to a non-indemnity trigger.[36] In that situation, there is no link between the depletion of the SPV's payment obligations to the investors and the actual loss suffered by the ceding sponsor as a result of the occurrence of the stipulated event. Investors may take a degree of comfort from the fact that this interpretation has the support of the UK insurance regulator, the Financial Services Authority.[37]

In the United States, this issue has been addressed in the *Special Purpose Reinsurance Vehicle Model Act 2001* released by the National Association of Insurance Commissioners. This Act, which is designed to facilitate the sponsorship of catastrophic risk securitisation transactions by US insurance and reinsurance companies, expressly provides a safe-harbour from State insurance laws for investors in CAT bonds.[38] In addition, the US Bond Market Association has recommended that where an issuer of CAT bonds believes that investors in those instruments are at risk of becoming subject to the insurance laws of a jurisdiction (a "non-permitted jurisdiction"), it should state in the offering document for the CAT bonds that only investors resident in a "permitted jurisdiction" may purchase the CAT bonds and require investors to execute a "purchaser's awareness letter" in which the investors confirm that they are resident in a permitted jurisdiction.[39]

LIFE INSURANCE SECURITISATION

Open block securitisations

[5.120] Open block securitisations are structurally similar to the whole of business securitisations discussed in Ch 8, in that in both cases the debt securities issued to investors in the capital markets are backed by the cash flows from a limited recourse loan made by the issuer to the transaction sponsor.[40]

Open block securitisations are employed by life insurance companies to crystallise the present value of the surplus[41] expected to emerge from a segregated portfolio or "block" of life insurance policies.[42] These transactions enable life insurance companies to originate blocks of business and then effectively sell that business to investors, freeing up capital that can be used to write new business and releasing the embedded profit in the securitised business. The block comprises the liabilities of the life insurance company under the designated life insurance policies and the revenues (premiums and fees) generated by those policies and the assets in which those revenues have been invested.

An SPV is established by the life insurance company sponsor for the purpose of making a loan to the sponsor and issuing debt securities to investors in the capital markets backed by principal and interest payments on the loan. In common with other securitisations, these debt securities may be credit tranched. The proceeds of the debt securities are lent on a secured, limited recourse basis to the sponsor. The sponsor's obligations to repay the principal amount of, and make interest payments on, the loan are contingent upon the emergence of, and limited to, the surplus on a segregated portfolio or block of life insurance polices. In addition, the sponsor's obligations under the loan are supported by a first-ranking security interest granted to the SPV over the revenues of the life insurance policies[43] and the assets in which those revenues have been invested.[44]

The structure of a generic open block securitisation transaction is set out below.

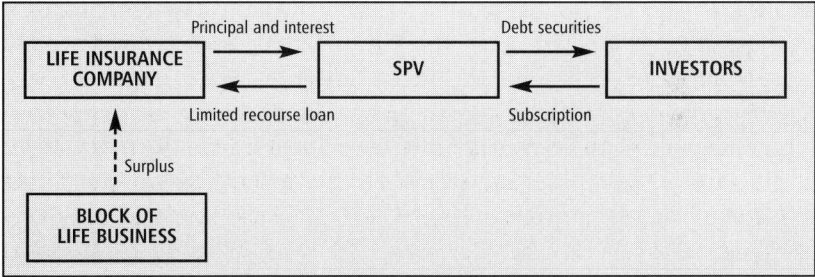

Viatical and life settlement securitisations

[5.130] Viatical and life settlement securitisations are, in contrast to block securitisations, structurally equivalent to conventional cash securitisations.[45] The subscription proceeds of the debt securities issued to the investors in the capital markets are employed by the issuer to acquire a pool of life insurance policies and the debt securities are serviced out of the cash flows (the death benefits and bonuses) generated by those policies.

A *viatical* settlement refers to the purchase of a life insurance policy at a discount to its face value in circumstances where the person insured is terminally ill. A *life settlement* is the purchase of life insurance policies at a discount to face value in all other circumstances.

An SPV is established for the purpose of acquiring life insurance policies and issuing debt securities to finance the acquisition of those policies and the payment of premiums on the policies (this last step is crucial, to keep the policies in force and ensure that the SPV can collect the death benefits under the policies on the death of the insured persons).

The structure of a generic viatical/life settlement securitisation transaction is set out below.

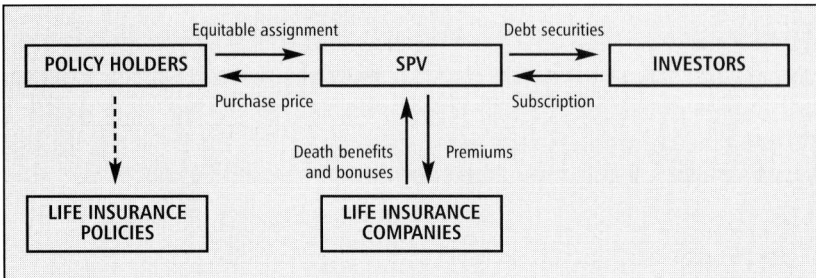

In common with conventional cash securitisations, the acquisition of the securitised life insurance policies is effected by an assignment in equity. In Australia the *Life Insurance Act 1995* (Cth) provides an exclusive regime for the legal assignment of life insurance policies, but does not preclude equitable assignments of life insurance policies.[46] However, a number of jurisdictions (eg Ontario) prohibit both the legal and equitable assignment of life insurance policies, thus making impossible the implementation of viatical and life settlement securitisations in those jurisdictions.[47] In addition, several US jurisdictions have enacted specific laws regulating viatical and life settlements, requiring secondary purchasers of life insurance policies to hold licences, imposing disclosure requirements on purchasers (eg a purchaser must inform the policyholder of possible alternatives to a viatical or life settlement) and restricting advertising for settlements.[48]

[1] See generally Culp CL, *The ART of Risk Management: Alternative Risk Transfer, Capital Structure, and the Convergence of Insurance and Capital Markets* (John Wiley & Sons, 2002) pp 333-336.

[2] See generally "Structured Finance and Catastrophe Risk" (Special Report, Fitch Ratings, 3 February 1997) p 2; Shann J, "The Art of Securitizing Catastrophe Risk" [1999] IFLR (August) 27-28; Ali PU, "GIO, Earthquakes and Hurricanes: An Overview of Catastrophe-Linked Securities and Other Innovations" (2000) 18 C&SLJ 62; Cox SH, Fairchild JR and Pedersen HW, "The Economics of Insurance Securitizations", *Contingencies* (Sept/Oct 2000).

[3] See "Securitising Terror: Terrorism Catastrophe Bonds", *Risk* (March 2003).

[4] See Froot K, "The Evolving Market for Catastrophic Event Risk" (Marsh & McLennan Securities, 1998) p 12; cf Lane MN and Beckwith RG, "Trends in the Insurance-Linked Securities Market", *Derivatives Quarterly* (Fall 2000).

[5] See Mathias A, "Why Not CAT Bonds?", *Environmental Finance* (March 2002); Guy Carpenter & Co, "Market Update: The Catastrophe Bond Market at Year-End 2002" (March 2003) pp 4 and 31; Mathias A, "Are CAT Bonds Changing Course?", *Environmental Finance* (April 2003).

[6] See Guy Carpenter & Co, "Market Update: The Catastrophe Bond Market at Year-End 2002" (March 2003) pp 6-7. A Taiwanese reinsurance company has recently sponsored a CAT bond transaction to lay off Taiwan earthquake risk to investors: see further "First Taiwan CAT Bond to offer Diversity for Hungry Investors", *Structured Finance International News* (9 May 2003).

[7] See Guy Carpenter & Co, "Market Update: The Catastrophe Bond Market at Year-End 2002" (March 2003) p 6.

[8] See Guy Carpenter & Co, "Market Update: The Catastrophe Bond Market at Year-End 2002" (March 2003) pp 8-9 and 32.

[9] See "Moody's Approach to the Rating of Catastrophe-Linked Notes" (Moody's Special Comment, 12 September 1997) pp 1 and 3; "Praying for a Catastrophe", *Euromoney* (February 1999); "Modelling Catastrophe Reinsurance Risk: Implications for the CAT Bond Market" (Special Report, Standard & Poor's, June 1999) pp 2-3 and 6; Paul-Choudhury S, "Quakes send Tremors through Insurance Industry", *Environmental Finance* (October 1999); Torre-Enciso IM and Laye JE, "Financing Catastrophe Risk in the Capital Markets" (2001) 1 Int J Emergency Manag 61 at 64; Andersen TJ, "Innovative Financial Instruments for Natural Disaster Risk Management" (Inter-American Development Bank, December 2002).

[10] See ISO, "Financing Catastrophe Risk: Capital Market Solutions – Executive Summary" (January 1999).

[11] See Murra F, "Saving Them for a Rainy Day", *International Securitisation Report* (May 1999); "The Operation and Evolution of Catastrophe-Linked Bonds" (Special Report, Fitch Ratings, 31 July 2001) p 3.

[12] See Bantwal VJ and Kunreuther HC, "A CAT Bond Premium Puzzle?" (Wharton Risk Management and Decision Processes Center, 1999).

[13] See Litzenberger RH, Beaglehole DR and Reynolds CE, "Assessing Catastrophe Reinsurance-Linked Securities as a New Asset Class", *Journal of Portfolio Management*, Special Issue 1996; Cantor MS, Cole JB and Sandor RL, "A New Asset Class for the Capital Markets and a New Hedging Tool for the Insurance Industry" (1997) 10 J App Corp Fin 69.

[14] See "The Operation and Evolution of Catastrophe-Linked Bonds" (Special Report, Fitch Ratings, 31 July 2001) p 1-2.

[15] See Guy Carpenter & Co, "Market Update: The Catastrophe Bond Market at Year-End 2002" (March 2003) pp 8-9.

[16] See generally Bernero RH, "Second-Generation OTC Derivatives and Structured Products: Catastrophe Bonds, Catastrophe Swaps, and Life Insurance Securitizations" in Himick M (ed), *Securitized Insurance Risk: Strategic Opportunities for Insurers and Investors* (Glenlake Publishing Co, 1998) pp 49-59; Ganapati S, Retik M, Puleo P and Starr B, "Catastrophe-Linked Securities" in Fabozzi FJ (ed), *Handbook of Structured Financial Products* (Frank J Fabozzi Associates, 1998) pp 277-279; Wang WHC, *Reinsurance Regulation: A Contemporary and Comparative Study* (Kluwer, 2003) pp 136-138.

[17] See Louverge H, Kellezi E and Gilli M, "Using Catastrophe-Linked Securities to Diversify Insurance Risk: A Financial Analysis of Cat Bonds" (1999) 22 J Ins Issues 125 at 130-131.

[18] See Guy Carpenter & Co, "Market Update: The Catastrophe Bond Market at Year-End 2002" (March 2003) pp 12-17.

¹⁹ See Culp CL, *The ART of Risk Management: Alternative Risk Transfer, Capital Structure, and the Convergence of Insurance and Capital Markets* (John Wiley & Sons, 2002) pp 472-473; "The Operation and Evolution of Catastrophe-Linked Bonds" (Special Report, Fitch Ratings, 31 July 2001) pp 5-6.

²⁰ See generally Belonsky G, Durbin D and Laster D, "Insurance-Linked Securities" in Shimpi P (ed), *Integrating Corporate Risk Management* (Texere, 2001) pp 178-184; Mocklow D, DeCaro J and McKenna M, "Catastrophe Bonds" in Lane MN (ed), *Alternative Risk Strategies* (Risk Books, 2002) pp 50-54; "Insurance-Linked Securities" (Swiss Re New Markets, 1999) pp 7-10.

²¹ See Guy Carpenter & Co, "Market Update: The Catastrophe Bond Market at Year-End 2002" (March 2003) pp 12-17.

²² See "The Operation and Evolution of Catastrophe-Linked Bonds" (Special Report, Fitch Ratings, 31 July 2001) p 7.

²³ See "The Operation and Evolution of Catastrophe-Linked Bonds" (Special Report, Fitch Ratings, 31 July 2001) p 7.

²⁴ Regarding tranching in general, see Kravitt JHP, *Securitization of Financial Assets* (2nd ed, Aspen Law & Business, 1996) at [3.05]; Lee D and Chen W, "Securitization: An Overview of Arbitrage and Tranching" (1998) 1 *Securitization Conduit* 5.

²⁵ *Insurance Act 1973* (Cth), s 12(1) and (2). Insurance companies (but not reinsurance companies) are also subject to the licensing and disclosure requirements of Chapter 7 of the *Corporations Act 2001* (Cth): ss 762A(2) and 764A(1)(d). Reinsurance contracts, in contrast, are not financial products: Corporations Act, s 765A(1)(g). Accordingly, the risk transfer arrangements that form the basis of nature-linked securities, under which an insurance company or reinsurance company cedes risk to the issuer of the securities if they are contracts of insurance, are arguably reinsurance contracts and therefore not subject to Chapter 7.

²⁶ *Insurance Act 1973* (Cth), ss 10(1) and 11.

²⁷ Unlike contracts of life insurance, there is no statutory protection for contracts of general insurance transacted by unauthorised insurers: *Life Insurance Act 1995* (Cth), s 230. There is, however, some judicial support for the continuing enforceability of such contracts of general insurance: *Yango Pastoral Co Pty Ltd v First Chicago Australia Ltd* (1978) 139 CLR 410.

²⁸ *Insurance Act 1973* (Cth), s 3(1).

²⁹ *Prudential Insurance Company v Commissioners of Inland Revenue* [1904] 2 KB 658. See further Birds J, *Modern Insurance Law* (4th ed, Sweet & Maxwell, 1997) pp 13-16; Legh-Jones N, Longmore A, Birds J and Owen D (eds), *MacGillivray on Insurance Law* (9th ed, Sweet & Maxwell, 1997) at [1-1]-[1-6]; Merkin R (ed), *Colinvaux's Law of Insurance* (7th ed, Sweet & Maxwell, 1997) at [1-03]-[1-07]; Lowry J and Rawlings P, *Insurance Law: Doctrines and Principles* (Hart, 1999) pp 3-4 and 10-11; Hodgin R, "Problems in Defining Insurance Contracts" [1980] LMCLQ 14.

³⁰ The traditional interpretation of this requirement is that the recipient of the contingent payment must have a legal or equitable interest in the subject matter of the contract: *Macaura v Northern Assurance Co Ltd* [1925] AC 619. More recently, the courts have taken the view that a proximate physical relationship to the subject matter, falling short of a legal or equitable interest, will suffice: *Petrofina (UK) Ltd v Magnaload Ltd* [1984] QB 127. See further Goodliffe J, "Insurable Interests – Traps for the Unwary" (1996) 4 Int Ins L Rev 101. This issue does not arise in Australia in relation to all insurance contracts other than contracts of marine insurance.

³¹ *Insurance Contracts Act 1984* (Cth), ss 16(1) and 17.

³² *Insurance Contracts Act 1984* (Cth), s 17.

³³ *British Traders Insurance Co Ltd v Monson* (1964) 111 CLR 86. See also Legh-Jones N, Longmore A, Birds J and Owen D (eds), *MacGillivray on Insurance Law* (9th ed, Sweet & Maxwell, 1997) at [1-10] and [1-12]; Merkin R (ed), *Colinvaux's Law of Insurance* (7th ed, Sweet & Maxwell, 1997) at [1-10]-[1-14]; Lowry J and Rawlings P, *Insurance Law: Doctrines and Principles* (Hart, 1999) pp 14-16

³⁴ See Ali PU, "GIO, Earthquakes and Hurricanes: An Overview of Catastrophe-Linked Securities and Other Innovations" (2000) 18 C&SLJ 62 at 64.

³⁵ See McMillan TV, "Securitization and the Catastrophe Bond: A Transactional Integration of Industries through a Capacity-Enhancing Product of Risk Management" (2001/2002) 8 Conn Ins LJ 131 at 170.

[36] See Wang WHC, *Reinsurance Regulation: A Contemporary and Comparative Study* (Kluwer, 2003) p 142.

[37] See Financial Services Authority, "Cross-Sector Risk Transfers" (May 2002) at [5.55].

[38] This Act has been adopted in Illinois and South Carolina. Both these States provide statutory safe-harbours for investors: "The securities issued by the SPRV under an SPRV insurance securitization shall not be deemed to be insurance or reinsurance contracts. An investor in securities issued pursuant to an SPRV insurance securitization or any holder of those securities shall not, by sole means of the investment or holding, be deemed to be transacting an insurance business in this State." See *Illinois Compiled Statutes*, Chapter 215, Act 5, Article XIE (Special Purpose Reinsurance Vehicle Law) at [179E-95]; *Code of Laws of South Carolina*, Title 38, Chapter 14 (Special Purpose Reinsurance Vehicle Model Act) at [38-14-190].

[39] Bond Market Association, "Recommended Policies and Procedures for Secondary Market Trading in Certain Book-Entry Risk-Linked Securities" (20 March 2001). See also "BMA Tries to Standardise CAT Bonds", *Structured Finance International* (13 June 2001).

[40] The first "open block" securitisation was executed in 1998 by National Provident Institution, a UK life insurance company. This chapter does not examine "closed block" securitisations. The closed block refers to the segregation and running-off of participating life insurance policies (policies that entitle the holder to "dividends", ie to share in the distribution by the life insurer of profits: eg *Life Insurance Act 1995* (Cth), s 15(2)(a)) effected by many demutualising life insurers in the United States. (Demutualisation describes the process by which a life insurer changes its corporate form from a "mutual society" or company limited by guarantee to a company limited by shares.) The establishment of a closed block ensures that the dividend expectations of the participating policyholders continue to be met, following the demutualisation of the insurer. See further Millette MJ, Kumar S, Chaudhary OJ, Keating JM and Schreiber SI, "Securitisation of Life Insurance Businesses" in Lane MN (ed), *Alternative Risk Strategies* (Risk Books, 2002) pp 403-410; "Insurance Capital Optimization: Reducing Risk through the Creation of a Closed Block", *RatingsDirect* (Standard & Poor's, 24 October 2001).

[41] The surplus is basically the excess of the value of the invested revenues from the life insurance policies over the value of the insured sums and bonuses paid out under the policies.

[42] See Millette MJ, Kumar S, Chaudhary OJ, Keating JM and Schreiber SI, "Securitisation of Life Insurance Businesses" in Lane MN (ed), *Alternative Risk Strategies* (Risk Books, 2002) pp 400-403; "Interest in Life Insurance Securitization Heats up", *RatingsDirect* (Standard & Poor's, 23 October 2001).

[43] A life insurance company does not own the policies owned by it (although it can, subsequently, become the assignee, either absolutely or by way of security, of the policy without there being a merger of interests under Australian law: *Life Insurance Act 1995* (Cth), s 200(6)). Accordingly, the security interest in question cannot (naturally) be granted over the policy; instead, it is granted over the choses in action constituted by the life insurance company's right to receive premiums and fees under the policy and the proceeds of those choses in action. For the analogous fallacy regarding the granting of a security interest over debentures by the issuer, see Cottrill VA, "The Effect of the 'Pledge' of a Debenture" (1990) 16 CBLJ 453 and the dismissal of the views expressed in that article in Goode RM, "Letter to the Editor" (1991) 17 CBLJ 463.

[44] A second security interest will be granted by the SPV over its assets (basically, the right to receive principal and interest on the loan and the benefit of the loan covenants and supporting security interest) to an independent trustee for the benefit of the investors.

[45] The first Australian life settlement securitisation was executed in 2001: see "The AM Securitised Traded Policies Trust No. 1" (Presale Report, Standard & Poor's, 28 February 2001).

[46] *Life Insurance Act 1995* (Cth), s 200(8)(a). Indeed, there is a "healthy" secondary market in life insurance policies in Australia: see Kachor M, "The Market for Traded Life Policies", *Policylink* (February 2001). On the topic of secondary sales of life insurance policies, see generally Doherty NA and Singer HJ, "The Benefits of a Secondary Market for Life Insurance Policies" (Wharton Financial Institutions Center, 2002).

[47] *Insurance Act RSO 1990* (Ont), s 115: "Any person who advertises or holds himself, herself or itself out as a purchaser of life insurance policies or of benefits thereunder, or who traffics or trades in life insurance policies for the purpose of procuring the sale, surrender, transfer, assignment, pledge or hypothecation thereof to himself, herself or itself or any

other person, is guilty of an offence." Given the broad terms in which this prohibition is expressed, it is doubtful whether in the event of a breach of the prohibition a court would be prepared to constitute the putative assignor a constructive trustee of the life insurance policy for the benefit of the putative assignee, despite valuable consideration having been exchanged. As regards the legal consequences of putative assignments of unassignable rights and assignments in breach of anti-assignment clauses, see Benzie S, "Charges over Non-assignable Contracts" [1999] JIBL 342; McCormack G, "Debts and Non-Assignment Clauses" [2000] JBL 422; Tijo H, "Assigning Unassignable Rights" [2000] JBL 465.

[48] The majority of US States have enacted laws based on the *National Association of Insurance Commissioners' Viatical Settlements Model Act 2001*. In addition, several US States have enacted laws based on the *National Conference of Insurance Legislators' Life Settlements Model Act 2000*. Stone Street Financial provides a regularly updated list of US jurisdictions with specific viatical and life settlement laws (http://www.stonestreetfinancial.com).

Chapter 6

HEDGE FUND SECURITISATION: REPACKAGING FUNDS OF HEDGE FUNDS

CFOS: INTRODUCTION AND BENEFITS

Hedge fund securitisation: an introduction

[6.10] Collateralised fund of hedge fund obligations (CFO) securitisation transactions offer investors an alternative to funds of hedge funds and managed discretionary accounts as a means of obtaining exposure to hedge fund investments.[1] They also enable the managers of hedge funds to lock in long-term financing and diversify their sources of finance.[2]

There are an estimated 1,900 hedge funds in operation worldwide, managing an estimated US$550-650 billion in investment assets and the hedge fund industry, as a whole, continues to enjoy strong growth in terms of the net in-flow of funds to hedge funds.[3] Although hedge funds are commonly portrayed as unregulated and highly speculative,[4] they invest in the same assets and use the same trading techniques as conventional managed investment funds[5] and increasingly are managed and promoted by the same financial institutions that manage and promote conventional managed investment funds.[6] However, what distinguishes hedge funds from their conventional counterparts is not the speculative character of the former, but the legal structure of the hedge fund and the considerable flexibility enjoyed by the managers of hedge funds in designing and implementing investment strategies and employing leverage.[7]

The first CFO (Diversified Strategies CFO), managed by Investcorp Management Services, a Bahrain-based hedge fund manager, and arranged by JP Morgan Chase, was executed in May 2002. This has been followed by five further CFO transactions.[8]

Benefits of CFOs

[6.20] CFOs are attractive to both hedge fund managers and investors.[9] For hedge fund managers, CFO debt securities enable hedge fund managers to obtain long-term financing at relatively low interest rates, facilitating the creation of leveraged positions by the hedge fund manager, compared to conventional sources of financing for hedge funds (eg prime brokers and securities loan and repo counterparties). For investors, CFO debt securities offer significant diversification benefits, namely the coupling of higher rates of return relative to conventional debt securities with an equivalent credit rating and the (arguably) weak correlation of those returns to the returns on conventional investment instruments.[10] In addition, institutional investors, such as superannuation funds and managed investment funds, are likely to be subject to fewer restrictions in their investment mandates on the purchase of rated CFO debt securities, particularly the senior and mezzanine tranches of CFO debt securities, in comparison to the purchase of direct, unlisted equity interests in a hedge fund or fund of hedge funds.[11]

CFOS: STRUCTURE AND UNDERLYING ASSET

Structure

CFO structure v CDO structure

[6.30] CFOs are structured in a similar manner to market value collateralised debt obligations, the key difference being the nature of the asset securitised: equity interests in a fund of hedge funds in the case of the former and loans and debt securities in the case of the latter. In a market value CDO, the debt securities issued to investors in the capital markets are serviced by the "trading profits" generated from the capital appreciation and the active trading of the securitised assets, as opposed to the cash flow generated by principal and interest payments on the securitised assets (as is the case with other CDOs and cash securitisations, such as RMBS, CMBS, auto loan and credit card securitisations).[12]

In a CFO, a bankruptcy-remote, off-balance sheet special purpose vehicle (SPV) is established for the purpose of investing in a fund of hedge funds and issuing debt securities to investors in the capital markets to finance the investment in the fund of hedge funds.[13] The subscription proceeds are invested by the SPV in the fund of hedge funds, which in turn invests them in a diversified portfolio of hedge funds (the fund of hedge funds will also have the capacity to transact total return swaps). The following diagram describes the structure of a generic CFO.

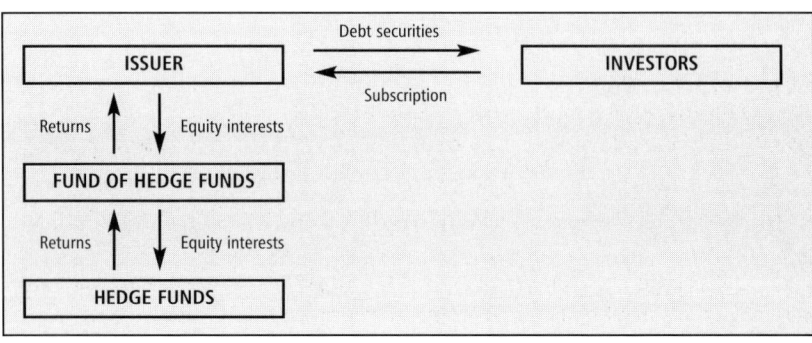

Principal and interest payments on the CFO debt securities are serviced principally out of redemptions of the equity interests held by the SPV in the fund of hedge funds. These in turn are funded by the active trading (ie redemption or secondary sale) by the fund of hedge funds of its equity interests in the underlying hedge funds (the ability of the manager of the fund of hedge funds to redeem those equity interests will, however, be subject to the limitations placed on redemption by the underlying hedge funds). On maturity, the CFO debt securities will be redeemed for cash out of the proceeds of redemption of the SPV's equity interests in the fund of hedge funds.[14]

The CFO debt securities are limited recourse securities and, accordingly, the SPV is not liable for any shortfall on the principal amount of the securities following the redemption of its equity interests in the fund of hedge funds and the distribution of the redemption proceeds to the investors in the CFO debt securities.[15]

Tranching of CFOs
[6.40] In common with other cash securitisations, the debt securities issued by the SPV may be credit tranched. Whereas the interest rate on the senior and mezzanine tranches of CFO debt securities will be the aggregate of a benchmark interest rate and a fixed margin, the "interest rate" on the junior or "equity" tranches will comprise a share of the increase in the value of the net assets of the fund of hedge funds over the interest payment period (ie the appreciation of the fund of hedge funds' equity interests in the underlying hedge funds).

The CFO debt securities may also include a principal-protected tranche, where the return of the principal amount of the debt securities to the CFO investors on maturity of those securities is guaranteed. This is usually achieved through the credit-wrapping of the debt securities with a monoline insurer providing credit insurance for the securities.[16]

Total return swaps
[6.50] As an alternative to making a direct investment in a hedge fund, the fund of hedge funds can obtain synthetic exposure to the hedge fund by transacting a total return swap and thereby obtain exposure to hedge funds that are closed to new investment and for which there is no liquid secondary market in which interests in the hedge funds can be purchased.[17] In CFO transactions, the underlying fund of hedge funds will have the capacity to create its portfolio of hedge funds either by investing directly in hedge funds or entering into total return swaps referencing hedge funds.[18]

The total return swaps used to synthesise exposure to hedge funds are the same as those used by banks and other financial institutions to lay off the credit risk on loans and debt securities.[19] Hence, the fund of hedge funds agrees to make periodic interest rate payments on a notional principal amount to the swap counterparty in exchange for the swap counterparty agreeing to pay it periodic amounts representing distributions by the reference hedge fund and, on maturity, an amount representing the increase in the net value of the assets of the reference hedge fund during the term of the swap.[20] If the net value of the reference hedge fund's assets has declined during the term of the swap, the fund of hedge funds will make a payment, on maturity, to the swap counterparty, equivalent to the decline in value.[21]

The total return swap not only delivers synthetic exposure to a hedge fund, it also replicates a leveraged investment in that hedge fund.[22] The fund of hedge funds has effectively obtained secured funding from the swap counterparty to acquire the exposure to the reference hedge fund: the fund of hedge funds pays an interest rate to the swap counterparty and its "loan" obligations have effectively been collateralised by the financed position in the reference hedge fund. The fund of hedge funds is entitled to the benefit of all distributions on the financed position and of any appreciation in the value of that position, but is liable for any depreciation in the value of the financed position.

Total return swap referenced to a hedge fund

```
                    Interest rate on notional principal
  ┌─────────────────┐  ───────────────▶  ┌─────────────────┐
  │ FUND OF HEDGE   │                    │ SWAP            │
  │ FUNDS           │  ◀───────────────  │ COUNTERPARTY    │
  └─────────────────┘   Hedge fund returns└─────────────────┘
                                                  │
                                                  ▼
                                         ┌─────────────────┐
                                         │ REFERENCE       │
                                         │ HEDGE FUND      │
                                         └─────────────────┘
```

Underlying asset

Funds of hedge funds: an introduction

[6.60] CFOs have been used to securitise funds of hedge funds, rather than single hedge funds. However, given the funding advantages for hedge funds offered by CFOs and continuing investor demand for hedge fund investments, the eventual securitisation of single hedge funds may involve the creation of debt securities with embedded options designed to capture the outperformance of the hedge fund for the CFO investors, in an analogous manner to "PEPS-style" converting securities.[23]

Funds of hedge funds are pooled investment vehicles (which, like the underlying hedge funds, can be structured as limited liability companies, limited partnerships, master trusts or managed discretionary accounts) that invest in the shares of or other equity interests in multiple hedge funds.[24] There are over 400 funds of hedge funds in operation worldwide, accounting for some 20% of the total funds under the management of hedge funds.[25]

Advantages of structure

[6.70] By making a single investment in a fund of hedge funds, investors can obtain exposure to several hedge funds. This structure offers significant benefits to investors, both those who have invested directly in a fund of hedge funds or those who have done so indirectly via a CFO.[26]

Access to hedge funds

A fund of hedge funds makes it possible to obtain exposure to a hedge fund, without the individual investor having to meet the minimum investment required by the hedge fund (in general, the minimum investment required by a fund of hedge funds will be substantially lower than that required by the vast majority of hedge funds).[27]

A fund of hedge funds can also be used to obtain exposure to a hedge fund that is closed to new investment. Investors can enter the fund of hedge funds and thus obtain exposure to the hedge funds in which that fund of hedge funds is invested, despite the underlying hedge funds not accepting new investors.[28]

Increased liquidity for hedge fund investments

A fund of hedge funds effectively creates a secondary market for interests in the underlying hedge funds, thus providing investors with increased liquidity. An investor can terminate its exposure to the underlying hedge fund by exiting its investment in the fund of hedge funds, whereas, had the investor invested directly in that hedge fund, it would not be able to exit its investment as readily (since hedge funds usually place strict conditions on the redemption of hedge fund interests).

In addition, many funds of hedge funds are listed on an official exchange, in marked contrast to single hedge funds, thus enabling investors to exit their investments by selling their interests, as opposed to redeeming them.

Diversification benefits

Funds of hedge funds offer diversification benefits. A fund of hedge funds enables investors in the fund to diversify their exposure to hedge funds, rather than having the entirety of their investment placed directly with a single hedge fund or small number of hedge funds.[29] Further, the funds invested in a fund of hedge funds will usually be allocated by the manager of the fund of hedge funds not only among several hedge funds, but also among different hedge fund investment strategies.

Monitoring of the underlying hedge funds

The fund of hedge funds structure introduces an independent third party, the manager of the fund of hedge funds, which is likely to be better placed, in terms of infrastructure or for relationship reasons, than individual investors to monitor the performance of the managers of the underlying hedge funds. Through this monitoring process, a fund of hedge funds manager can identify departures from an underlying hedge fund's stated investment strategy (known as "style drift"), which may undermine the diversification benefits offered by the fund of hedge funds. In particular, the duplication of positions within the underlying hedge funds (which the selection of hedge funds pursuing different investment strategies is intended to avoid) will undermine the putative diversification benefits offered by the fund of hedge funds.[30]

Disadvantages of structure

[6.80] There are disadvantages associated with investing in funds of hedge funds rather than in single hedge funds.[31]

Funds of hedge funds are expensive

The investors in the fund of hedge funds will, in addition to bearing the fees payable to the fund managers of the underlying hedge funds, be paying a second set of fees to the fund manager of the fund of hedge funds.[32]

Illusory liquidity benefits

The introduction of a fund of hedge funds between the investor and the underlying hedge funds may not necessarily promote the ability of the investor to exit its investment, particularly in a market meltdown or other financial crisis where all investors in that market, and in vehicles that invest in that market, are seeking to sell or redeem their investments. The liquidity benefits offered by a fund of hedge funds may therefore only be sustainable in more generalised, less volatile market conditions.

In addition, the liquidity benefits offered by funds of hedge funds carry their own cost. In order for an unlisted fund of hedge funds to be able to offer investors greater liquidity (ie more relaxed entry and exit conditions) than the underlying hedge funds, it will usually be necessary for the fund manager of the fund of hedge funds to maintain a cash buffer to fund redemptions.[33] This is likely to act as a "cash drag" on the investment returns of the fund of hedge funds. Moreover, if the fund of hedge funds attempts to enhance liquidity by focusing on individual hedge funds with more relaxed entry and exit conditions, that may lead to an over-selection of hedge funds investing in the same highly liquid instruments and markets (since such funds tend to impose less strict conditions on post-lock-up redemption than hedge funds that invest in less liquid instruments). This, in turn, may lead to a strong positive correlation of returns among the underlying funds, undermining the diversification benefits of obtaining exposure to hedge funds.[34]

Illusory diversification benefits
Investing in a fund of hedge funds will lead to smoother or less volatile returns, but may also limit the investor's ability to capture the full outperformance of an individual hedge fund or particular hedge fund investment strategy (since the inclusion of several hedge funds in the fund of hedge funds' portfolio means diluted exposure to individual hedge funds and investment strategies). Also, the inclusion of too many hedge funds in the fund of hedge funds' portfolio will further dilute the performance contribution of individual hedge funds and may ultimately destroy the rationale for obtaining exposure to hedge funds.[35]

HEDGE FUNDS

Rationale for investing in hedge funds
[6.90] The major attraction of hedge funds for investors concerns the putative diversification benefits of hedge fund investments, namely that the inclusion of hedge funds in an investment portfolio will either generate a higher return for the portfolio without raising the collective investment risk of the portfolio or, alternatively, reduce the portfolio's investment risk without reducing the aggregate returns on the portfolio.[36]

This is predicated upon hedge fund returns not being strongly correlated to the returns of the other (conventional) constituents of the investment portfolio, such as shares and bonds. The extent to which investment returns can be maximised for a given level of risk or the collective risk of a portfolio can be minimised for a given level of returns depends upon the correlation of the returns between the various instruments in the portfolio.

Correlation is the measure of the extent to which different instruments produce similar returns in similar market conditions. According to modern portfolio theory, the lower or weaker the correlation between different instruments, the greater their combined potential to increase the aggregate returns of the portfolio or reduce the collective risk of the portfolio. Consequently, the inclusion of hedge fund investments in a portfolio should produce diversification benefits if the returns on the hedge fund investments are weakly or negatively correlated to the returns on the other portfolio constituents.

Whether hedge funds do, in fact, produce such diversification benefits has been called into question by a recent study of hedge fund returns, which argues that the returns of equity-oriented hedge funds are weakly correlated to share returns in a bull market, but are strongly positively correlated to such returns in a bear market.[37] Further, a financial crisis may result in otherwise uncorrelated assets becoming strongly positively correlated.[38]

Hedge fund: definition, structure, market
[6.100] The term "hedge fund" does not have a precise legal definition. Instead, that term is used to describe broadly a wide range of pooled investment structures, including limited liability companies, limited partnerships, master trusts and managed discretionary accounts,[39] that pursue disparate investment strategies from high-risk, opportunistic directional strategies to lower risk, arbitrage relative value strategies.[40] However, there are a number of key structural features common to the hedge funds that are marketed to investors in the US and other mature hedge fund markets and which distinguish hedge funds from conventional investment funds.[41]

First, hedge funds are deliberately structured to take advantage of the licensing safe-harbours and reduced disclosure obligations provided for the securities laws of their home markets, and are usually jurisdictionally bifurcated from their managers.[42] The hedge fund manager will typically be located in a major financial centre (such as Frankfurt, Hong Kong, London, New York or Tokyo), while the hedge fund will be domiciled in an off-shore jurisdiction (principally, the Cayman Islands, British Virgin Islands, Bermuda and the Bahamas, in that order).[43] The four most popular off-shore domiciles for funds of hedge funds are the British Virgin Islands, Bermuda, Cayman Islands and Netherlands Antilles (in that order).[44]

Hedge funds are also marketed principally to high net worth individuals and institutional investors (including superannuation funds, mutual funds, life insurance companies and charitable endowments and foundations).[45] Retail investors are usually only able to invest in hedge funds indirectly, via funds of hedge funds.

Hedge funds: additional features
[6.110] In the case of investors in CFO securities, there are five additional attributes of hedge funds that need to be borne in mind.[46]

Hedge funds enjoy broad and flexible investment mandates
Hedge fund managers are subject to few or no restrictions with regard to investment strategies and the classes of assets in which hedge funds may invest.[47] Although, in practice, most hedge funds will invest according to a single, dominant investment strategy, the hedge fund manager will invariably have the authority to change that strategy or blend it with other strategies as the manager sees fit.

Hedge funds use leverage to boost returns

Hedge fund managers enjoy a wide discretion to employ leverage, eg by transacting derivatives (which are inherently leveraged) or raising funds via margin loans, securities loans or repo transactions to purchase investments.[48] While leveraged investing is by no means unique to hedge funds, the manager of a hedge fund will be subject to fewer constraints on the use of leverage compared to the managers of conventional managed investment funds.

Hedge funds have limited liquidity

Conventional managed investment funds are characterised by the constant in-flow and out-flow of cash, ie investors are constantly entering the fund by exchanging cash for interests in the fund and exiting the fund by redeeming their interests for cash.[49] This creates transaction costs for the fund. Also, the incoming investors dilute the existing investors' interests in the fund, while the realisation of fund assets to finance redemptions may crystallise a taxable gain that will be borne by the remaining (but not the exiting) investors. In addition, this pattern of continuous redemptions makes it imperative for the fund manager to maintain a "cash buffer" to finance redemptions, which, in turn, acts as a "cash drag" on the performance of the fund, since that cash is held in either relatively low-yield cash or demand deposits or invested in highly liquid, highly rated, and thus low-yield, cash instruments.

In contrast, hedge funds impose strict limits on investor entry and exit.[50] Investors can only subscribe for interests in a hedge fund during the initial offer period (for "closed-end" hedge funds) or during specified entry windows (for the less common "open-end" hedge funds). Investments in a hedge fund will also be subject to a "lock-up" period, during which investors cannot redeem their interests in the hedge fund or otherwise withdraw the funds committed by them to the hedge fund. In addition, hedge funds usually place strict restrictions on redemptions following the expiry of lock-up periods: investors must give advance notice of their intention to redeem their interests and such interests will only be redeemed during specified exit windows (and even with advance notice, many hedge funds permit withdrawals only quarterly or annually).

Hedge fund managers are investors too

In contrast to the managers of conventional investment funds, hedge fund managers invest in their hedge funds alongside outside investors.[51] This alignment of interests should mitigate the agency costs and moral hazard associated with the relatively high performance fees levied by hedge fund managers.[52]

Hedge funds are relatively expensive
The management fees (often 1-2%) and performance fees (often 20% of investment returns) charged by hedge fund managers are considerably higher than the fees charged by the managers of conventional investment funds.[53]

Hedge fund investment strategies
[6.120] The subscription proceeds of CFOs are invested via a fund of hedge funds in a diversified portfolio of hedge funds, pursuing a range of investment strategies.[54] This "blending of strategies" is designed to smooth out the investment returns from the hedge funds to which the subscription proceeds have been allocated.[55]

Hedge fund investment strategies can be divided into:[56]
- *relative value strategies* – where the hedge fund seeks to generate investment returns by exploiting the price differential or spread between similar market-traded instruments (see **[6.130]**); and
- *directional strategies* – where the hedge fund seeks to generate trading profits from directional movements in the price of individual market-traded and the over-the-counter instruments, sectors of a market or an entire market (see **[6.160]**).

Of these two main categories of hedge fund investment strategies, CFOs tend to favour relative value strategies, eg the Diversified Strategies CFO may allocate up to 80% of its funds to directional strategies but only up to 40% to directional strategies.[57] Similarly, both the Man Glenwood Alternative Strategies CFOs permit a greater proportion of their funds to be allocated to relative value strategies such as "long/short" hedge fund investment strategies as opposed to directional strategies, such as short biased investment strategies.[58]

Hedge funds do not, despite their name, uniformly engage in "hedging" (ie purchasing portfolio insurance or put options or engaging in short selling for the purpose of locking in investment gains or limiting downside risk), but rather invariably do the opposite, employing leverage to magnify the exposure of the hedge fund to certain instruments or markets.[59]

Relative value strategies
[6.130] The vast majority of hedge funds employ relative value investment strategies.[60] The purpose of relative value strategies is to generate a profit from disparities in the pricing relationship between similar instruments but without, in contrast to directional strategies, unduly exposing the hedge fund to the risk of an adverse movement in the prices of the individual instruments.[61]

The most common relative value strategies are (in order of "popularity"):[62]
- long/short equity (see **[6.140]**);
- event-driven (see **[6.150]**);
- convertible arbitrage (see **[6.150]**);
- equity market neutral (see **[6.150]**); and
- fixed income arbitrage (see **[6.150]**).

Long/short equity strategies

[6.140] Long/short equity hedge funds are the most common type of hedge fund.[63] A manager of a long/short equity hedge fund will establish a "long" position in shares considered to be under-valued relative to other shares (typically, by purchasing the former shares), while also establishing a short position in the latter shares (by borrowing these shares for the purpose of selling them in anticipation of being able to repurchase an equivalent number of shares at a later date for a lower price).[64]

If the manager's valuations prove to be correct, the hedge fund will receive profits from both positions: from the increase in the price of shares underlying the long position and the fall in the price of the shares underlying the short position.[65] Alternatively, if only one of the valuations proves to be correct, the hedge fund may still make a profit if the gain on one position exceeds the loss incurred on the other. In addition, long/short equity hedge funds will adopt either a net long position (where the value of the long position exceeds than that of the short position) or a net short position, depending upon the manager's view of the prevailing conditions in the market or markets in which the shares are traded. In a "bull market", a long/short equity hedge fund will maintain a net long position, in an attempt to benefit from the upward movement of the entire market; in a "bear market", a long/short equity hedge fund will do the opposite, maintaining a net short position.

Other relative value strategies

[6.150] Hedge funds that follow *event-driven* strategies seek to profit from the mispricing of instruments due to the occurrence, or created by anticipation, of significant events in the "life cycle" of the issuer (most commonly, changes in control or capital restructurings). This is well illustrated by "merger arbitrage" (or "risk arbitrage"), one of the most common event-driven strategies.[66]

In a *merger arbitrage* strategy, the hedge fund will, either in anticipation of a takeover bid being made for a target company or following the announcement of such a bid, establish a long position in the voting shares of the target and a wholly or partially off-setting short position in the voting shares of the intending acquirer.[67] The intention is to profit from any increase in the price of the target's voting shares (since these shares will generally trade at a discount to the bid price, reflecting the risk that the bid may not succeed) and any decrease in the price of the bidder's voting shares following the announcement of the bid (since the market may perceive that the bidder is paying too high a premium for the target shares).

The other relative value strategies, convertible arbitrage, equity market neutral and fixed income arbitrage, are similar to long/short equity strategies. In the case of *convertible arbitrage* strategies, the hedge fund invests in a long position in the convertible securities of an issuer and establishes an off-setting position in the ordinary shares underlying the convertible securities.[68] In *equity market neutral* strategies[69] and *fixed income arbitrage* strategies,[70] the hedge fund will establish long and short positions in equity securities and debt securities respectively. However, while a long/short equity hedge fund will switch between net long and net short positions, in the case of each of these three strategies, the hedge fund will maintain balanced positions with the short positions offsetting the long positions. Thus, hedge funds following these strategies will seek to generate investment returns entirely relative to movements in the price of the instruments underlying the long and short positions, without any contribution from an across-the-board rise or fall in the prices of those instruments attributable to general market conditions.

Directional strategies
[6.160] Hedge funds that employ directional strategies, in contrast to those funds that have adopted relative value strategies (see **[6.130]**), rely predominantly upon directional movements in the price for instruments such as securities, derivatives and foreign exchange instruments to generate returns. The most common directional strategy employed by hedge funds is the *global macro* strategy.[71] Hedge funds that pursue global macro strategies seek to profit from opportunistic trades (in other words, by making aggressive, leveraged bets) on the basis of macro-economic data, such as budget balances, exchange rates, foreign exchange reserves, Gross Domestic Products, interest rates, trade balances and unemployment rates.[72]

CHAPTER 6 • HEDGE FUND SECURITISATION: REPACKAGING FUNDS OF HEDGE FUNDS

1. See "Fund of Fund CDOs test the Cutting 'Hedge' of CDO Technology", *Bond Week* (18 November 2002); "Fund-backed Bonds Headed to Market", *Asset-Backed Alert* (30 May 2003); "Hedge Funds make Leeway into CDO Market", *Asset Securitization Report* (30 June 2003); "JPM, Man Roll out Hedge Fund CFO with Master Fund", *Structured Finance International News* (1 August 2003). The majority of retail investors already have indirect exposure to hedge funds via their superannuation funds: see, for example, "The Hedge Fund Dilemma", *APRA Insight* (2nd quarter 2003).
2. See "Hedge Funds: A New Class in Structured Finance" (Special Report, Fitch Ratings, 6 September 2001) p 1; "Global Hedge Fund CFO Securitizations spark Market Interest", *RatingsDirect* (Standard & Poor's, 26 September 2002).
3. See generally Ali PU, Stapledon G and Gold M, *Corporate Governance and Investment Fiduciaries* (Thomson Legal & Regulatory, 2003) Ch 5.
4. See, for example, Temple P, *Hedge Funds: Courtesans of Capitalism* (John Wiley & Sons, 2001). Many investors are also attracted to the deliberately cultivated "mystique" of hedge funds: see Serwer A, "Where the Money's Really Made", *Fortune* (31 March 2003).
5. See Purcell D and Crowley P, "The Reality of Hedge Funds", *Journal of Investing* (Fall 1999).
6. See Anson MJP, "Should Hedge Funds be Institutionalized?", *Journal of Investing* (Fall 2001).
7. See Ali PU, Stapledon G and Gold M, *Corporate Governance and Investment Fiduciaries* (Thomson Legal & Regulatory, 2003) at [5.7]-[5.14].
8. Man Glenwood Alternative Investment Strategies (May 2002); Premier I (July 2002); Premier II (July and November 2002); Premier III (February 2003); and Man Glenwood Alternative Investment Strategies II (July 2003). The hedge fund managers are Man-Glenwood and, as regards the Premier CFOs, the Partners Group, both based in Switzerland. See further "Diversified Strategies CFO, SA" (Presale Report, Fitch Ratings, 21 February 2002); "Diversified Strategies CFO SA Collateralised Fund of Hedge Funds" (Presale Report, Moody's, 28 February 2002); "Diversified Strategies CFO SA" (ABS Multiple Class Presale Report, Standard & Poor's, 4 April 2002); "Man Glenwood Alternative Investment Strategies I Collateralised Fund of Hedge Funds Obligations" (Presale Report, Moody's, 6 May 2002); "Man Glenwood Alternative Investment Strategies II Ltd" (Presale Report, Fitch Ratings, 25 July 2003); "Man Glenwood Alternative Investment Strategies II Ltd/Man Glenwood Alternative Investment Strategies II LLC" (Credit Ratings, Standard & Poor's, 7 August 2003).
9. See generally Mahadevan S and Schwartz D, "Hedge Fund Collateralized Fund Obligations", *Journal of Alternative Investments* (Fall 2002).
10. See also "Moody's Approach to Rating Collateralized Funds of Hedge Fund Obligations" (Rating Methodology, Moody's, 10 July 2003) p 2.
11. See Cheng C, "Securitization & Hedge Funds: Creating a More Efficient Market" (22 August 2002) p 4.
12. See "Moody's Approach to Rating Market-Value CDOs" (Special Report, Moody's, 3 April 1998); "Market Value CBO/CLO Rating Criteria" (Special Report, Fitch Ratings, 1 June 1999).
13. See Ali PU, Stapledon G and Gold M, *Corporate Governance and Investment Fiduciaries* (Thomson Legal & Regulatory, 2003) at [5.34]; "Diversified Strategies CFO SA Collateralised Fund of Hedge Funds" (Presale Report, Moody's, 28 February 2002) p 2; "Man Glenwood Alternative Investment Strategies I Collateralised Fund of Hedge Funds Obligations" (Presale Report, Moody's, 6 May 2002) p 2; "Man Glenwood Alternative Investment Strategies II Ltd" (Presale Report, Fitch Ratings, 25 July 2003) pp 2-3.
14. Alternatively, the debt securities may be redeemed in specie for the fund of hedge fund's equity interests in the underlying hedge funds: see "New Convertible Backed by Hedge Fund", *Bond Week* (7 July 2002).
15. Also, in common with other securitisations, the CFO debt securities will be supported by a first-ranking security interest granted by the SPV over its assets (principally, its equity interests in the fund of hedge funds).
16. See Lhabitant FS, *Hedge Funds: Myths and Limits* (John Wiley & Sons, 2002) pp 218-221; Wachovia Securities, "Understanding Hedge Fund Linked Principal-Protected Securities" (12 May 2003) p 6. As regards monoline insurers, see generally Morgan Stanley Dean Witter, "Monoline Bond Insurers: Are All AAAs Created Equal?" (January 2000).
17. See McCrary SA, *How to Create and Manage a Hedge Fund: A Professional's Guide* (John Wiley & Sons, 2002) p 120.
18. See, for example, "Man Glenwood Alternative Investment Strategies II Ltd" (Presale Report, Fitch Ratings , 25 July 2003) p 4.

[19] See, for example, Henderson SK, "Credit Derivatives" in Hudson A (ed), *Credit Derivatives: Law, Regulation and Accounting Issues* (Sweet & Maxwell, 1999) pp 4-6.

[20] This swap can be also physically settled, with the swap counterparty agreeing to deliver on maturity equity interests in the reference hedge fund to the fund of hedge funds, in exchange for the fund of hedge funds making a payment representing the value of the equity interests on the inception of the swap.

[21] The total return swap can also be customised to provide the fund of hedge funds with a currency-hedged return on the reference hedge fund.

[22] See Ali PU, "Unbundling Credit Risk: The Nature and Regulation of Credit Derivatives" (2000) 11 JBFLP 73 at 76-77.

[23] See Cheng C, "Securitization & Hedge Funds: Creating a More Efficient Market" (22 August 2002) p 8. PEPS-style (premium exchangeable participating securities) convertible securities are typically issued at the prevailing market price for the underlying ordinary shares (the "offering price"). The investor may convert the securities at any time prior to maturity into ordinary shares at a fixed premium to the offering price (the "conversion price"). On maturity, in contrast to conventional convertible securities, the above securities will be mandatorily converted into ordinary shares (or their cash equivalent, at the election of the issuer); the applicable ratio will be determined by the then market price for the ordinary shares. Since mandatory conversion entails the investors assuming greater downside risk on maturity, as the market price may be less than the offering price, these convertible securities carry a higher rate of return than conventional convertible securities. In addition, the former securities will also incorporate significant hard call protection so that, usually, the issuer will not have the option to exchange the securities for ordinary shares before maturity: see Morgan Stanley Dean Witter, *Guide to PEPS: Premium Exchangeable Participating Securities* (December 1998) pp 13-15; Coxe TA, "Convertible Structures: Evolution Continues" in Nelken I (ed), *Handbook of Hybrid Instruments* (John Wiley & Sons, 2000) pp 36-41; Ali PU, "Alphabet Soup: An Overview of Exotic Convertible Securities" (2000) 18 C&SLJ 579.

[24] Funds of hedge funds should be distinguished from "master-feeder funds", which act as a conduit between on-shore investors, and a single off-shore hedge fund or family of hedge funds: see Cullen I, "Hedge Funds: Structure and Documentation" in Cullen I and Parry H (eds), *Hedge Funds: Law and Regulation* (Sweet & Maxwell, 2001) pp 11-12.

[25] See Ineichen AM, *Absolute Returns* (John Wiley & Sons, 2002) p 40.

[26] See Ali PU, Stapledon G and Gold M, *Corporate Governance and Investment Fiduciaries* (Thomson Legal & Regulatory, 2003) at [5.16]-[5.17]; Fothergill M and Coke C, "Funds of Hedge Funds: An Introduction to Multi-Manager Funds", *Journal of Alternative Investments* (Fall 2001).

[27] See Lhabitant FS, *Hedge Funds: Myths and Limits* (John Wiley & Sons, 2002) p 199.

[28] Lhabitant FS, *Hedge Funds: Myths and Limits* (John Wiley & Sons, 2002) p 200.

[29] Lhabitant FS, *Hedge Funds: Myths and Limits* (John Wiley & Sons, 2002) pp 196-199; Ineichen AM, *Absolute Returns* (John Wiley & Sons, 2002) pp 405-407.

[30] See Lhabitant FS, *Hedge Funds: Myths and Limits* (John Wiley & Sons, 2002) p 205.

[31] See Ali PU, Stapledon G and Gold M, *Corporate Governance and Investment Fiduciaries* (Thomson Legal & Regulatory, 2003) at [5.18].

[32] See Lhabitant FS, *Hedge Funds: Myths and Limits* (John Wiley & Sons, 2002) pp 202-203; Ineichen AM, *Absolute Returns* (John Wiley & Sons, 2002) pp 409-411; Brown SJ, Goetzmann WN and Liang B, "Fees on Fees in Funds of Funds" (Yale International Center for Finance, September 2002).

[33] See Lhabitant FS, *Hedge Funds: Myths and Limits* (John Wiley & Sons, 2002) p 203.

[34] See Lhabitant FS, *Hedge Funds: Myths and Limits* (John Wiley & Sons, 2002) p 204; Ineichen AM, *Absolute Returns* (John Wiley & Sons, 2002) p 417; Jaeger L, "The Significance of Liquidity and Transparency for Multi-Manager Portfolios of AIS" (Partners Group, 15 July 2002) pp 5-7.

[35] Amin GS and Kat HM, "Portfolios of Hedge Funds: What Investors Really Invest in" (ISMA Centre, University of Reading, January 2002) consider that a portfolio of 15 hedge funds would provide most of the diversification benefits, while Lhabitant FS and Learned M, "Hedge Fund Diversification: How Much is Enough?" (FAME – International Center for Financial Asset Management and Engineering, July 2002) contend that holding five to ten hedge funds is sufficient. The underlying fund of hedge funds of CFOs typically invest in considerably more hedge funds. For example, the fund of hedge funds underlying the Diversified Strategies CFO is required to invest in a minimum of 25 hedge funds (see

"Diversified Strategies CFO, SA" (Presale Report, Fitch Ratings, 21 February 2002) p 3), while the underlying fund of hedge funds for the Man Glenwood Alternative Strategies II CFO is required to invest in a minimum of 35 hedge funds (see "Man Glenwood Alternative Investment Strategies II Ltd" (Presale Report, Fitch Ratings, 25 July 2003) p 4).

[36] See Ali PU, Stapledon G and Gold M, *Corporate Governance and Investment Fiduciaries* (Thomson Legal & Regulatory, 2003) at [5.48]-[5.54]; Amin G and Kat HM, "Who Should Buy Hedge Funds? The Effects of Including Hedge Funds in Portfolios of Stocks and Bonds" (ISMA Centre, University of Reading, March 2002).

[37] See Agarwal V and Naik NY, "Risks and Portfolio Decisions Involving Hedge Funds" (Georgia State University and London Business School, July 2002).

[38] See Lo AW, "Risk Management for Hedge Funds: Introduction and Overview", *Financial Analysts Journal* (Nov/Dec 2001).

[39] See McCrary SA, *How to Create and Manage a Hedge Fund: A Professional's Guide* (John Wiley & Sons, 2002) pp 91-102.

[40] See Lavinio S, *The Hedge Fund Handbook: A Definitive Guide for Analysing and Evaluating Alternative Investments* (McGraw-Hill, 2000) pp 1-5; Lhabitant FS, *Hedge Funds: Myths and Limits* (John Wiley & Sons, 2002) pp 14-20; Ali PU, Stapledon G and Gold M, *Corporate Governance and Investment Fiduciaries* (Thomson Legal & Regulatory, 2003) at [5.4].

[41] See Ali PU, Stapledon G and Gold M, *Corporate Governance and Investment Fiduciaries* (Thomson Legal & Regulatory, 2003) at [5.4]-[5.14].

[42] See McCrary SA, *How to Create and Manage a Hedge Fund: A Professional's Guide* (John Wiley & Sons, 2002) pp 177-193; Ali PU, Stapledon G and Gold M, *Corporate Governance and Investment Fiduciaries* (Thomson Legal & Regulatory, 2003) at [5.11]-[5.12]; "Hedge Funds: A New Class in Structured Finance" (Special Report, Fitch Ratings, 6 September 2001) p 2.

[43] See Ali PU, Stapledon G and Gold M, *Corporate Governance and Investment Fiduciaries* (Thomson Legal & Regulatory, 2003) at [5.12].

[44] See Ineichen AM, *Absolute Returns* (John Wiley & Sons, 2002) p 385.

[45] See McCrary SA, *How to Create and Manage a Hedge Fund: A Professional's Guide* (John Wiley & Sons, 2002) pp 50-60; Ali PU, Stapledon G and Gold M, *Corporate Governance and Investment Fiduciaries* (Thomson Legal & Regulatory, 2003) at [5.9].

[46] See Ali PU, "Hedge Fund Investments and the Prudent Investor Rule" (2003) 17 TLI 74 at 75-77.

[47] See Anson MJP, "Should Hedge Funds be Institutionalized?", *Journal of Investing* (Fall 2001) p 35; Ali PU, Stapledon G and Gold M, *Corporate Governance and Investment Fiduciaries* (Thomson Legal & Regulatory, 2003) at [5.7].

[48] See Benjamin J, *Interests in Securities: A Proprietary Law Analysis of the International Securities Markets* (Oxford University Press, 2000) pp 235-238; McCrary SA, *How to Create and Manage a Hedge Fund: A Professional's Guide* (John Wiley & Sons, 2002) pp 116-125 and 128-132; Ali PU, Stapledon G and Gold M, *Corporate Governance and Investment Fiduciaries* (Thomson Legal & Regulatory, 2003) at [5.8].

[49] See Lhabitant FS, *Hedge Funds: Myths and Limits* (John Wiley & Sons, 2002) pp 16-17; Ali PU, Stapledon G and Gold M, *Corporate Governance and Investment Fiduciaries* (Thomson Legal & Regulatory, 2003) at [5.10].

[50] See Ali PU, Stapledon G and Gold M, *Corporate Governance and Investment Fiduciaries* (Thomson Legal & Regulatory, 2003) at [5.10]; "Hedge Funds: A New Class in Structured Finance" (Special Report, Fitch Ratings, 6 September 2001) pp 6-7; "Moody's Approach to Rating Collateralized Funds of Hedge Fund Obligations" (Rating Methodology, Moody's, 10 July 2003) p 3.

[51] See Ali PU, Stapledon G and Gold M, *Corporate Governance and Investment Fiduciaries* (Thomson Legal & Regulatory, 2003) at [5.14].

[52] See Fung W and Hsieh DA, "A Primer on Hedge Funds" (1999) 6 J of Empirical Finance 309 at 316; Ackermann C, McEnally R and Ravenscraft D, "The Performance of Hedge Funds: Risk, Return, and Incentives" (1999) 54 J of Finance 833 at 836-838; Brown SJ, Goetzmann WN and Park J, "Careers and Survival: Competition and Risk in the Hedge Fund and CTA Industry" (2001) 56 J of Finance 1869 at 1877-1879.

[53] See McCrary SA, *How to Create and Manage a Hedge Fund: A Professional's Guide* (John Wiley & Sons, 2002) pp 13-16; Ali PU, Stapledon G and Gold M, *Corporate Governance and Investment Fiduciaries* (Thomson Legal & Regulatory, 2003) at [5.12]; "Big Money", *Economist* (25 January 2003). The payment of performance fees to a hedge fund manager will

usually be subject to a "high water mark" ie the payment of performance fees is conditional upon the hedge fund manager achieving a rate of return on the fund's investments above a stipulated threshold (after recouping any accumulated losses). There is, however, a risk that a manager, rather than trying to recoup past losses, will simply wind up the fund and start a new fund: see Loomis CJ, "Doing the Hedge Fund Hustle", *Fortune* (31 March 2003).

[54] See "Moody's Approach to Rating Collateralized Funds of Hedge Fund Obligations" (Rating Methodology, Moody's, 10 July 2003) p 5.

[55] See "Man Glenwood Alternative Investment Strategies II Ltd" (Presale Report, Fitch Ratings, 25 July 2003) pp 4-5.

[56] See generally Anson MJP, "Should Hedge Funds be Institutionalized?", *Journal of Investing* (Fall 2001) pp 14-35; McCrary SA, *How to Create and Manage a Hedge Fund: A Professional's Guide* (John Wiley & Sons, 2002) pp 33-43; Ali PU, "Hedge Fund Investments and the Prudent Investor Rule" (2003) 17 TLI 74 at 77-80; "Hedge Funds: A New Class in Structured Finance" (Special Report, Fitch Ratings, 6 September 2001) pp 8-11.

[57] See "Diversified Strategies CFO, SA" (Presale Report, Fitch Ratings, 21 February 2002) p 4.

[58] See "Man Glenwood Alternative Investment Strategies I Collateralised Fund of Hedge Funds Obligations" (Presale Report, Moody's, 6 May 2002) p 5; "Man Glenwood Alternative Investment Strategies II Ltd" (Presale Report, Fitch Ratings, 25 July 2003) p 5.

[59] See Asness C, Krail R and Liew J, "Do Hedge Funds Hedge?", *Journal of Portfolio Management* (Fall 2001).

[60] See Ali PU, Stapledon G and Gold M, *Corporate Governance and Investment Fiduciaries* (Thomson Legal & Regulatory, 2003) at [5.21].

[61] See Nicholas JG, *Market Neutral Investing: Long/Short Hedge Fund Strategies* (Bloomberg Press, 2000) pp 5-17 and 40-52.

[62] See Ali PU, Stapledon G and Gold M, *Corporate Governance and Investment Fiduciaries* (Thomson Legal & Regulatory, 2003) at [5.21].

[63] Ali PU, Stapledon G and Gold M, *Corporate Governance and Investment Fiduciaries* (Thomson Legal & Regulatory, 2003) at [5.24].

[64] Both the long and short positions can be established "synthetically" without buying or selling the physical instruments, by trading equity swaps or other equity derivatives: see further Ali PU, "Mimicking Shares: The Nature and Regulation of Equity Swaps" (1999) 17 C&SLJ 436 at 437-438.

[65] See Jaeger L, *Managing Risk in Alternative Investment Strategies* (Prentice-Hall, 2002) pp 82-84; Ineichen AM, *Absolute Returns* (John Wiley & Sons, 2002) pp 288-290; Jacobs BI and Levy KN, "Long/Short Equity Investing", *Journal of Portfolio Management* (Fall 1993); Jacobs BI and Levy KN, "The Long and Short on Long-Short", *Journal of Investing* (Spring 1997); Jacobs BI, Levy KN and Starer D, "Long-Short Portfolio Management: An Integrated Approach", *Journal of Portfolio Management* (Winter 1999).

[66] See Ali PU, Stapledon G and Gold M, *Corporate Governance and Investment Fiduciaries* (Thomson Legal & Regulatory, 2003) at [5.25].

[67] See Ineichen AM, *Absolute Returns* (John Wiley & Sons, 2002) pp 252-257.

[68] See Anson MJP, "Should Hedge Funds be Institutionalized?", *Journal of Investing* (Fall 2001) pp 19-22; Ineichen AM, *Absolute Returns* (John Wiley & Sons, 2002) pp 202-206.

[69] See Nicholas JG, *Market Neutral Investing: Long/Short Hedge Fund Strategies* (Bloomberg Press, 2000) pp 203-217 and 221-230; Jaeger L, *Managing Risk in Alternative Investment Strategies* (Prentice-Hall, 2002) pp 53-56; Ineichen AM, *Absolute Returns* (John Wiley & Sons, 2002) pp 236-237.

[70] See Nicholas JG, *Market Neutral Investing: Long/Short Hedge Fund Strategies* (Bloomberg Press, 2000) pp 89-101 and 107-110; Ineichen AM, *Absolute Returns* (John Wiley & Sons, 2002) pp 221-22.

[71] See Ali PU, Stapledon G and Gold M, *Corporate Governance and Investment Fiduciaries* (Thomson Legal & Regulatory, 2003) at [5.26].

[72] See Burstein G, *Macro Trading and Investment Strategies: Macroeconomic Arbitrage in Global Markets* (John Wiley & Sons, 1999); de Brouwer G, *Hedge Funds in Emerging Markets* (Cambridge University Press, 2001) pp 21-26; Anson MJP, "Should Hedge Funds be Institutionalized?", *Journal of Investing* (Fall 2001) pp 17-18; Jaeger L, *Managing Risk in Alternative Investment Strategies* (Prentice-Hall, 2002) pp 78-80; Ineichen AM, *Absolute Returns* (John Wiley & Sons, 2002) pp 319-322. Global macro hedge funds can now make use of "economic derivatives" to take long or short positions in respect of national and regional unemployment rates: see "Doomsday Derivatives", *Economist* (17 October 2002).

Chapter 7

INTELLECTUAL PROPERTY SECURITISATION: CRYSTALLISING THE VALUE OF BRAND NAMES AND IDEAS

INTELLECTUAL PROPERTY: INTRODUCTION

Intellectual property rights

[7.10] Companies that operate in the knowledge-based or information industries – such as bio-technology, communications, computer, entertainment, media and pharmaceutical companies – often possess valuable intellectual property rights. For many of these companies, particularly those that fall within the high-technology subset of the information industry, their intellectual property rights may be their most valuable or principal asset.[1]

The chief means of extracting value from intellectual property rights is through the generation of fees from the licensing of such rights or royalties from the sale of the subject matter of the intellectual property rights. However, increasing use is being made of a third alternative: raising funds from banks and investors on the security of intellectual property rights, with those funds being employed to finance further research and development, and the creation of additional intellectual property rights.[2]

This is typically accomplished by the company either obtaining a loan from a bank or other financier on a secured basis or securitising its intellectual property rights. The first method involves the company granting a security interest over its intellectual property rights to the bank or financier in support of the loan. The second method involves the company sequestering its intellectual property rights and raising funds by issuing securities supported by those rights to investors in the capital markets. This chapter discusses the second of these techniques and also provides an overview of four landmark intellectual property securitisations: the securitisation of copyright (as exemplified by the "Bowie Bonds" securitisation: see **[7.70]**), patent (BioPharma: see **[7.80]**) and trademark royalties (Guess?: see **[7.90]**) and software (Tokimeki Memorial Game Fund: see **[7.100]**).

SECURITISATION OF INTELLECTUAL PROPERTY RIGHTS

How does an intellectual property securitisation work?

[7.20] In a generic intellectual property securitisation, debt securities are issued backed by the cash flows generated from the originator's intellectual property rights and associated licences, with those rights and licences providing credit support to the issuer's payment obligations under the debt securities. This is typically achieved in one of the following ways:

1. The intellectual property rights and associated licences are sequestered in the issuing vehicle via a "true sale" equitable assignment[3] and, in common with conventional asset backed securitisations, the issuer grants a first-ranking security interest over those rights and licences to a security trustee for the benefit of the investors.
2. The intellectual property rights and associated licences are retained by the originator (or, more commonly, a special purpose intermediary established to hold those rights and licences) with the issuer's payment obligations under the debt securities being supported by a combination of a guarantee and a first-ranking security interest over the rights and licences granted by the originator or intermediary to a security trustee for the benefit of the investors.

IP securitisations: distinguishing features

[7.30] The techniques used to securitise conventional assets, such as residential and commercial mortgages or corporate loans, can readily be applied to securitise intellectual property rights. There are, however, a number of key characteristics that distinguish intellectual property rights from the other types of intangible property that are securitised or employed as collateral in securitisation transactions.[4]

First, intellectual property rights are "non-rivalrous": one person's use of intellectual property rights does not diminish the ability of another person to use those rights contemporaneously.

Secondly, intellectual property rights are infinitely replicable. The creation of fresh subject matter in which intellectual property rights subsist does not detract from the original or earlier subject matter of those rights or the validity of those rights. In contrast, in the case of other intangible property, the creation of fresh intangible property pre-supposes the conversion or destruction of the original property (eg the conversion of inventory into receivables on the sale of the former or the extinguishment of receivables on collection and their replacement with proceeds).

Thirdly, intellectual property rights are less susceptible to control than other types of intangible property. Since intellectual property rights are non-rivalrous and infinitely replicable, the holder of those rights may not effectively be able to exclude others from exploiting those rights (eg via piracy or passing-off).

Key legal IP risks
[7.40] There are three key legal risks that may affect the securitisability of intellectual property rights.[5]

Validity of the originator's claim to the intellectual property rights
The extent of the originator's interest in the intellectual property rights determines its claim to the royalties generated by those intellectual property rights (eg the securitisability of intellectual property rights will be diminished where not all of the owners of the rights participate in the securitisation, since the quantum of the royalties available to service the debt securities will be reduced).[6] In addition, a successful challenge to the originator's putative ownership of the intellectual property rights or the validity or scope of those rights may result in the cessation, or a reduction in the quantum, of the royalties generated from the rights.[7]

Infringement of intellectual property rights
The value of intellectual property rights depends upon them not being infringed upon.[8] For example, the value of a copyright and the royalties generated by that copyright are likely to be undermined by piracy of the copyrighted work. Equally, brand recognition and thus the value of the relevant trademark or service mark and its associated goodwill will be eroded by passing-off.

Finite duration
Intellectual property rights have a finite "legal life" (ranging from six years for designs,[9] eight years for innovation patents,[10] ten years for trademarks[11] and 20 years for standard patents[12] to 50 years after the death of the author in the case of copyright in literary, dramatic, musical and artistic – other than photographic – works[13]). However, the exploitable life of the originator's intellectual property rights may fall short of their legal life: technological advances may result in the development of superior substitutes rendering those rights redundant or in more cost-effective methods of production, making it no longer economically feasible to continue the maintenance or exploitation of the rights.

Licence of IP rights
[7.50] The originator will generally own the intellectual property rights the cash flows of which are being securitised. If, however, the originator is not the owner of the intellectual property rights, but is only a licensee of the rights, the availability of securitisation as a financing option will depend upon whether the licence is transferable, as opposed to being

purely personal to the licensee.[14] In the latter case, the originator will be unable to transfer the licence to the issuing vehicle or create a valid security interest over the licence for the benefit of the investors.[15]

Even where the licence held by the originator is transferable, it is likely that the terms of the licence will permit transfers only with the prior consent of the licensor. An assignment of the licence to the issuing vehicle in breach of such a contractual limitation on assignment may be void if the limitation is construed as a condition.[16] In addition, there appears to be judicial support for differentiating between the contract (ie the licence) and the "fruits" of the contract (ie the revenue generated by the originator from the exploitation of the licensed intellectual property rights).[17] Arguably, a contractual provision that, without more, prohibits or limits the assignment of the contract may not affect the transfer of royalties, as fruits of the contract, from the originator to the issuing vehicle.[18]

SECURITY INTERESTS OVER INTELLECTUAL PROPERTY

Legislative requirements

[7.60] A typical intellectual property securitisation transaction involves the issuance of debt securities with the payment obligations under those securities supported by a perfected security interest over the intellectual property rights,[19] associated goodwill (in the case of trademark and service mark securitisations)[20] and the benefit of intellectual property licences.

Mortgages (legal and equitable) and charges (fixed and floating) over patents, trademarks, service marks, copyright and registered designs and goodwill must be registered under the *Corporations Act 2001* (Cth) within 45 days of the date of the creation of the mortgage or charge.[21] Failure to register such a security interest within the prescribed time will render the security interest void as against the liquidator or administrator of the grantor of the security interest.[22]

In addition to being registered under the Corporations Act, these security interests must comply with the "form and content" and, except in the case of copyright security interests, the registration requirements prescribed by the various Australian intellectual property statutes.[23] It is, however, arguable that such requirements apply only to mortgages and charges over trademarks and service marks[24] and mortgages of patents,[25] copyright[26] and registered designs.[27]

In contrast, security interests over the two remaining types of intellectual property (rights in integrated circuits and plant breeders' rights) recognised by Australian statutory law are not required to be registered under the Corporations Act. Mortgages – but not charges – of such rights will, nonetheless, need to comply with the "form and content" requirements of the *Circuit Layouts Act 1989* (Cth)[28] and the "form and content" and registration requirements of the *Plant Breeder's Rights Act 1994* (Cth).[29]

Finally, note that the "code of priorities" contained in Chapter 2K of the Corporations Act, governing contests between registrable charges, does not apply to mortgages or charges over patents, trademarks, service marks, copyright and registered designs (although Chapter 2K's priority rules will apply to mortgages and charges over goodwill).[30] Mortgages and charges over rights in integrated circuits and plant breeders' rights (which are not registrable under the Corporations Act) likewise fall outside the scope of the Chapter 2K rules of priority. Thus, the relative priority ranking of competing security interests over intellectual property is a matter for the general law.[31]

CASE STUDIES

Jones/Tintoretto Entertainment (Bowie bonds) – US$55 million copyright securitisation (February 1997)

[7.70] The Jones/Tintoretto Entertainment Co LLC is the owner of the music catalogue of David Bowie, a popular musician.[32]

This transaction involved the securitisation of the cash flows generated from the copyright in a catalogue of David Bowie's 25 pre-1993 albums (approximately 300 songs). These cash flows comprised publishing royalties (ie income from the licensing and performance of the copyrighted songs) and recording royalties (ie moneys paid by record companies for the right to use the copyrighted songs).[33]

A bankruptcy-remote special purpose vehicle (Issuer) was established to issue debt securities backed by the above copyright royalties. The proceeds of issuance were applied by the Issuer to acquire the copyright to, and associated licensing rights in, the above albums from the originator, with the Issuer's principal and interest obligations being serviced primarily out of future royalty payments.[34] Those obligations are, in addition, supported by a first-ranking security interest created by the Issuer over the copyright and copyright licences in favour of a security trustee for the benefit of the investors.

In the event that the Issuer defaults in the performance of its obligations, the investors will be entitled to recoup the moneys owing to them by directing the security trustee to enforce the security interest over the Issuer's intellectual property rights and licences.

BioPharma Royalty Trust – US$115 million patent securitisation (August 2000)

[7.80] Yale University owns a patent for Zerit, a HIV/AIDS medicine. Zerit is produced, marketed and distributed by Bristol-Myers Squibb Co (Licensee) under an exclusive patent licensing agreement between the Licensee and the originator.

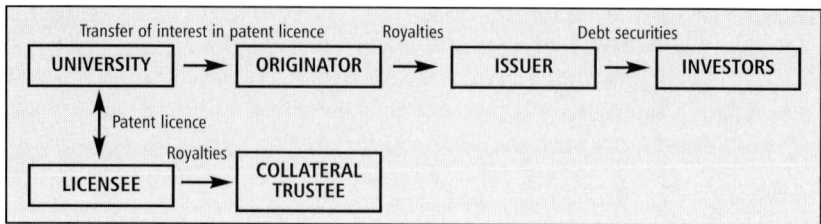

This transaction involved the securitisation of a majority of the cash flows generated from the university's patent licence.[35]

The royalties generated from the licence are divided between the university (70%) and the two inventors of Zerit (30%). The university's 70% share of the patent licence royalties was "monetised" by the originator – the originator paid the university US$115 million to purchase its share of the royalties, in the expectation that a 70% of the actual royalties generated by Zerit would ultimately be greater than the amount paid to the university. (The university, in exchange, is able to hedge the risk of commercialisation of patent by receiving a guaranteed amount in place of the variable royalties.)

A bankruptcy-remote special purpose vehicle, the BioPharma Royalty Trust (Issuer), was established to issue debt securities backed by the originator's 70% share of the patent licence royalties. The proceeds of the issuance were applied by the Issuer to acquire the benefit of the originator's 70% interest in the royalties, with the Issuer's principal and interest obligations under the debt securities being serviced primarily out of future royalty payments.

The royalties generated from the sale of Zerit are paid directly to an independent trustee (Collateral Trustee), which then distributes the unsecuritised 30% of the royalties to the university and the securitised 70% to the investors (and other creditors of the Issuer).

Guess? Royalty Finance – US$75 million trademark securitisation (January 2003)

[7.90] The originator, Guess? Inc, designs apparel and accessories for sale in its own retail outlets and also those of third party distributors. These products are marketed under various "Guess?" trademarks. The originator has also granted exclusive non-transferable trademark licences to third parties to manufacture and distribute a wide range of products that complement its core products.

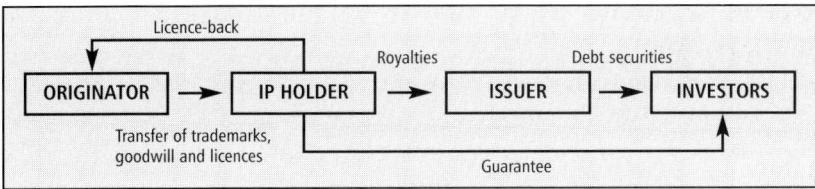

This transaction involved the securitisation of the cash flows generated from the originator's material trademark licences.[36] As a first step, all income-generating Guess? trademarks and associated goodwill, together with the material licence agreements, were placed in a bankruptcy-remote special purpose vehicle (IP Holder). The IP Holder then granted a licence-back to the originator, to enable the originator to continue to the use the Guess? trademarks in carrying on its business. This licence-back also contained non-competition clauses restraining the originator from competing with any of the licensees the trademark licences of which had been transferred to the IP Holder.

A second bankruptcy-remote special purpose vehicle (Issuer) was established to issue debt securities backed by the royalties generated on the trademark licences (other than the licence-back to the originator) held by the IP Holder. The proceeds of the issuance were applied by the Issuer to acquire the benefit of the royalties generated on the above trademark licences, with the Issuer's principal and interest obligations under the debt securities being serviced primarily out of future royalty payments. Those obligations are, in addition, supported by a guarantee from the IP Holder – which has granted a first-ranking security interest over the trademarks, goodwill and trademark licences, in favour of a security trustee for the benefit of the investors. Thus, should the Issuer default in the performance of its obligations, the investors will be entitled to recoup the moneys owed to them by directing the security trustee to enforce the security interest against the IP Holder's trademarks, goodwill and trademark licences.

Tokimeki Memorial Game Fund – JPY1.1 billion software-linked units (October 2000)

[7.100] Konami, a software developer, resorted to securitisation to finance the development and marketing of two computer games, "Tokimeki Memorial 3" and a new Tokimeki-like game. Funds were raised by selling units in a trust to retail investors.[37]

The return on the units is the variable principal amount which the investors receive on maturity.[38] The repayment of principal is linked to the quantum of sales of the two games. If, for example, fewer than 150,000 copies of the two games are sold, investors will receive only 50% of the face value of their units. On the other hand, if more than 400,000 copies of one game and more than 350,000 copies of the other game are sold, the return will be 150% of the face value of the units.[39]

[1] See Dickerson AM, "From Jeans to Genes: The Evolving Nature of Property of the Estate" (1999) 15 Bankruptcy Develop J 285 at 298; Chertok M and Agin WE, "Restart.com: Identifying, Securing and Maximizing the Liquidation Value of Cyber-Assets in Bankruptcy Proceedings" (2000) 8 American Bankruptcy Inst L Rev 255 at 261-263. As to the tradeability and implicit securitisation potential of "ideas", see Bell TW, "Gambling for the Good, Trading for the Future: The Legality of Markets in Science Claims" (2002) 5 Chapman L Rev 159.

[2] See Conley JG and Szobocsan J, "Snow White Shows the Way", *Managing Intellectual Property* (June 2001).

[3] For a general discussion of such equitable assignments, see Fitzgerald J and Firth A, "Equitable Assignments in Relation to Intellectual Property" [1999] 2 IPQ 228.

[4] See Maskus KE, *Intellectual Property Rights in the Global Economy* (Institute for International Economics, 2001) p 146.

[5] See also Eisbruck JH, "Credit Analysis of Intellectual Property Securitization: A Rating Agency Perspective" in Berman B (ed), *From Ideas to Assets: Investing Wisely in Intellectual Property* (John Wiley & Sons, 2002) pp 447-448.

[6] See Fairfax LM, "When You Wish Upon a Star: Explaining the Cautious Growth of Royalty-Backed Securitization" (1999) Colum Bus L Rev 441 at 472-476.

[7] It is possible to obtain "patent validity insurance", which provides for a lump-sum payment to be made to the originator in the event that a court holds a patent to be invalid. Alternatively, a put option over intellectual property rights can be purchased, permitting the option-holder to sell the covered rights to the option-writer at a fixed price and thus protecting the option-holder against any deterioration in the value of the intellectual property rights: see "Writing Options for Brainwaves", *Risk* (June 2000).

[8] It is also possible to obtain infringement insurance, covering lost profits and royalties, as well as associated legal costs due to patent, trademark or copyright infringement. The value of the intellectual property rights may also be eroded by, for instance, third parties "designing around" the originator's patent: see further Lipton JD, "Security over 'Information Products'" (2000) 11 AIPJ 23 at 34.

[9] *Designs Act 1906* (Cth), s 27A(8).

[10] *Patents Act 1990* (Cth), s 68.

[11] *Trade Marks Act 1995* (Cth), s 72(3).

[12] *Patents Act 1990* (Cth), s 67.

[13] *Copyright Act 1968* (Cth), s 33(2). Copyright in photographs, sound recordings, cinematograph films, television broadcasts and sound broadcasts subsists for 50 years (ss 33(6), 93, 94(1) and 95(1)), while copyright in published editions of works subsists for 25 years (s 96).

[14] Even where the originator is the owner of the intellectual property rights, it may not be economically feasible for it to transfer those rights to the issuing vehicle, eg the originator will need to retain ownership of its patents to ensure the availability of cross-licensing arrangements with third parties (such arrangements reduce the cost of licensing patents since the licensee, by making available its own portfolio of patents to the licensor, will be able to negotiate a reduction in the licensing fee). As to the different types of intellectual property licences, see further Bell I, "Securitisation of Intellectual Property Rights" in Borrows J (ed), *Current Issues in Securitisation* (Sweet & Maxwell, 2002) pp 86-87.

[15] However, a purported assignment of such an unassignable licence may arguably render the assignor the trustee of the licence for the benefit of the assignee: *Don King Productions Inc v Warren* [1999] 3 WLR 276. See also Benzie S, "Charges Over Non-Assignable Contracts" [1999] JIBL 342.

[16] *Linden Gardens Trust Ltd v Lenesta Sludge Disposals Ltd* [1994] 1 AC 85; *Re Turner Corp Ltd* (1995) 17 ACSR 761; *Westgold Resources NL v St George Bank Ltd* (1998) 29 ACSR 396. The result depends upon the construction of the clause; if it is a warranty, the breach will sound only in damages: *Anning v Anning* (1907) 4 CLR 1049. See further McCormack G, "Debts and Non-Assignment Clauses" [2000] JBL 422.

[17] See *Helstan Securities Ltd v Hertfordshire County Council* [1978] 3 All ER 262; *Linden Gardens Trust Ltd v Lenesta Sludge Disposals Ltd* [1994] 1 AC 85; Tjio H, "Alienating Unassignable Rights" [2000] JBL 465. An Australian (or UK) court may, however, in the aftermath of *Agnew v CIR* [2001] 3 WLR 454 take the view that while the fruits of a contract are legally distinguishable from the contract itself, they cannot be enjoyed in specie.

[18] The attractiveness of such a structure to investors is likely to be diminished by the inability of the originator or the issuing vehicle to make available the underlying licence in support of the issuer's payment obligations under the debt securities.

[19] See generally Lipton JD, *Security over Intangible Property* (LBC Information Services, 2000)

Chs 9 and 11; Swinson JV, "Security Interests in Intellectual Property" in Mallesons Stephen Jaques, *Australian Finance Law* (5th ed, Lawbook Co., 2002) Ch 21; McGuiness P, *Intellectual Property Commercialisation* (Butterworths, 2003) pp 326-331; Lipton JD, "Secured Finance Law and Practice in the Global Information Age" (2000) 11 JBFLP 17; Knopf HP, "Security Interests in Intellectual Property: An International Comparative Approach" (9th Annual Fordham Intellectual Property Law and Policy Conference, New York, 19-20 April 2001); Swinson JV, "Security Interests in Intellectual Property in Australia" (2002) 14 Bond L Rev 86; Nguyen XTN, "Commercial Law Collides with Cyberspace: The Trouble with Perfection – Insecurity Interests in the New Corporate Asset" (2002) 59 Wash & Lee L Rev 37; Nguyen XTN, "Exploring Emerging Issues: New Intellectual Property, Information Technology, and Security in Borderless Commerce" (2002) 8 Texas Wesleyan L Rev 489.

[20] Not all types of goodwill can support a security interest: *Commissioner of Taxation v Krakos Investments Pty Ltd* (1995) 61 FCR 489. In addition, the utility of taking a discrete security interest over goodwill is questionable, given that those types of goodwill (ie "premises", "competition" and "name" goodwill) that can support a security interest are capable of transfer only in conjunction with the intellectual property rights with which that goodwill is associated: cf Lipton JD, "Security Interests in Business Goodwill" (1998) 26 ABLR 25. As to the feasibility of business reputation as a discrete, tradeable asset, see Tadelis S, "What's in a Name? Reputation as a Tradeable Asset" (Stanford University, February 1998).

[21] *Corporations Act 2001* (Cth), s 262(1)(e).

[22] *Corporations Act 2001* (Cth), s 266(1)(c)(i).

[23] The relief from double registration provided for in ss 273A and 273B of the *Corporations Act 2001* (Cth) does not apply to these security interests.

[24] The *Trade Marks Act 1995* (Cth) makes reference only to assignments of intellectual property rights, arguably limiting dual compliance to mortgages of trademarks: ss 107(1) and 109(1). However, the registration provisions of that Act extend to all interests and rights in respect of trademarks, arguably subjecting both mortgages and charges to the registration requirements of the Trade Marks Act: ss 113(1)(a) and 117(1)(b). The consequences of non-registration under this Act are unclear given the inconsistency between s 22(1) and (2). It is arguable that any dealing with a registered trademark by its holder will be subject to all existing registered or unregistered interests. See further Ali PU, *The Law of Secured Finance: An International Survey of Security Interests over Personal Property* (Oxford University Press, 2002) pp 148-149.

[25] In the case of patents, an assignment (including a mortgage) of a patent will not be effective unless it is in writing executed by or on behalf of both the assignor and the assignee: *Patents Act 1990* (Cth), s 14(1). Assignments must be registered: s 187. Failure to register means that the assignor will be entitled to deal with the patent as if it were the absolute owner (s 189(1)) and further that the assignment will be defeated by a transferee in good faith for value of the patent (s 189(3)).

[26] Under the *Copyright Act 1968* (Cth), an assignment (including a mortgage) of copyright will not be effective unless it is in writing executed by or on behalf of the assignor: s 196(3).

[27] An assignment (including a mortgage) of a registered design will not be effective unless it is in writing executed by or on behalf of the assignor: *Designs Act 1906* (Cth), s 25C(3). In addition, assignments and mortgages must be registered (s 38A) and failure to register means that the assignment or mortgage will not be admissible in evidence in court proceedings: s 38B.

[28] Assignments (including mortgages) of rights in an integrated circuit layout will not be effective unless in writing executed by or on behalf of the assignor: s 45(3).

[29] Assignments (including mortgages) of plant breeders' rights will not be effective unless in writing executed by or on behalf of both the assignor and the assignee: s 20(2). Further, such assignments must be registered within 30 days after the assignment: s 21(1). See further Mahoney B, "The Suitability of Plant Breeders' Rights as Security Collateral" (2000) 11 JBFLP 257.

[30] *Corporations Act 2001* (Cth), s 279(5) provides that this "code" does not affect the operation of the *Copyright Act 1968* (Cth), *Designs Act 1906* (Cth), *Patents Act 1952* (Cth) or *Trade Marks Act 1955* (Cth). Those Acts are, however, only relevant to the issue of the validity, as opposed to the priority-ranking, of security interests over intellectual property.

[31] As to the applicable general law rules of priority, see further Ali PU, *The Law of Secured Finance: An International Survey of Security Interests over Personal Property* (Oxford University Press, 2002) pp 206-214. It is difficult to characterise intellectual property rights as choses in action stricto sensu (notwithstanding the statutory conferral of the status of personal property on intellectual property rights in Australia). Arguably, intellectual

property rights are merely monopoly rights and fall short of proprietary status in the same manner as the right in tort "not to be defamed or not to be assaulted": see Sykes EI and Walker S, *The Law of Securities* (5th ed, Law Book Co, 1993) p 759. This issue has significant implications for the relative status of competing interests in intellectual property rights and, consequently, for the financing of intellectual property rights. In particular, it raises doubts as to whether the rule in *Dearle v Hall* (1828) 3 Russ 1 – which governs contests between competing assignees in equity of choses in action – is the appropriate mechanism for ranking competing equitable interests in intellectual property rights. The rule in *Dearle v Hall* is often expressed as applying to competing equitable assignments. It would not, on this basis, apply to fixed charges since such charges do not depend upon an assignment of an equitable interest to the secured party. However, the better view is that this rule applies to priority contests between consensual equitable interests over choses in action: see Ferran E, *Company Law and Corporate Finance* (Oxford University Press, 1999) p 536, where the rule is applied to contests between consecutive charges. Smith LD, *The Law of Tracing* (Oxford University Press, 1997) p 359 notes that it is doubtful that the rule applies to charges (viz equitable liens) and other equitable interests arising by operation of law. The rule in *Dearle v Hall* does not apply to contests between legal and equitable assignees: see Oditah F, "Priorities: Equitable Versus Legal Assignments of Book Debts" (1989) 9 OJLS 513.

[32] For an overview of this and other music royalty securitisations, see "Moody's Approach to Rating Music Royalty and Intellectual Property-Backed Transactions: There's no Business Like Show Business" (Special Report, Moody's, 2 July 1999); "DCR Comments on Music Royalty Securitizations" (Special Report, Duff & Phelps, September 1999). See also Chu N, "Bowie Bonds: A Key to Unlocking the Wealth of Intellectual Property" (1999) 21 Hastings Communication & Entertainment LJ 469; Sylva JB, "Bowie Bonds Sold for Far More than a Song: The Securitization of Intellectual Property as a Super-Charged Vehicle for High Technology Financing" (1999) 15 Santa Clara Computer & High Tech LJ 195; Grant A, "Ziggy Stardust Reborn: A Proposed Modification of the Bowie Bond" (2001) 22 Cardozo L Rev 1291.

[33] See Kerr TN, "Bowie Bonding in the Music Biz: Will Music Royalty Securitization be the Key to the Gold for Music Industry Participants?" (2000) 7 UCLA Entertainment L Rev 367 at 383-387.

[34] See Mullen JT, Long JL and Kiriakos TS, "Has David Bowie Started a New Era of Celebrity Securitizations?" (1998) 1 *Securitization Conduit* 13 at 14.

[35] See Fischer BH, "New Patent Issue: BioPharma Royalty Trust" in Berman B (ed), *From Ideas to Assets: Investing Wisely in Intellectual Property* (John Wiley & Sons, 2002) pp 487-492.

[36] See "Guess? Royalty Finance LLC" (Presale Report, Moody's, 17 January 2003); "Guess? Royalty Finance LLC" (Presale Report, Standard & Poor's, 22 January 2003).

[37] See "Konami Announces Securitisation Scheme" (Konami, 25 October 2000).

[38] As an added incentive, investors who purchased ten or more units would be listed in the game's credits (displayed at the end of the game) and those who purchased 20 or more units would also receive a special edition of the game.

[39] The break-even amount is in the region of 150,000 copies for one game and 200,000 copies for the other game: see further "ABS Market in Japan – Review of FY2000" (Mizhuo Securities, April 2001).

Chapter 8

WHOLE OF BUSINESS SECURITISATION: UNLOCKING THE WEALTH WITHIN

WOBS: INTRODUCTION AND EXAMPLES

Whole of business securitisations: an introduction
[8.10] In the last few years, whole of business securitisation (WOBS), an offshoot of conventional securitisation, has emerged as a popular financing method for various businesses. As the title suggests, WOBS encompasses a conventional securitisation arrangement with cash flows derived from the operating revenues of the whole business.

This chapter provides an overview of the main WOBS deals and the advantages of securitisation. It explains the mechanics of conventional securitisation and addresses the bankruptcy remoteness issue. It further explores the differences between WOBS and conventional securitisation, including the creation of the security package and, finally, a discussion of suitable business candidates for WOBS.

Key WOBS industries
[8.20] The key WOBS deals fall within five main industries (discussed below), although newer industries are surfacing, signalling its growing trend and familiarity among market participants. An example is the recent note issuance by a forestry company supported by operating revenues derived essentially from the sale of felling rights of forestry lands.[1]

The entertainment/leisure industry experienced three major WOBS deals. The Tussauds group consists of a complex trans-national business with operating revenues generated from different jurisdictions.[2] Its securitisation of intellectual property rights, including trademarks (the Tussauds name), copyrights and design rights (the waxworks moulds) and offer of leisure venues (waxworks museum and theme parks) as security, constituted a major breakthrough in UK securitisation.[3]

Similarly, Formula One issued bonds backed largely by intangible assets, such as trademarks, broadcasting technology and television broadcasting contracts, the last item providing its main revenue.[4] This transaction highlighted an innovative synthetic initial public offering (IPO) structure whereby Formula One's owner sold company *shares* to a special purpose vehicle (SPV), the purchase of which relied on proceeds from a *bond* issuance (via a second SPV). Having sold shares, Formula One's owner achieved non-recourse financing and is unaffected by that company's debts.[5]

The Really Useful Theatres deal involved a WOBS of its portfolio of theatres.[6] Operating revenues were generated from the group's theatre ownerships and theatrical productions (including contracts with production companies), retail sales at the theatres and ticket sales.

Pubs also feature strongly in the WOBS market, encouraged by its industry structure in the UK – the "tie" between the pub owner-company and the long-term pub lessee, whereby the latter operates the pub, but pays rent to and purchases beer from the former (beer-tie).[7] The securitised portfolio of leased pubs[8] provides a steady income stream needed to support payment of interest and principal to noteholders.

The €5.6 billion UK Anglian Water Services transaction in the water sector, which combined new bonds issuance and refinancing of existing bonds, was the largest European WOBS issuance in 2002.[9] Its success depended on several factors, namely the water industry being a regulated business and Anglian being the monopoly provider of essential water and sewerage services, thereby yielding stable operating revenues.

Healthcare entities are also familiar in the WOBS market. In one transaction, the number-two UK private healthcare provider generated a predictable stream of receivables by providing private acute care hospital services.[10] Another healthcare WOBS transaction is the Craegmoor deal, which involved a portfolio of care homes.[11] In that case, the notes issued were backed substantially by proceeds received for providing care services under governmental care contracts.

Infrastructure financings

[8.30] Infrastructure financings, traditionally associated with project finance, also utilise WOBS techniques. The London City Airport transaction marked its first use.[12] There, proceeds from the notes issuance were lent to the airport operator. This loan was repaid using revenues generated from its aviation, commercial and transportation activities. Following closely is the recent €1.35 billion bonds issuance by Aeroporti di Roma SpA backed by operating revenues of its two Italian airports.[13]

Another notable WOBS infrastructure deal is the funding of stadia development by football clubs, with operating revenues originating from ticket sales, shirt sponsorships and merchandising sales.[14]

Securitisation: advantages summarised

[8.40] The advantages of securitisation are well known. It transforms illiquid assets to liquid assets, thereby raising working capital efficiently. It allows off-balance sheet financing by de-recognising the transaction as a liability on the balance sheet. Debt-to-equity ratios or leverage therefore remains unaffected.[15] By selling its assets, the asset-owner also enjoys non-recourse financing.[16]

Compared to bank finance, securitisation offers the asset-owner cost-competitive and flexible long-term financing. Further, investors receive greater yield from highly rated securities than from government issues of similar maturities.[17] Moreover, the lower-cost funding afforded by securitisation generates social and economic benefits when performed on a broader scale.[18]

CASH SECURITISATIONS

Mechanics of conventional securitisations

[8.50] In conventional securitisation, the company asset-owner (the originator) sells income-producing assets to a thinly capitalised SPV-company or an SPV-trust, which finances this purchase by issuing credit-rated securities to investors in the capital markets. Debt obligations (payment of principal and interest) on securities are serviced using cash flows generated from those assets; hence, the common parlance "asset-backed securities".

The SPV grants a security interest over the assets to a security trustee under a security trust deed for the benefit of secured creditors, principally the investors. The security interest performs two roles: ensuring that the investors have priority in terms of recourse to the assets of the SPV and effecting the segregation of the SPV's assets where different series of securities are backed by different pools of assets. In addition, where the securities have been issued in registered (as opposed to bearer or negotiable) form, the trust structure overcomes the problem of privity (since the only contract is that in respect of the global security issued by the SPV to the security registrar) in that the investor receives the benefit of the covenant made by the SPV in favour of the security trustee to pay interest and principal on the registered securities.[19]

In an SPV-trust structure, investors are likewise protected when the trustee[20] similarly covenants with the security trustee, the benefit of which is held on their behalf.[21] Moreover, these investors become secured creditors and have a direct security interest (via the security trustee) over the assets for any unperformed debt obligations without relying on the trustee's right of indemnity for trust liabilities from trust assets, which pertains only to properly incurred trust debts and not to breaches of trust.[22]

Conventional securitisation commonly features fee-receiving participants: the manager provides management services to the SPV; the servicer monitors cash flows and their collection, including taking enforcement measures; swap counterparties provide hedging facilities when the payment characteristics of the assets and securities differ, creating timing mismatches and reinvestment risk; the credit enhancer offers credit support if the underlying obligors default in their payment obligations whilst the liquidity facility provider ensures continued payments on the securities in the event of market disruptions.

True sale of securitised assets
[8.60] An effective securitisation must address the central issue: the SPV's bankruptcy remoteness. The SPV should not become insolvent or be adversely affected by the originator's insolvency. To achieve this, the assets are *legally* isolated through a "true sale", so as to exclude them from the originator's bankruptcy estate, thus avoiding any recharacterisation of the sale as a secured loan[23] and enabling the issuance of securities with a higher credit rating (and thus lower servicing costs) than that attainable by the originator itself. The investors' recourse is limited to the SPV's assets, but those assets are unavailable for satisfaction of debts owing to the originator's creditors.[24]

To abate the risk of SPV insolvency, the SPV-company's constitution or SPV-trust's trust deed or transaction documents will contain conditions restricting the SPV's business activities, debt limitation clauses and undertakings by secured creditors not to wind up the SPV.[25]

To insulate against the originator's insolvency risk, the SPV should:
- appoint an independent director to consider the investors' interests, thereby acting as a check on its board;[26]
- comply with separateness covenants to distinguish itself from the originator;[27] and
- have a charitable trust hold its shares to prevent insolvency risk from arising through consolidation on the originator's balance sheet.[28]

The assets, which are choses in action representing third party obligations to the originator, are invariably isolated by an equitable assignment to the SPV, leaving the originator as the bare trustee of the assets.[29] There are two major advantages of an equitable assignment. First, an equitable assignment effected via a "Clayton's contract" (written offer, acceptance via conduct) will avoid the imposition of ad valorem stamp duty. Secondly, the efficacy of the assignment is not dependent upon notice of the assignment being given to the underlying obligors. In contrast, legal assignments require the service of notices of assignment on the obligors, possibly disrupting long-standing relationships between the parties.

Moreover, equitable assignments may facilitate debt recovery, since the originator remains the legal creditor of record with regard to the obligors.

WHOLE OF BUSINESS SECURITISATIONS

WOBS: distinguishing features

[8.70] The hallmark distinction of WOBS is its secured loan structure.[30] Here, the SPV makes a loan, funded by the issuance of rated securities, to an operating company (the borrower). This loan is secured by the borrower's core assets and repaid using its business income.[31] In other words, the entire income stream of the originator is securitised unlike conventional securitisation, which involves the securitisation of particular assets. The WOBS structure also involves similar fee-receiving participants.

Two sets of security interest are created: a security trustee is granted fixed[32] and floating[33] charges over substantially all of the borrower's assets for the SPV's benefit; the SPV, in turn, grants security over all its assets (namely, its chose in action for any unpaid principal and interest under the loan and the benefit of its security interest) to the same or another security trustee for the benefit of the secured creditors (including investors). This allows the same security trustee or the security trustee in respect of the secured loan (if separately appointed) to appoint a receiver upon the borrower's default, thus staving off administration[34] and enabling uninterrupted management of the core assets and income flows needed to service debt obligations on securities. The SPV's beneficial interest in the security interests is thereby subordinated to that of the secured creditors, giving the latter a first-ranking claim to any recoveries.

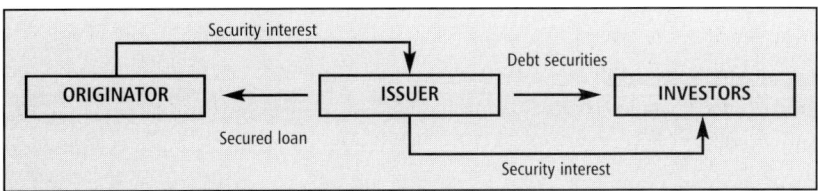

Whole of business securitisation

Also, the SPV is often a member of the borrower's corporate group rather than an orphan company,[35] as off-balance sheet financing is not the raison d'être of WOBS, unlike conventional securitisation.

Further, since managing an entire business in WOBS is more complicated than managing specific asset pools in conventional securitisation, the loan covenants relating to business operations and cash flows between the borrower and SPV must confer greater management flexibility, albeit within certain defined parameters.[36]

Finally, the WOBS structure is a hybrid of conventional securitisation and secured corporate debt. Like the former, WOBS utilises similar structural reinforcements and isolates the assets that secure the debt from the borrower's insolvency. Resembling the latter, the debt reflects the borrower's liabilities and the borrower retains ownership of the assets, which are secured in favour of investors.

SECURITY PACKAGE

Group company shares
[8.80] This section briefly examines the creation of security interests in assets likely to form the security package.

A legal or equitable mortgage may be created over the shares in the group's operating subsidiaries (including those held in the Clearing House Electronic Sub-register system (CHESS) where the shares are listed on the Australian Stock Exchange). Although a legal mortgage is not registrable as contemplated by s 262(1)(g)(ii) of the *Corporations Act 2001* (Cth), compliance with certain statutory formalities[37] and transfer requirements stipulated in each company's constitution remain necessary. The legal title holder may acquire greater control, but faces considerable burdens flowing from its membership of the company, thereby making this option unattractive.[38]

To create an equitable mortgage, the share certificates (including those derived from the conversion of uncertificated CHESS shares)[39] with the executed transfers in blank are deposited with the mortgagee. Statutory registration is again unnecessary, unless an equitable mortgage is created over uncertificated CHESS shares, as that constitutes a mortgage *not* created by the deposit of title documents.[40]

Intangible assets
[8.90] Trademarks and goodwill typify intangible property and possess commercial value by embodying the business identity and reputation respectively. They are generally inter-linked because goodwill requires attachment to other business intangibles, such as the associated trademark, and a trademark is usually worthless without the inherent goodwill.[41]

Registered trademarks with associated goodwill may form the subject of a legal mortgage or floating charge. The absence of a document of title for depositing arrangements makes the grant of an equitable mortgage difficult.[42] Complying with assignment formalities under the *Trade Marks Act 1995* (Cth) creates a legal mortgage,[43] which also constitutes a registrable charge under s 262(1)(e) of the *Corporations Act 2001* (Cth). As the trademarks remain functional to the business, the mortgagee must permit licence-back arrangements.⁴⁴ Their freedom of use will continue uncurtailed if a floating charge (bearing a restrictive covenant) is granted⁴⁵ by registering the mortgagee's interest under s 113 of the *Trade Marks Act 1995* (Cth) and s 262(1)(e) of the *Corporations Act 2001* (Cth). By obviating the need to comply with the assignment provisions, the mortgagee avoids administrative inconvenience and saves cost. Also, future trademarks are automatically captured under the mortgage.

Well-developed businesses usually develop databases (whether paper-based or computerised) containing comprehensive and structured data paramount to business functionality. Databases are generally protected as "literary works" under s 10 of the *Copyright Act 1968* (Cth)⁴⁶ and therefore may be mortgaged or charged. The collateral is likely to be the structured data, rather than the data management system (the computer program), as copyright in the latter usually already subsists in third parties. For this reason, security interests over databases may present difficulties in terms of their valuation and "on-sales" upon default.⁴⁷

Statutory formalities exist for the creation of a legal mortgage over copyright in existing⁴⁸ and arguably future databases,⁴⁹ which is registrable under s 262(1)(e) of the *Corporations Act 2001* (Cth). An equitable mortgage will result upon failure to comply with these formalities.⁵⁰ If the copyright is essential for business activities, licence-back arrangements must be in place. Alternatively, for ease of use and automatic capture of future copyright, a floating charge may be granted. Section 262(1)(e) of the *Corporations Act 2001* (Cth) similarly applies. It is further suggested that the goodwill inherent in the database may form the subject of a floating charge registrable under s 262(1)(a).

Finally, these businesses may also hold valuable trade secrets.⁵¹ Because of their nebulous nature and dependency on the shroud of secrecy maintained by the owner and imposed on others, trade secrets convey no exclusive rights beyond this.⁵² Subsequent discovery and use are therefore not protected. In fact, legal protection is often directed instead to the behaviour of parties privy to the secret. As such, trade secrets are generally not considered as "property" and cannot properly be offered as collateral.

Cash and receivables

[8.100] As the cash income is likely to be needed for the chargor's working capital, a floating charge (instead of a fixed charge) registrable under s 262(1)(a) of the *Corporations Act 2001* (Cth) may be created over the bank account into which the cash income is deposited. The charge instrument should, for reasons of prudence, restrict the chargor from creating another charge ranking with, or in priority to, the floating charge without the chargee's consent and contain an automatic crystallisation clause. Further, flawed asset arrangements, whereby the chargor forgoes the right of repayment of deposit until fulfilment of certain conditions, should be in place to prevent any set-off from arising from the mutuality of debts between the bank and the chargor before crystallisation of the floating charge.[53]

Receivables generated under agreements with obligors may be assigned by way of security.[54] Such an assignment constitutes a charge over book debts and is registrable under s 262(1)(f) of the *Corporations Act 2001* (Cth). Present receivables are assignable at *law*, although the notification requirement may prove inefficient and commercially unviable. Future receivables are only assignable in *equity*, if supported by consideration from the assignee and an agreement to assign. Upon the latter coming into existence, equity will immediately vest the equitable estate in the receivables in the assignee.[55] Importantly, the equitable assignment relates back to the point of the agreement to assign and the assignor is from that time deemed to hold the receivables on trust for the assignee.[56]

WOBS: CONCLUSION

Suitable WOBS candidates

[8.110] Not every business will be suitable for WOBS. Yet, no exact formula exists to determine their suitability.[57] Nevertheless, general suitability criteria can be gleaned from recent WOBS deals:[58]

- the business should generate predictable and continuous cash flows necessary to discharge debt obligations represented by the securities issued to investors;
- business operations should occur in a regulated or protected industry, like healthcare and water, where high barriers to entry reduce competition and ensure income stability;
- the business should have a well-established market position; and
- the business ought to be considerably recession-proof (eg pubs).

By satisfying the above criteria, the prospective WOBS candidate presents optimum conditions to credit rating agencies. This will bolster credit ratings conferred on securities issued and, accordingly, promote the efficacy of raising funds using WOBS, as opposed to traditional, financing techniques.

[1] "Tornator Finance plc" (Presale Report, Standard & Poor's, 14 November 2002); "2002 Review and 2003 Outlook European WOBS: Issuance Up 37% in 2002 with Strong Growth Expected for 2003" (Special Report, Moody's, 21 January 2003) p 5. WOBS has also been used to finance: (a) buy-outs, eg Rank Hovis McDougall, a food company (August 2000); Dignity Finance, a funeral home operator (April 2003); and (b) equipment leases, eg Xerox Financial Services (July 2003). Regarding the former, see further "Dignity Finance Plc" (Fitch Ratings, 23 April 2003).

[2] See Downey C, "Whole Business Securitization Comes of Age" (1999) 18(9) IFLR 8.

[3] See Downey C, "Whole Business Securitization Comes of Age" (1999) 18(9) IFLR 8 at 8 and 10.

[4] See Mannix R, "Morgan Stanley Answers Formula One Critics" (1999) 18(8) IFLR 11.

[5] See Mannix R, "Combining the Benefits of Debt and Equity" (1999) 18(8) IFLR 12 at 12-13.

[6] "Really Useful Theatres Finance Limited Asset Backed Notes" (Presale Report, Moody's, 16 October 2000).

[7] "Whole Business Securitisations: A Unique Opportunity for UK Assets" (Special Report, Moody's, 19 October 2000) p 4. For an overview of UK pub WOBS transactions from 1998-2002 see "One for the Road – A Crawl through UK Pub Securitisations" (Special Report, Fitch Ratings, 15 January 2003).

[8] "Punch Funding II Ltd Secured Notes" (Presale Report, Moody's, 24 May 2000); "Punch Taverns Finance plc" (Presale Report, Moody's, 4 October 2000); "The Unique Pub Finance Co plc" (Standard & Poor's, 30 September 2002); "Pubmaster Finance Ltd" (Presale Report, Moody's, 15 November 2002). For a securitised portfolio of wholly managed pubs, see "Spirit Funding Ltd" (Standard & Poor's, 2 August 2002).

[9] "Anglian Water Services Financing plc" (Presale Report, Moody's, 9 May 2002). Four other UK water utilities have subsequently raised funds via WOBS structures: Mid Kent Water (December 2002); Bristol Water (April 2003); Dwr Cymru (April 2003); Southern Water (July 2003). See also Albagli D, Barnard C, Borrows J and Turtle T, "Securitisation by Water Companies" in Borrows J (ed), *Current Issues in Securitisation* (Sweet & Maxwell, 2002) pp 77-78; "Anglian Water – Redesigning an Industry", *Structured Finance International* (August 2002); "2002 Review and 2003 Outlook European WOBS: Issuance Up 37% in 2002 with Strong Growth Expected for 2003" (Special Report, Moody's, 21 January 2003) p 3.

[10] See "UK Hospitals No. 1 S.A." (Presale Report, Standard & Poor's, 28 June 2002).

[11] See "Craegmoor Funding plc Asset-Backed Floating Rate Notes" (Presale Report, Moody's, 30 October 2000); "Craegmoor Funding (No. 2) Limited" (Presale Report, Fitch Ratings, 25 June 2003). Other recent healthcare WOBS transactions include Priory Finance (July 2003): see "Priory Finance Co Ltd" (Presale Report, Standard & Poor's, 16 July 2003); "Priory Finance Company Limited (Presale Report, Fitch Ratings, 18 July 2003).

[12] See Petkovic D, "New Structures: 'Whole Business' Securitisations of Project Cash Flows" (2000) 15 JIBL 187. Other related developments are the securitisation of electricity transmission (Moyle Interconnector, April 2003) and "motorway service areas", which are businesses providing bundled accommodation, catering, fuel and gaming services adjacent to motorways (RoadChef, July 2003). See "RoadChef Finance Ltd" (Fitch Ratings, 1 July 2003).

[13] "Romulus Finance S.r.I." (Presale Report, Standard & Poor's, 29 November 2002). See also "Whole Business Securitisation Takes Wing", *Structured Finance International* (April 2003).

[14] See Brinkworth S, "Football Turns to Securitization to Fund Growth" (2002) 21(2) IFLR 13.

[15] See Schwarcz SL, "The Alchemy of Asset Securitization" (1994) 1 Stan J L Bus & Fin 133 at 142-143. This is less pertinent in WOBS since no assets sales occur and the issuer and operating company are usually group members.

[16] See Schwarcz SL, "The Alchemy of Asset Securitization" (1994) 1 Stan J L Bus & Fin 133 at 136. This is unlike WOBS, given the secured loan structure.

[17] See European Securitisation Forum, "European Securitisation: A Resource Guide" (1999) p 6.

[18] See European Securitisation Forum, "European Securitisation: A Resource Guide" (1999) pp 6-7.

[19] See Clayton Utz, *A Guide to the Law of Securitisation in Australia* (3rd ed, 2003) p 6.

[20] Being a non-separate legal entity, a trust cannot owe debt obligation and requires the trustee to contract with third parties: see Clayton Utz, "A Guide to the Law of Securitisation in Australia" (3rd ed, 2003) p 51.

[21] See Clayton Utz, *A Guide to the Law of Securitisation in Australia* (3rd ed, 2003) p 6.

[22] See further Clayton Utz, *A Guide to the Law of Securitisation in Australia* (3rd ed, 2003) pp

51-52.

[23] See Gordon TJ, "Securitization of Executory Future Flows as Bankruptcy-Remote True Sales" (2000) 67 U Chi L Rev 1317 at 1327.

[24] See European Securitisation Forum, "European Securitisation: A Resource Guide" (1999) p 2.

[25] See Indelicato MS, "Securitization Provides Means to Protect Assets" 227(32) *New York Law Journal* 9; " Structured Finance Criteria Introduced for Australian and New Zealand Special-Purpose Entities" (Standard & Poor's, 22 May 2001) pp 1-2.

[26] Gordon TJ, "Securitization of Executory Future Flows as Bankruptcy-Remote True Sales" (2000) 67 U Chi L Rev 1317 at 1324. Many Australian SPV-companies are single-director companies. The presence of an independent director (or a majority of independent directors) also minimises the risk of the SPV being consolidated with the Originator as a controlled entity of the Originator.

[27] See "Structured Finance Criteria Introduced for Australian and New Zealand Special-Purpose Entities" (Standard & Poor's, 22 May 2001) p 3

[28] See Wood PR, *Title Finance, Derivatives, Securitisations, Set-off and Netting* (Sweet and Maxwell, 1995) p 41. Another advantage of a charitable trust (and a purpose trust) is that the objects of the trust are purposes, not persons, thus avoiding the risk that the beneficiaries of the trust could compel the transfer in specie of the trust estate (the shares in the SPV-company) to them pursuant to the rule in *Saunders v Vautier* (1841) 41 ER 482.

[29] It is considered that the use of a Clayton's contract does not offend the requirement in *Conveyancing Act 1919* (NSW), s 23C(1)(c) and its counterparts for dispositions of equitable interests to be made in writing: see further Ali PU and Tisdell M, "Collateralised Debt Obligations, with an Overview of the CONDOR Securitisation Programme" (2000) 18 C&SLJ 371 at 374.

[30] See generally Lambie C, "Whole Business Securitisation: Maximising Your Assets" (2000) XI(11) PLC 41 at 43-44; Hill CA, "Whole Business Securitization in Emerging Markets" (2002) 12 Duke J Comp & Int'l L 521 at 524-525; "Whole Business Securitisations: A Unique Opportunity for UK Assets" (Special Report, Moody's, 19 October 2000) pp 2-3. The secured loan securitisation structure has also been utilised in the field of inventory securitisation, in relation to champagne (Marne et Champagne Finance (March 2000) and FCC Cote des Noires (January 2002)) and diamond inventories (Rosy Blue Carat, January 2002): see further "Debut of Inventory Securitisation in Europe: Moody's Rating Approach" (Special Report, Moody's, 21 May 2002).

[31] See also Kothari V, "Whole Business Securitization: Secured Lending Repackaged?" (2002) 12 Duke J Comp & Int'l L 537 at 537-538.

[32] Fixed charges should support fully the debt obligations of the securities: see Petkovic D, "New Structures: 'Whole Business' Securitisations of Project Cash Flows" (2000) 15 JIBL 187 at 189.

[33] This would be encompassed within the residual floating charge over assets not subject to fixed charges.

[34] *Corporations Act 2001* (Cth), s 441A.

[35] "Structured Finance Research" (ICICI Ltd, July 2002) p 10.

[36] Lambie C, "Whole Business Securitisation: Maximising Your Assets" (2000) XI(11) PLC 41 at 45-46.

[37] *Corporations Act 2001* (Cth), Pt 7.13, Div 2.

[38] See Lipton JD, *Security Over Intangible Property* (LBC Information Services, 2000) p 72.

[39] See Allen, Allen & Hemsley, "CHESS and Security Over Shares" (1996) 7 JBFLP 63 at 64-67; Dwyer E, "Shares as Security in Australia's CHESS System" [1998] JIBL 258 at 261.

[40] *Corporations Act 2001* (Cth), s 262(1)(g)(i).

[41] See Lipton JD, *Security Over Intangible Property* (LBC Information Services, 2000) pp 90 and 94. See also Lipton JD, "Security Interests in Trade Marks and Associated Business Goodwill" (1999) 10 AIPJ 157.

[42] The certificate of registration of the trademark is not such a document: see Lipton JD, *Security Over Intangible Property* (LBC Information Services, 2000) p 113.

[43] *Trade Marks Act 1995* (Cth), ss 106-111.

[44] See Lipton JD, *Security Over Intangible Property* (LBC Information Services, 2000) pp 110-111.

[45] See *Re Cosslett (Contractors) Ltd* [1998] Ch 495; *Re Westmaze Ltd* [1999] BCC 441.

[46] See Lipton JD, *Security Over Intangible Property* (LBC Information Services, 2000) p 196. See also Lipton JD, "Security Interests in Electronic Databases" (2001) 9 IJL&IT 65 for the English position.

[47] See Lipton JD, "Security Interests in Electronic Databases" (2001) 9 IJL&IT 65 at 69.

[48] *Copyright Act 1968* (Cth), s 196.

[49] *Copyright Act 1968* (Cth), s 197(1).

[50] See Lipton JD, *Security Over Intangible Property* (LBC Information Services, 2000) p 150.

[51] See Lipton JD, *Security Over Intangible Property* (LBC Information Services, 2000) pp 170-173.

[52] See Smith LS, "Trade Secrets in Commercial Transactions and Bankruptcy" (2000) 40 IDEA 549 at 570-574; Jacoby MB and Zimmerman DL, "Foreclosing on Fame: Exploring the Uncharted Boundaries of the Right of Publicity" (2002) 77 NYULR 1322 at 1345, where it is considered that trade secrets are assets.

[53] See Derham SR, *Set-Off* (2nd ed, Oxford University Press, 1996) pp 334-335 and 606-608.

[54] For the effects of non-assignability clauses, see *Linden Gardens Trust Ltd v Lenesta Sludge Disposals Ltd* [1994] 1 AC 85; cf *Don King Productions Inc v Warren* [1998] 2 All ER 608 (HC) and [1999] 2 All ER 218 (CA). See further McCormack G, "Debts and Non-Assignment Clauses" [2000] JBL 422. As to the nature of security interests over receivables, see generally Berg A, "Brumark Investments Ltd and the 'Innominate Charge'" [2001] JBL 532; McKnight A, "Brumark: the Difference Between Fixed and Floating Charges" [2001] JIBL 157; Gregory R and Walton P, "Fixed and Floating Charges – A Revelation" [2001] LMCLQ 123.

[55] *Holroyd v Marshall* (1862) 10 HL Cas 191; *Tailby v Official Receiver* (1888) 13 App Cas 523.

[56] *Palette Shoes Pty Ltd v Krohn* (1937) 58 CLR 1 at 27 (per Dixon J).

[57] See Colomer N, "One Size Won't Fit All: Looking at the Evolution of Whole Business Deals", *Asset Securitization Report* (17 June 2002).

[58] See also "Structured Finance Research" (ICICI Ltd, July 2002) pp 11-12.

Appendix

About this Appendix: forms included

[A.10] The following documents from the International Swaps and Derivatives Association (ISDA) are reproduced as a guide only. The documents may be subject to change as developments occur. Regular reference should be made to the ISDA website (http://www.isda.org) for the most up-to-date documents and information.

Master Confirmation: Asia-Pacific

[A.20] This ISDA form is available to download from the ISDA website (http://www.isda.org).

2003 MASTER CREDIT DERIVATIVES CONFIRMATION AGREEMENT

This 2003 Master Credit Derivatives Confirmation Agreement ("Master Confirmation Agreement") is dated as of [_____] between [_____] ("Party A") and [_____] ("Party B").

The parties wish to facilitate the process of entering into and confirming Credit Derivative Transactions and accordingly agree as follows:

1. Credit Derivatives Definitions. This Master Confirmation Agreement hereby incorporates by reference the 2003 ISDA Credit Derivatives Definitions as supplemented by the May 2003 Supplement to the 2003 ISDA Credit Derivatives Definitions (together, the "Credit Derivatives Definitions"). Any capitalized term not otherwise defined herein shall have the meaning assigned to such term in the Credit Derivatives Definitions.

2. Confirmation Process. The parties intend to enter into separate Credit Derivative Transactions (each a "Transaction") with respect to each Reference Entity set out in a Transaction Supplement substantially in the form attached as Annex 1 (a "Transaction Supplement"). The confirmation applicable to each Transaction, which shall constitute a "Confirmation" for the purposes of, and will supplement, form a part of, and be subject to, the ISDA Master Agreement between Party A and Party B dated as of [_____], as amended and supplemented from time to time (the "Master Agreement"), shall consist of this Master Confirmation Agreement including the form of General Terms Confirmation attached as Exhibit A (the "General Terms Confirmation"), as supplemented by the trade details applicable to such Transaction as set forth in the Transaction Supplement.[1]

    In the event of any inconsistency between (i) this Master Confirmation Agreement, including the form of General Terms Confirmation and a Transaction Supplement and/or (ii) the Credit Derivatives Definitions and a Transaction Supplement, the Transaction Supplement shall govern for the purpose of the relevant Transaction. The Transaction Supplement shall set forth, at a minimum, all of the information set out in the applicable form of Transaction Supplement attached hereto as Annex 1.

3. Non-Exclusive. The parties acknowledge and agree that the execution of this Master Confirmation Agreement does not require them to document Transactions in accordance with this Master Confirmation Agreement.

4. Preparation of Transaction Supplements. The preparation of a Transaction Supplement shall be the responsibility of the Seller in respect of the Transaction to which the relevant Transaction Supplement relates.

5   Miscellaneous.

   (a) Entire Agreement. This Master Confirmation Agreement constitutes the entire agreement and understanding of the parties with respect to its subject matter and supersedes all oral communication and prior writings with respect specifically thereto.

   (b) Amendments. An amendment, modification or waiver in respect of this Master Confirmation Agreement will only be effective if in writing (including a writing evidenced by a facsimile transmission) and executed by each of the parties or confirmed by an exchange of telexes or by an exchange of electronic messages on an electronic messaging system.

   (c) Counterparts. This Master Confirmation Agreement and each Transaction Supplement documented hereunder may be executed in counterparts, each of which will be deemed an original.

   (d) Headings. The headings used in this Master Confirmation Agreement are for convenience of reference only and shall not affect the construction of or be taken into consideration in interpreting this Master Confirmation Agreement.

   (e) Governing Law. This Master Confirmation Agreement and each Transaction confirmed by a Confirmation documented hereunder will be governed by and construed in accordance with the law specified in the Master Agreement.

N WITNESS WHEREOF the parties have executed this document with effect from the date specified on the first page of this document.

[_____]   [_____]

By: By:_____

Name: Name:

Title: Title:

Date: Date:

[1] If the parties have not yet executed an ISDA Master Agreement, the following language shall be included: "The confirmation applicable to each Transaction shall consist of this Master Confirmation Agreement including the form of General Terms Confirmation attached as Exhibit A (the "General Terms Confirmation"), as supplemented by the trade details applicable to such Transaction as set forth in the Transaction Supplement and shall constitute a "Confirmation" as referred to in the ISDA Master Agreement specified below. The Confirmation applicable to each Transaction will evidence a complete and binding agreement between the parties as to the terms of the Transaction to which such Confirmation relates. In addition, the parties agree to use all reasonable efforts promptly to negotiate, execute and deliver an agreement in the form of an ISDA Master Agreement, with such modifications as the parties in good faith agree. Upon execution by the parties of such an agreement (the "Master Agreement"), each Confirmation already executed in connection with this Master Confirmation Agreement and all future Confirmations executed in connection with this Master Confirmation Agreement will supplement, form a part of, and be subject to, that Master Agreement. All provisions contained in or incorporated by reference in that Master Agreement upon its execution will govern each Confirmation except as expressly modified below. Until the parties execute and deliver that Master Agreement, each Confirmation confirming a Transaction entered into between the parties in connection with this Master Confirmation Agreement (notwithstanding anything to the contrary in a Confirmation), shall supplement, form a part of, and be subject to, an agreement in the form of the 2002 ISDA Master Agreement as if the parties had executed an agreement in such form (but without any Schedule except for the election of [New York Law] [English Law] as the governing law) on the Trade Date of the first such Transaction between the parties in connection with this Master Confirmation Agreement. In the event of any inconsistency between the provisions of that agreement and a Confirmation, the Confirmation will prevail for purposes of the relevant Transaction."

SYNTHETIC, INSURANCE AND HEDGE FUND SECURITISATIONS

[Date]

Re: General Terms Confirmation

Dear Sir or Madam,

The purpose of this General Terms Confirmation (this "General Terms Confirmation") is to confirm certain general terms and conditions of the Credit Derivative Transactions entered into between us under the 2003 Master Credit Derivatives Confirmation Agreement between us dated as of [   ] ("Master Confirmation Agreement").

This General Terms Confirmation hereby incorporates by reference the 2003 ISDA Credit Derivatives Definitions as supplemented by the May 2003 Supplement to the 2003 ISDA Credit Derivatives Definitions (together, the "Credit Derivatives Definitions"). In the event of any inconsistency between the Credit Derivatives Definitions and this General Terms Confirmation, this General Terms Confirmation will govern.

All provisions contained in the Master Agreement govern each Confirmation (each as defined in the Master Confirmation Agreement) except as expressly modified below The general terms of each Transaction to which this General Terms Confirmation relates are as follows, as supplemented by the Transaction Supplement related to such Transaction:

1. **General Terms:**

Trade Date:	As shown in the Transaction Supplement
Effective Date:	As shown in the Transaction Supplement
Scheduled Termination Date:	As shown in the Transaction Supplement
Transaction Type:	As shown in the Transaction Supplement
Floating Rate Payer:	As shown in the Transaction Supplement (the "Seller")
Fixed Rate Payer:	As shown in the Transaction Supplement (the "Buyer")
Calculation Agent:	Seller
Calculation Agent City:	As shown in the Transaction Supplement
Business Day:	If the Transaction Type indicated in the Transaction Supplement is:
	Japan: New York, London and Tokyo (and TARGET Settlement Day if the Floating Rate Payer Calculation Amount is in EUR)
	Australia and New Zealand: If the Reference Entity indicated in the Transaction Supplement is: (i) an Australian Entity, New York, London[, Tokyo] and Sydney (and TARGET Settlement Day if the Floating Rate Payer Calculation Amount is in EUR); or (ii) a New Zealand Entity; New York, London[, Tokyo] and Auckland (and TARGET Settlement Day if the Floating Rate Payer Calculation Amount is in EUR)
	Asia: New York [and][,] London [and Tokyo] (and TARGET Settlement Day if the Floating Rate Payer Calculation Amount is in EUR)
	Singapore: New York, London[, Tokyo] and Singapore (and TARGET Settlement Day if the Floating Rate Payer Calculation Amount is in EUR)
Business Day Convention:	Following (which, subject to Sections 1.4 and 1.6 of the Credit Derivatives Definitions, shall apply to any date referred to in this General Terms Confirmation or in the related Transaction Supplement that falls on a day that is not a Business Day).
Reference Entity:	As shown in the Transaction Supplement
Reference Obligation(s):	As shown in the Transaction Supplement
Reference Price:	100% All Guarantees: Applicable

2. **Fixed Payments:**

Fixed Rate Payer Calculation Amount:	The Floating Rate Payer Calculation Amount
Fixed Rate Payer Payment Dates:	As shown in the Transaction Supplement
Fixed Rate:	As shown in the Transaction Supplement
Fixed Rate Day Count Fraction:	Actual/360

APPENDIX

3. **Floating Payment:**

Floating Rate Payer
Calculation Amount: As shown in the Transaction Supplement

Conditions to Settlement:
- Credit Event Notice

  Notifying Parties: Buyer or Seller

  If the Transaction Type indicated in the Transaction Supplement is Japan, "Greenwich Mean Time" in Section 3.3 of the Credit Derivatives Definitions shall be replaced by "Tokyo time".

  If the Transaction Type indicated in the Transaction Supplement is Japan, Section 3.9 of the Credit Derivatives Definitions shall not apply.

- Notice of Physical Settlement
- Notice of Publicly Available Information: Applicable

Credit Event: The following Credit Events shall apply to this Transaction:

Bankruptcy

Failure to Pay

Grace Period Extension:	Not Applicable
Payment Requirement:	If the Transaction Type indicated in the Transaction Supplement is Japan and the Floating Rate Payer Calculation Amount is in JPY, JPY 100,000,000 or its equivalent in the relevant Obligation Currency as of the occurrence of the relevant Failure to Pay
	In all other cases, USD 1,000,000 or its equivalent in the relevant Obligation Currency as of the occurrence of the relevant Failure to Pay

Restructuring: If indicated as applicable in the Transaction Supplement, the following terms shall apply:

Restructuring Maturity Limitation and Fully Transferable Obligation:	If the Transaction Type indicated in the Transaction Supplement is: Japan: Not Applicable Australia and New Zealand: Applicable Asia: Not Applicable Singapore: Not Applicable
Modified Restructuring Maturity Limitation and Conditionally Transferable Obligation:	If the Transaction Type indicated in the Transaction Supplement is: Japan: Not Applicable Australia and New Zealand: Not Applicable Asia: Not Applicable Singapore: Not Applicable
Multiple Holder Obligation:	If the Transaction Type indicated in the Transaction Supplement is: Japan: Not Applicable Australia and New Zealand: Applicable Asia: Applicable Singapore: Applicable
Default Requirement:	If the Transaction Type indicated in the Transaction Supplement is Japan and the Floating Rate Payer Calculation Amount is in JPY, JPY 1,000,000,000 or its equivalent in the relevant Obligation Currency as of the occurrence of the relevant Credit Event
	In all other cases, USD 10,000,000 or its equivalent in the relevant Obligation Currency as of the occurrence of the relevant Credit Event

Obligation(s): For the purposes of the tables below:

"Yes" shall mean that the relevant selection is applicable; and

"No" shall mean that the relevant selection is not applicable.

1) If the Transaction Type indicated in the Transaction Supplement is Japan, the following table shall apply for the purposes of the Transaction supplemented by such Transaction Supplement:

Obligation Categories: (Select only one)		Obligation Characteristics: (Select all that apply)	
No	Payment	Yes	Not Subordinated
Yes	Borrowed Money	No	Specified Currency – Standard Specified Currencies
No	Reference Obligation(s) Only	No	Not Sovereign Lender
No	Bond	No	Not Domestic Currency
No	Loan	No	Not Domestic Law
No	Bond or Loan	No	Listed
		No	Not Domestic Issuance

2) If the Transaction Type indicated in the Transaction Supplement is Australia and New Zealand, the following table shall apply for the purposes of the Transaction supplemented by such Transaction Supplement:

Obligation Categories: (Select only one)		Obligation Characteristics: (Select all that apply)	
No	Payment	No	Not Subordinated
Yes	Borrowed Money	No	Specified Currency – Standard Specified Currencies
No	Reference Obligation(s) Only	No	Not Sovereign Lender
No	Bond	No	Not Domestic Currency
No	Loan	No	Not Domestic Law
No	Bond or Loan	No	Listed
		No	Not Domestic Issuance

3) If the Transaction Type indicated in the Transaction Supplement is Asia, the following table shall apply for the purposes of the Transaction supplemented by such Transaction Supplement:

Obligation Categories: (Select only one)		Obligation Characteristics: (Select all that apply)	
No	Payment	Yes	Not Subordinated
No	Borrowed Money	No	Specified Currency – Standard Specified Currencies
No	Reference Obligation(s) Only	Yes	Not Sovereign Lender
No	Bond	Yes	Not Domestic Currency
No	Loan	Yes	Not Domestic Law
Yes	Bond or Loan	No	Listed
		Yes	Not Domestic Issuance

APPENDIX

4) If the Transaction Type indicated in the Transaction Supplement is Singapore, the following table shall apply for the purposes of the Transaction supplemented by such Transaction Supplement:

Obligation Categories: (Select only one)		Obligation Characteristics: (Select all that apply)	
No	Payment	Yes	Not Subordinated
No	Borrowed Money	Yes	Specified Currency – Standard Specified Currencies and Domestic Currency
No	Reference Obligation(s) Only	Yes	Not Sovereign Lender
No	Bond	No	Not Domestic Currency
No	Loan	No	Not Domestic Law
Yes	Bond or Loan	No	Listed
		No	Not Domestic Issuance

4. **Settlement Terms:**

Settlement Method: Physical Settlement

Settlement Currency: The currency of denomination of the Floating Rate Payer Calculation Amount

Terms Relating to Physical Settlement:

Physical Settlement Period: Thirty (30) Business Days

Deliverable Obligations: Exclude Accrued Interest

Deliverable Obligation Category and Characteristics: For the purposes of the tables below:

"**Yes**" shall mean that the relevant selection is applicable; and

"**No**" shall mean that the relevant selection is not applicable.

1) If the Transaction Type indicated in the Transaction Supplement is Japan, the following table shall apply for the purposes of the Transaction supplemented by such Transaction Supplement:

Deliverable Obligation Categories: (Select only one)		Deliverable Obligation Characteristics: (Select all that apply)	
No	Payment	Yes	Not Subordinated
No	Borrowed Money	Yes	Specified Currency – Standard Specified Currencies
No	Reference Obligation(s) Only	No	Not Sovereign Lender
No	Bond	No	Not Domestic Currency
No	Loan	No	Not Domestic Law
Yes	Bond or Loan	No	Listed
		Yes	Not Contingent
		No	Not Domestic Issuance
		Yes	Assignable Loan
		Yes	Consent Required Loan
		No	Direct Loan Participation
		Yes	Transferable
		Yes – 30 years	Maximum Maturity
		No	Accelerated or Matured
		Yes	Not Bearer

187

2) If the Transaction Type indicated in the Transaction Supplement is Australia and New Zealand, the following table shall apply for the purposes of the Transaction supplemented by such Transaction Supplement:

Deliverable Obligation Categories: (Select only one)		**Deliverable Obligation Characteristics:** (Select all that apply)	
No	Payment	Yes	Not Subordinated
No	Borrowed Money	Yes	Specified Currency – Standard Specified Currencies and Domestic Currency
No	Reference Obligation(s) Only	No	Not Sovereign Lender
No	Bond	No	Not Domestic Currency
No	Loan	No	Not Domestic Law
Yes	Bond or Loan	No	Listed
		Yes	Not Contingent
		No	Not Domestic Issuance
		Yes	Assignable Loan
		Yes	Consent Required Loan
		No	Direct Loan Participation
		Yes	Transferable
		Yes – 30 years	Maximum Maturity
		No	Accelerated or Matured
		Yes	Not Bearer

3) If the Transaction Type indicated in the Transaction Supplement is Asia, the following table shall apply for the purposes of the Transaction supplemented by such Transaction Supplement:

Deliverable Obligation Categories: (Select only one)		**Deliverable Obligation Characteristics:** (Select all that apply)	
No	Payment	Yes	Not Subordinated
No	Borrowed Money	Yes	Specified Currency – Standard Specified Currencies
No	Reference Obligation(s) Only	Yes	Not Sovereign Lender
No	Bond	No	Not Domestic Currency
No	Loan	Yes	Not Domestic Law
Yes	Bond or Loan	No	Listed
		Yes	Not Contingent
		Yes	Not Domestic Issuance
		Yes	Assignable Loan
		No	Consent Required Loan
		No	Direct Loan Participation
		Yes	Transferable
		Yes – 30 years	Maximum Maturity
		No	Accelerated or Matured
		Yes	Not Bearer

APPENDIX

4) If the Transaction Type indicated in the Transaction Supplement is Singapore, the following table shall apply for the purposes of the Transaction supplemented by such Transaction Supplement:

Deliverable Obligation Categories: (Select only one)		Deliverable Obligation Characteristics: (Select all that apply)	
No	Payment	Yes	Not Subordinated
No	Borrowed Money	Yes	Specified Currency – Standard Specified Currencies and Domestic Currency
No	Reference Obligation(s) Only	Yes	Not Sovereign Lender
No	Bond	No	Not Domestic Currency
No	Loan	No	Not Domestic Law
Yes	Bond or Loan	No	Listed
		Yes	Not Contingent
		No	Not Domestic Issuance
		Yes	Assignable Loan
		No	Consent Required Loan
		No	Direct Loan Participation
		Yes	Transferable
		Yes – 30 years	Maximum Maturity
		No	Accelerated or Matured
		Yes	Not Bearer

Excluded Deliverable
Obligations: None

Partial Cash Settlement
of Consent Required Loans: Not Applicable

Partial Cash Settlement
of Assignable Loans: Not Applicable

Partial Cash
Settlement of Participations: Not Applicable

Escrow: [Applicable] [Not Applicable]

5. **Notice and Account Details:**

Notice and Account Details for Party A:
Notice and Account Details for Party B:

189

[Buyer Contact Information:]
[Seller Contact Information:]

TRANSACTION SUPPLEMENT

Transaction Type: [Japan][Australia and New Zealand][Asia][Singapore]

This Transaction Supplement is entered into between the Buyer and Seller listed below on the Trade Date set forth below.

The purpose of this communication is to confirm the terms and conditions of the Credit Derivative Transaction entered into between us on the Trade Date specified below (the "Transaction"). This Transaction Supplement is entered into under the 2003 Master Credit Derivatives Confirmation Agreement dated as of [_____] and, together with the 2003 Master Credit Derivatives Confirmation Agreement and the General Terms Confirmation attached thereto, constitutes a "Confirmation" as referred to in the Master Agreement between the parties, as amended and supplemented from time to time.

The terms of the Transaction to which this Transaction Supplement relates are as follows:

Reference Entity:

[Reference Obligation,	[The obligation[s] identified as follows:
If applicable:	Primary Obligor: [ ]
	Guarantor: [ ]
	Maturity: [ ]
	Coupon: [ ]
	CUSIP/ISIN: [ ]]]

Trade Date:

Effective Date:

Scheduled Termination Date:

Floating Rate Payer:	[ ] (the "Seller")
Fixed Rate Payer:	[ ] (the "Buyer")
Calculation Agent City:	[ ]
Fixed Rate Payer Payment Dates:	
Fixed Rate:	_____%
Floating Rate Payer Calculation Amount:	[ ]
Restructuring Credit Event:	[Applicable] [Not Applicable]
[Additional Terms:	[ ]]

Please confirm your agreement to be bound by the terms of the foregoing by executing a copy of this Transaction Supplement and returning it to us [at the contact information listed above].

[_____]   [_____]

By: _____   By: _____
Name: Name:
Title: Title:

APPENDIX

Master Confirmation: US and Europe

[A.30] This ISDA form is available to download from the ISDA website (http://www.isda.org).

June 6, 2003

2003 MASTER CREDIT DERIVATIVES CONFIRMATION AGREEMENT

This 2003 Master Credit Derivatives Confirmation Agreement ("Master Confirmation Agreement") is dated as of [_____] between [_____] ("Party A") and [_____] ("Party B").

The parties wish to facilitate the process of entering into and confirming Credit Derivative Transactions and accordingly agree as follows:

1. Credit Derivatives Definitions. This Master Confirmation Agreement hereby incorporates by reference the 2003 ISDA Credit Derivatives Definitions as supplemented by the May 2003 Supplement to the 2003 ISDA Credit Derivatives Definitions (together, the "Credit Derivatives Definitions"). Any capitalized term not otherwise defined herein shall have the meaning assigned to such term in the Credit Derivatives Definitions.

2. Confirmation Process. The parties intend to enter into separate Credit Derivative Transactions (each a "Transaction") with respect to each Reference Entity set out in a Transaction Supplement substantially in the form attached as Annex 1 (a "Transaction Supplement"). The confirmation applicable to each Transaction, which shall constitute a "Confirmation" for the purposes of, and will supplement, form a part of, and be subject to, the ISDA Master Agreement between Party A and Party B dated as of [_____], as amended and supplemented from time to time (the "Master Agreement"), shall consist of this Master Confirmation Agreement including the form of General Terms Confirmation attached as Exhibit A (the "General Terms Confirmation"), as supplemented by the trade details applicable to such Transaction as set forth in the Transaction Supplement.[1]

   In the event of any inconsistency between (i) this Master Confirmation Agreement, including the form of General Terms Confirmation and a Transaction Supplement and/or (ii) the Credit Derivatives Definitions and a Transaction Supplement, the Transaction Supplement shall govern for the purpose of the relevant Transaction. The Transaction Supplement shall set forth, at a minimum, all of the information set out in the applicable form of Transaction Supplement attached hereto as Annex 1.

3. Non-Exclusive. The parties acknowledge and agree that the execution of this Master Confirmation Agreement does not require them to document Transactions in accordance with this Master Confirmation Agreement.

4. Preparation of Transaction Supplements. The preparation of a Transaction Supplement shall be the responsibility of the Seller in respect of the Transaction to which the relevant Transaction Supplement relates.

5 Miscellaneous.

   (a) Entire Agreement. This Master Confirmation Agreement constitutes the entire agreement and understanding of the parties with respect to its subject matter and supersedes all oral communication and prior writings with respect specifically thereto.

(b) Amendments. An amendment, modification or waiver in respect of this Master Confirmation Agreement will only be effective if in writing (including a writing evidenced by a facsimile transmission) and executed by each of the parties or confirmed by an exchange of telexes or by an exchange of electronic messages on an electronic messaging system.

(c) Counterparts. This Master Confirmation Agreement and each Transaction Supplement documented hereunder may be executed in counterparts, each of which will be deemed an original.

(d) Headings. The headings used in this Master Confirmation Agreement are for convenience of reference only and shall not affect the construction of or be taken into consideration in interpreting this Master Confirmation Agreement.

(e) Governing Law. This Master Confirmation Agreement and each Transaction confirmed by a Confirmation documented hereunder will be governed by and construed in accordance with the law specified in the Master Agreement.

IN WITNESS WHEREOF the parties have executed this document with effect from the date specified on the first page of this document.

[_____]   [_____]

By:_____   By:_____

Name: Name:

Title: Title:

Date: Date:

---

[1] If the parties have not yet executed an ISDA Master Agreement, the following language shall be included: "The confirmation applicable to each Transaction shall consist of this Master Confirmation Agreement including the form of General Terms Confirmation attached as Exhibit A (the "General Terms Confirmation"), as supplemented by the trade details applicable to such Transaction as set forth in the Transaction Supplement and shall constitute a "Confirmation" as referred to in the ISDA Master Agreement specified below. The Confirmation applicable to each Transaction will evidence a complete and binding agreement between the parties as to the terms of the Transaction to which such Confirmation relates. In addition, the parties agree to use all reasonable efforts promptly to negotiate, execute and deliver an agreement in the form of an ISDA Master Agreement, with such modifications as the parties in good faith agree. Upon execution by the parties of such an agreement (the "Master Agreement"), each Confirmation already executed in connection with this Master Confirmation Agreement and all future Confirmations executed in connection with this Master Confirmation Agreement will supplement, form a part of, and be subject to, that Master Agreement. All provisions contained in or incorporated by reference in that Master Agreement upon its execution will govern each Confirmation except as expressly modified below. Until the parties execute and deliver that Master Agreement, each Confirmation confirming a Transaction entered into between the parties in connection with this Master Confirmation Agreement (notwithstanding anything to the contrary in a Confirmation), shall supplement, form a part of, and be subject to, an agreement in the form of the 2002 ISDA Master Agreement as if the parties had executed an agreement in such form (but without any Schedule except for the election of [New York Law] [English Law] as the governing law) on the Trade Date of the first such Transaction between the parties in connection with this Master Confirmation Agreement. In the event of any inconsistency between the provisions of that agreement and a Confirmation, the Confirmation will prevail for purposes of the relevant Transaction."

APPENDIX

[Date]

Re: **General Terms Confirmation**

Dear Sir or Madam,

The purpose of this General Terms Confirmation (this "General Terms Confirmation") is to confirm certain general terms and conditions of the Credit Derivative Transactions entered into between us under the 2003 Master Credit Derivatives Confirmation Agreement between us dated as of [   ] ("Master Confirmation Agreement").

This General Terms Confirmation hereby incorporates by reference the 2003 ISDA Credit Derivatives Definitions as supplemented by the May 2003 Supplement to the 2003 ISDA Credit Derivatives Definitions (together, the "Credit Derivatives Definitions"). In the event of any inconsistency between the Credit Derivatives Definitions and this General Terms Confirmation, this General Terms Confirmation will govern.

All provisions contained in the Master Agreement govern each Confirmation (each as defined in the Master Confirmation Agreement) except as expressly modified below. The general terms of each Transaction to which this General Terms Confirmation relates are as follows, as supplemented by the Transaction Supplement related to such Transaction:

1. **General Terms:**

Trade Date:	As shown in the Transaction Supplement
Effective Date:	As shown in the Transaction Supplement
Scheduled Termination Date:	As shown in the Transaction Supplement
Transaction Type:	As shown in the Transaction Supplement
Floating Rate Payer:	As shown in the Transaction Supplement (the "Seller")
Fixed Rate Payer:	As shown in the Transaction Supplement (the "Buyer")
Calculation Agent:	Seller
Calculation Agent City:	If the Transaction Type indicated in the Transaction Supplement is: European: London North American: New York
Business Day:	If the Floating Rate Payer Calculation Amount indicated in the Transaction Supplement is denominated in: EUR:　　London and TARGET Settlement Day USD:　　London and New York GBP:　　London CHF:　　London and Zurich
Business Day Convention:	Following (which, subject to Sections 1.4 and 1.6 of the Credit Derivatives Definitions, shall apply to any date referred to in this General Terms Confirmation or in the related Transaction Supplement that falls on a day that is not a Business Day)
Reference Entity:	As shown in the Transaction Supplement
Reference Obligation(s):	As shown in the Transaction Supplement
Reference Price:	100%
All Guarantees:	If the Transaction Type indicated in the Transaction Supplement is: European: Applicable North American: Not Applicable

2. **Fixed Payments:**

Fixed Rate Payer Calculation Amount:	The Floating Rate Payer Calculation Amount
Fixed Rate Payer Payment Dates:	As shown in the Transaction Supplement
Fixed Rate:	As shown in the Transaction Supplement
Fixed Rate Day Count Fraction:	Actual/360

3. **Floating Payment:**

Floating Rate Payer Calculation Amount:	As shown in the Transaction Supplement

Conditions to Settlement:	• Credit Event Notice
	Notifying Parties: Buyer or Seller
	• Notice of Physical Settlement
	• Notice of Publicly Available Information: Applicable

Credit Event: The following Credit Events shall apply to this Transaction:

Bankruptcy

Failure to Pay

Grace Period Extension: Not Applicable

	Payment Requirement:	USD 1,000,000 or its equivalent in the relevant Obligation Currency as of the occurrence of the relevant Failure to Pay

Restructuring: If indicated as applicable in the Transaction Supplement, the following terms shall apply:

	Restructuring Maturity Limitation and Fully Transferable Obligation:	If the Transaction Type indicated in the Transaction Supplement is: European: Not Applicable North American: Applicable
	Modified Restructuring Maturity Limitation and Conditionally Transferable Obligation:	If the Transaction Type indicated in the Transaction Supplement is: European: Applicable North American: Not Applicable
	Default Requirement:	USD 10,000,000 or its equivalent in the relevant Obligation Currency as of the occurrence of the relevant Credit Event

Obligation(s): For the purposes of the table below:

"**Yes**" shall mean that the relevant selection is applicable; and

"**No**" shall mean that the relevant selection is not applicable.

Obligation Categories: (Select only one)		**Obligation Characteristics:** (Select all that apply)	
No	Payment	Yes	Not Subordinated
Yes	Borrowed Money	No	Specified Currency – Standard Specified Currencies
No	Reference Obligation(s) Only	No	Not Sovereign Lender
No	Bond	No	Not Domestic Currency
No	Loan	No	Not Domestic Law
No	Bond or Loan	No	Listed
		No	Not Domestic Issuance

4. Settlement Terms:

Settlement Method:	Physical Settlement
Settlement Currency:	The currency of denomination of the Floating Rate Payer Calculation Amount
Terms Relating to Physical Settlement:	
Physical Settlement Period:	If the Transaction Type indicated in the Transaction Supplement is: European: thirty (30) Business Days North American: as defined in Section 8.6 of the Credit Derivatives Definitions, but in no event longer than thirty (30) Business Days
Deliverable Obligations:	Exclude Accrued Interest

APPENDIX

Deliverable Obligation
Category and Characteristics: For the purposes of the table below:
"**Yes**" shall mean that the relevant selection is applicable; and
"**No**" shall mean that the relevant selection is not applicable.

Deliverable Obligation Categories: (Select only one)		**Deliverable Obligation Characteristics:** (Select all that apply)	
No	Payment	Yes	Not Subordinated
No	Borrowed Money	Yes	Specified Currency – Standard Specified Currencies
No	Reference Obligation(s) Only	No	Not Sovereign Lender
No	Bond	No	Not Domestic Currency
No	Loan	No	Not Domestic Law
Yes	Bond or Loan	No	Listed
		Yes	Not Contingent
		No	Not Domestic Issuance
		Yes	Assignable Loan
		Yes	Consent Required Loan
		No	Direct Loan Participation
		Yes	Transferable
		Yes – 30 years	Maximum Maturity
		No	Accelerated or Matured
		Yes	Not Bearer

Partial Cash Settlement
of Consent Required Loans: Not Applicable

Partial Cash Settlement
of Assignable Loans: Not Applicable

Partial Cash Settlement
of Participations: Not Applicable

Escrow: [Applicable] [Not Applicable]

5. **Notice and Account Details:**

Notice and Account Details for Party A:

Notice and Account Details for Party B:

SYNTHETIC, INSURANCE AND HEDGE FUND SECURITISATIONS

ANNEX 1

[Buyer Contact Information:]
[Seller Contact Information:]

TRANSACTION SUPPLEMENT

Transaction Type: [European] [North American]

This Transaction Supplement is entered into between the Buyer and Seller listed below on the Trade Date set forth below.

The purpose of this communication is to confirm the terms and conditions of the Credit Derivative Transaction entered into between us on the Trade Date specified below (the "Transaction"). This Transaction Supplement is entered into under the 2003 Master Credit Derivatives Confirmation Agreement dated as of [_____] and, together with the 2003 Master Credit Derivatives Confirmation Agreement and the General Terms Confirmation attached thereto, constitutes a "Confirmation" as referred to in the Master Agreement between the parties, as amended and supplemented from time to time.

The terms of the Transaction to which this Transaction Supplement relates are as follows:

Reference Entity:

[Reference Obligation: [The obligation[s] identified as follows:

                                      Primary Obligor: [   ]
                                      Guarantor: [   ]
                                      Maturity: [   ]
                                      Coupon: [   ]
                                      CUSIP/ISIN: [   ]]

Trade Date:
Effective Date:
Scheduled Termination Date:
Floating Rate Payer: [   ] (the "Seller")
Fixed Rate Payer: [   ] (the "Buyer")
Fixed Rate Payer Payment Dates:
Fixed Rate: _____%
Floating Rate Payer Calculation Amount: [   ]
Restructuring Credit Event: [Applicable] [Not Applicable]

[Additional Terms: [   ]]

Please confirm your agreement to be bound by the terms of the foregoing by executing a copy of this Transaction Supplement and returning it to us [at the contact information listed above].

[_____]   [_____]

By: _____   By: _____
Name: Name:
Title: Title:

ISDA standard credit default swap

[A.40] This ISDA form is available to download from the ISDA website (http://www.isda.org).

EXHIBIT A to 2003 ISDA Credit Derivatives Definitions

[Headed paper of Party A]

Date:

To: [Name and Address or Facsimile Number of Party B]

From: [Party A]

Re: Credit Derivative Transaction

Dear   :

The purpose of this [letter] (this "Confirmation") is to confirm the terms and conditions of the Credit Derivative Transaction entered into between us on the Trade Date specified below (the "Transaction"). This Confirmation constitutes a "Confirmation" as referred to in the ISDA Master Agreement specified below.

The definitions and provisions contained in the 2003 ISDA Credit Derivatives Definitions (the "Credit Derivatives Definitions"), as published by the International Swaps and Derivatives Association, Inc., are incorporated into this Confirmation. In the event of any inconsistency between the Credit Derivatives Definitions and this Confirmation, this Confirmation will govern.

[This Confirmation supplements, forms a part of, and is subject to, the ISDA Master Agreement dated as of [date], as amended and supplemented from time to time (the "Agreement"), between you and us. All provisions contained in the Agreement govern this Confirmation except as expressly modified below.][1]

The terms of the Transaction to which this Confirmation relates are as follows:

1. General Terms:

   Trade Date: [   ]

   Effective Date: [   ]

   Scheduled Termination Date: [   ]

   Floating Rate Payer: [Party A][Party B] (the "Seller").

   Fixed Rate Payer: [Party A][Party B] (the "Buyer").

   Calculation Agent:[2]   [   ]

   Calculation Agent City:[3]   [   ]

   Business Day:[4]   [   ]

   Business Day Convention: [Following][Modified Following][Preceding] (which, subject to Sections 1.4 and 1.6 of the Credit Derivatives Definitions, shall apply to any date referred to in this Confirmation that falls on a day that is not a Business Day[5]).

   Reference Entity: [   ]

   [Reference Obligation(s):][6]   [   ]

   [The obligation[s] identified as follows:

   Primary Obligor: [   ]

   Guarantor: [   ]

   Maturity: [   ]

   Coupon: [   ]

   CUSIP/ISIN: [   ]

	All Guarantees:	[Applicable][Not Applicable]
	Reference Price:	[%][7]

2. **Fixed Payments:**

	[Fixed Rate Payer Calculation Amount:[8]	[ ]]
	[Fixed Rate Payer Period End Date:[9]	[ ]]
	Fixed Rate Payer Payment Date[s]:	[ ], [ ], [ ] and [ ]
	[Fixed Rate:	[ ]][10]
	[Fixed Rate Day Count Fraction:[11]	[ ]]
	[Fixed Amount:	[ ]]

3. **Floating Payment:**

	Floating Rate Payer Calculation Amount:[12]	[ ]
	Conditions to Settlement:	Credit Event Notice
		Notifying Party: Buyer [or Seller]
		[Notice of Physical Settlement][13]
		[Notice of Publicly Available Information Applicable][14]
		[Public Source(s):[ ]][15]
		[Specified Number:[ ]][16]
	Credit Events:	The following Credit Event[s] shall apply to this Transaction:
		[Bankruptcy]
		[[Failure to Pay]
		[Grace Period Extension Applicable][17]
		[Grace Period:][18]
		Payment Requirement: [ ]][19]
		[Obligation Default]
		[Obligation Acceleration]
		[Repudiation/Moratorium]
		[Restructuring]
		[[Restructuring Maturity Limitation and Fully Transferable Obligation: Applicable][20]]
		[[Modified Restructuring Maturity Limitation and Conditionally Transferable Obligation: [Applicable][21]]
		[[Multiple Holder Obligation:][22] [Applicable]]
		[Default Requirement: [ ]][23]

APPENDIX

Obligation(s):

Obligation Categories: (Select only one)		Obligation Characteristics: (Select all that apply)	
[ ]	Payment	[ ]	Not Subordinated
[ ]	Borrowed Money	[ ]	Specified Currency: [ ][25]
[ ]	Reference Obligations Only[24]	[ ]	Not Sovereign Lender
[ ]	Bond	[ ]	Not Domestic Currency [Domestic Currency means: [ ]][26]
[ ]	Loan	[ ]	Not Domestic Law
[ ]	Bond or Loan	[ ]	Listed
		[ ]	Not Domestic Issuance

[and:]

[Specify any other obligations of a Reference Entity.]

[Excluded Obligations:][27]   [   ]

4. **Settlement Terms:**

Settlement Method: [Cash Settlement] [Physical Settlement]

[[Terms Relating to Cash Settlement:][28]

[Valuation Date:][29]   [Single Valuation Date:
                        [   ] Business Days][30]

                        [Multiple Valuation Dates:
                        [   ] Business Days[31]; and
                        each [   ] Business Days thereafter[32]
                        Number of Valuation Dates: [   ]][33]

[Valuation Time:][34]

[Quotation Method: [Bid][Offer][Mid-market]][35]

[Quotation Amount: [   ][Representative Amount][36]

[Minimum Quotation Amount:][37]

[Dealer(s):   ][38]

[Settlement Currency:][39]

[Cash Settlement Date: [   ] Business Days][40]

[Cash Settlement Amount:][41]

[Quotations: [Include Accrued Interest][Exclude Accrued Interest]][42]

[Valuation Method:[43]   [Market] [Highest][44]

                         [Average Market] [Highest] [Average Highest][45]

                         [Blended Market] [Blended Highest][46]

                         [Average Blended Market] [Average Blended Highest]][47]

[Terms Relating to Physical Settlement:][48]

[Physical Settlement Period: [   ] Business Days][49]

[Deliverable Obligations: [Include Accrued Interest] [Exclude Accrued Interest][50]

Deliverable Obligation Categories: (Select only one)		Deliverable Obligation Characteristics: (Select all that apply)	
[ ]	Payment	[ ]	Not Subordinated
[ ]	Borrowed Money	[ ]	Specified Currency: [ ][52]
[ ]	Reference Obligations Only[51]	[ ]	Not Sovereign Lender
[ ]	Bond	[ ]	Not Domestic Currency [Domestic Currency means:[ ]][53]
[ ]	Loan	[ ]	Not Domestic Law
[ ]	Bond or Loan	[ ]	Listed
		[ ]	Not Contingent
		[ ]	Not Domestic Issuance
		[ ]	Assignable Loan
		[ ]	Consent Required Loan
		[ ]	Direct Loan Participation Qualifying Participation Seller: [ ][54]
		[ ]	Transferable
		[ ]	Maximum Maturity [ ][55]
		[ ]	Accelerated or Matured
		[ ]	Not Bearer

[and:]

[Specify any other obligations of a Reference Entity.]

[Excluded Deliverable Obligations:][56]

[   ]

[Partial Cash Settlement of Consent Required Loans Applicable][57]

[Partial Cash Settlement of Assignable Loans Applicable][58]

[Partial Cash Settlement of Participations Applicable][59]

Escrow: [Applicable][Not Applicable]

5. **Notice and Account Details:**
   Telephone and/or
   Facsimile Numbers and
   Contact Details for Notices: Buyer: [   ]   Seller: [   ]
   Account Details   Account Details of Buyer: [   ]
   Account Details of Seller: [   ]

[6. **Offices**[60]   Seller: [   ]   Buyer: [   ]]

Closing

Please confirm your agreement to be bound by the terms of the foregoing by executing a copy of this Confirmation and returning it to us [by facsimile].

Yours sincerely,
PARTY A]
By: _____
Name: Title:

Confirmed as of the date
first above written:
[PARTY B]
By: _____
Name: Title:

APPENDIX

THE FOOTNOTES TO THIS CONFIRMATION ARE PROVIDED FOR CLARIFICATION ONLY AND DO NOT CONSTITUTE ADVICE AS TO THE STRUCTURING OR DOCUMENTATION OF A CREDIT DERIVATIVE TRANSACTION.

ISDA has not undertaken to review all applicable laws and regulations of any jurisdiction in which the Credit Derivatives Definitions may be used. Therefore, parties are advised to consider the application of any relevant jurisdiction's regulatory, tax, accounting, exchange or other requirements that may exist in connection with the entering into and documenting of a privately negotiated credit derivative transaction.

[1] Include if applicable. If the parties have not yet executed, but intend to execute, an ISDA Master Agreement include, instead of this paragraph, the following: "This Confirmation evidences a complete and binding agreement between you and us as to the terms of the Transaction to which this Confirmation relates. In addition, you and we agree to use all reasonable efforts promptly to negotiate, execute and deliver an agreement in the form of an ISDA Master Agreement, with such modifications as you and we will in good faith agree. Upon the execution by you and us of such an agreement, this Confirmation will supplement, form part of, and be subject to that agreement. All provisions contained in or incorporated by reference in that agreement upon its execution will govern this Confirmation except as expressly modified below. Until we execute and deliver that agreement, this Confirmation, together with all other documents referring to an ISDA Master Agreement (each a "Confirmation") confirming transactions (each a "Transaction") entered into between us (notwithstanding anything to the contrary in a Confirmation), shall supplement, form a part of, and be subject to, an agreement in the form of the 1992 ISDA Master Agreement (Multicurrency – Cross Border) if any Confirmation dated prior to the date of this Confirmation refers to that ISDA Master Agreement and otherwise the 2002 ISDA Master Agreement as if we had executed an agreement in such form (but without any Schedule except for the election of [English Law][the laws of the State of New York] as the governing law and [specify currency] as the Termination Currency) on the Trade Date of the first such Transaction between us. In the event of any inconsistency between the provisions of that agreement and this Confirmation, this Confirmation will prevail for the purpose of this Transaction."

[2] If the Calculation Agent is a third party, the parties may wish to consider any documentation necessary to confirm its undertaking to act in that capacity. If a person is not specified, the Credit Derivatives Definitions provide that the Calculation Agent will be the Seller.

[3] If a city is not specified, the Credit Derivatives Definitions provide that the Calculation Agent City will be the city in which the office through which the Calculation Agent is acting for purposes of the Credit Derivative Transaction is located.

[4] The Credit Derivatives Definitions provide a fallback to days on which commercial banks and foreign exchange markets are generally open to settle payments in the jurisdiction of the currency of the Floating Rate Payer Calculation Amount.

[5] The Credit Derivatives Definitions provide a fallback to the Following Business Day Convention.

[6] Specify if required. A Reference Obligation must be specified for Credit Derivative Transactions to which Cash Settlement applies. If a Reference Obligation is specified for Credit Derivative Transactions to which Physical Settlement applies then, subject to the second paragraph of Section 2.20(b)(i) and Sections 2.32(a) and 2.33(a), such Reference Obligation is a Deliverable Obligation even though at the time of delivery it does not fall into the Obligation Category or lacks any or all Deliverable Obligation Characteristics.

[7] If a percentage is not so specified, the Credit Derivatives Definitions provide that the Reference Price will be one hundred per cent.

[8] If an amount is not specified, the Credit Derivatives Definitions provide that the Fixed Rate Payer Calculation Amount will be the Floating Rate Payer Calculation Amount.

[9] If a date is not specified, the Credit Derivatives Definitions provide that the Fixed Rate Payer Period End Date will be each date specified in the related Confirmation as a Fixed Rate Payer Payment Date.

[10] The Credit Derivatives Definitions provide that the Fixed Rate means a rate, expressed as a decimal, equal to the per annum rate specified here.

[11] If a Fixed Rate Day Count Fraction is not specified, the Credit Derivatives Definitions provide a fallback to Actual/360 as the Fixed Rate Day Count Fraction.

[12] Specify an amount or, for amortizing Transactions, refer to amounts listed in an amortization schedule.

[13] Notice of Physical Settlement is a required Condition to Settlement in respect of Credit Derivative Transactions to which Physical Settlement is applicable. It is not applicable in relation to Credit Derivative Transactions to which Cash Settlement is applicable.

[14] If Notice of Publicly Available Information is intended to be a Condition to Settlement, the parties should include a reference to it here.

[15] If Notice of Publicly Available Information has been selected by the parties and a Public Source is not specified, the Credit Derivatives Definitions provide that the Public Sources will be Bloomberg Service, Dow Jones Telerate Service, Reuter Monitor Money Rates Services, Dow Jones News Wire, Wall Street Journal, New York Times, Nihon Keizai Shinbun, Asahi Shinbun, Yomiuri Shinbun, Financial Times, La Tribune, Les Echos and The Australian Financial Review (and successor publications), the main source(s) of business news in the jurisdiction in which the Reference Entity is organized and any other internationally recognized published or electronically displayed news sources.

[16] If Notice of Publicly Available Information has been selected by the parties and a number of Public Sources is not specified, the Credit Derivatives Definitions provide that the Specified Number will be two.

[17] Specify whether the parties intend Grace Period Extension to apply. If Grace Period Extension is not specified here as being applicable, Grace Period Extension will not apply to the Credit Derivative Transaction.

[18] If Grace Period Extension is applicable, the parties may also wish to specify the number of days in the Grace Period. Parties should specify whether the Grace Period is to be measured in calendar days. If a number of days is not so specified, Grace Period will be the lesser of the applicable grace period with respect to the relevant Obligation and thirty calendar days. If at the later of the Trade Date and the date as of which an Obligation is issued or incurred, no grace period with respect to payments or a grace period with respect to payments of less than three Grace Period Business Days is applicable under the terms of that Obligation, a Grace Period of three Grace Period Business Days shall be deemed to apply to that Obligation. Unless Grace Period Extension is specified as applicable to a Credit Derivative Transaction, this deemed Grace Period will expire no later than the Scheduled Termination Date.

[19] Payment Requirement is relevant to the Failure to Pay Credit Event. If a Payment Requirement is not specified, the Credit Derivatives

Definitions provide that the Payment Requirement will be USD 1,000,000 or its equivalent in the relevant Obligation Currency as of the occurrence of the relevant Failure to Pay.

[20] Specify whether the parties intend Restructuring Maturity Limitation and Fully Transferable Obligation, as set forth in Section 2.32 of the Credit Derivatives Definitions, to apply. If Restructuring Maturity Limitation and Fully Transferable Obligation are specified as applicable, the Restructuring Maturity Limitation Date is the date that is the earlier of 30 months following the Restructuring Date and the latest final maturity date of any Restructured Bond or Loan (but in no event a date earlier than the Scheduled Termination Date or a date later than 30 months following the Scheduled Termination Date) and only Fully Transferable Obligations may constitute Deliverable Obligations. The parties cannot specify that Restructuring Maturity Limitation and Fully Transferable Obligation and Modified Restructuring Maturity Limitation and Conditionally Transferable Obligation both apply. If Restructuring Maturity Limitation is not specified as being applicable, Restructuring Maturity Limitation will not apply to the Credit Derivative Transaction.

[21] Specify whether the parties intend Modified Restructuring Maturity Limitation and Conditionally Transferable Obligation, as set forth in Section 2.33 of the Credit Derivatives Definitions, to apply. If Modified Restructuring Maturity Limitation and Conditionally Transferable Obligation are specified as applicable, the Modified Restructuring Maturity Limitation Date is the later of (x) 60 months for a Restructured Bond or Loan (and 30 months for other Deliverable Obligations) following the Restructuring Date and (y) the Scheduled Termination Date, and only Conditionally Transferable Obligations may constitute Deliverable Obligations. The parties cannot specify that Restructuring Maturity Limitation and Fully Transferable Obligation and Modified Restructuring Maturity Limitation and Conditionally Transferable Obligation both apply. If Modified Restructuring Maturity Limitation is not specified as being applicable, Modified Restructuring Maturity Limitation will not apply to the Credit Derivative Transaction.

[22] Unless Not Applicable is specified, the Credit Derivatives Definitions provide that Restructurings are limited to Multiple Holder Obligations.

[23] Default Requirement is relevant to the Obligation Acceleration, Obligation Default, Repudiation/Moratorium and Restructuring Credit Events. If a Default Requirement is not specified, the Credit Derivatives Definitions provide that the Default Requirement will be USD 10,000,000 or its equivalent in the relevant Obligation Currency as of the occurrence of the relevant Credit Event.

[24] If Reference Obligations Only is specified as the Obligation Category, no Obligation Characteristics should be specified.

[25] Specify Currency. The Credit Derivatives Definitions provide that, if no currency is so specified, Specified Currency means the lawful currencies of any of Canada, Japan, Switzerland, the United Kingdom and the United States of America and the euro (and any successor currency to any such currency). The Credit Derivatives Definitions provide that these currencies may be referred to collectively in a Confirmation as the "Standard Specified Currencies".

[26] If no currency is specified, the Credit Derivatives Definitions provide that Domestic Currency will be the lawful currency and any successor currency of (a) the relevant Reference Entity, if the Reference Entity is a Sovereign, or (b) the jurisdiction in which the relevant Reference Entity is organized, if the Reference Entity is not a Sovereign. In no event shall Domestic Currency include any successor currency if such successor currency is the lawful currency of any of Canada, Japan, Switzerland, the United Kingdom or the United States of America or the euro (or any successor currency to any such currency).

[27] Unless specified here as an Excluded Obligation, the Reference Obligation will be an Obligation.

[28] Include if Cash Settlement applies.

[29] Include if the Cash Settlement Amount is not a fixed amount. The Credit Derivatives Definitions provide that if neither Single Valuation Date nor Multiple Valuation Dates is specified here, Single Valuation Date will apply.

[30] If the number of Business Days is not specified, the Credit Derivatives Definitions provide that this will be five Business Days.

[31] If the number of Business Days is not specified, the Credit Derivatives Definitions provide that this will be five Business Days.

[32] If the number of Business Days is not specified, the Credit Derivatives Definitions provide that this will be five Business Days.

[33] If the number of Valuation Dates is not specified, the Credit Derivatives Definitions provide that there will be five Valuation Dates.

[34] If no time is specified, the Credit Derivatives Definitions provide that the Valuation Time will be 11:00 a.m. in the principal trading market for the Reference Obligation.

[35] If no Quotation Method is specified, the Credit Derivatives Definitions provide that Bid shall apply.

[36] Specify either an amount in a currency or Representative Amount. If no Quotation Amount is specified, the Credit Derivatives Definitions provide that the Quotation Amount will be the Floating Rate Payer Calculation Amount.

[37] If no amount is specified, the Credit Derivatives Definitions provide that the Minimum Quotation Amount will be the lower of (i) USD 1,000,000 (or its equivalent in the relevant Obligation Currency) and (ii) the Quotation Amount.

[38] Specify the Dealers. If no Dealers are specified here, the Calculation Agent will select the Dealers in consultation with the parties.

[39] If no currency is specified, the Credit Derivatives Definitions provide that the Settlement Currency will be the currency of denomination of the Floating Rate Payer Calculation Amount.

[40] If a number of Business Days is not specified, the Credit Derivatives Definitions specify three Business Days.

[41] If no amount is so specified, the Credit Derivatives Definitions provide that the Cash Settlement Amount will be the greater of (a) (i) Floating Rate Payer Calculation Amount multiplied by (ii) the Reference Price minus the Final Price and (b) zero.

[42] If neither Include Accrued Interest nor Exclude Accrued Interest is specified with respect to Quotations, the Credit Derivatives Definitions provide that the Calculation Agent will determine, after consultation with the parties, based on then current market practice in the market of the Reference Obligation, whether such Quotations shall include or exclude accrued but unpaid interest.

[43] Include if the Cash Settlement Amount is not a fixed amount.

[44] One of these Valuation Methods may be specified for a Credit Derivative Transaction with only one Reference Obligation and only one Valuation Date. If no Valuation Method is specified in such circumstances, the Credit Derivatives Definitions provide that the Valuation Method shall be Highest.

[45] One of these three Valuation Methods may be specified for a Credit Derivative Transaction with only one Reference Obligation and more than one Valuation Date. If no Valuation Method is specified in such circumstances, the Credit Derivatives Definitions provide

that Average Highest shall apply.

[46] One of these Valuation Methods may be specified for a Credit Derivative Transaction with more than one Reference Obligation and only one Valuation Date. If no Valuation Method is specified in such circumstances, the Credit Derivatives Definitions provide that Blended Highest shall apply.

[47] One of these Valuation Methods may be specified for a Credit Derivative Transaction with more than one Reference Obligation and more than one Valuation Date. If no Valuation Method is specified in such circumstances, the Credit Derivatives Definitions provide that Average Blended Highest shall apply.

[48] Include if Physical Settlement applies. Subject to contrary agreement between the parties, the Partial Cash Settlement Terms contained in the Credit Derivatives Definitions apply automatically in the context of events rendering it impossible or illegal for Buyer to Deliver or for Seller to accept Delivery of the Deliverable Obligations on or prior to the Latest Permissible Physical Settlement Date. This should be distinguished from the Partial Cash Settlement of Consent Required Loans, Partial Cash Settlement of Assignable Loans and Partial Cash Settlement of Participations provisions, which are elective. If applicable for any reason, the Partial Cash Settlement Terms will apply in the form prescribed in the Credit Derivatives Definitions unless contrary provision is made by the parties in the Confirmation.

[49] If a number of Business Days is not specified, the Credit Derivatives Definitions provide that the Physical Settlement Period will be, with respect to a Deliverable Obligation, the maximum number of Business Days for settlement in accordance with then current market practice of such Deliverable Obligation, as determined by the Calculation Agent after consultation with the parties.

[50] Specify whether, in respect of Deliverable Obligations with an outstanding principal balance, the Deliverable Obligation is to include or exclude accrued but unpaid interest. If neither "Include Accrued Interest" nor "Exclude Accrued Interest" is specified here, the Credit Derivatives Definitions provide that the Deliverable Obligations shall exclude accrued but unpaid interest.

[51] If Reference Obligations Only is specified as the Deliverable Obligation Category, no Deliverable Obligation Characteristics should be specified.

[52] Specify Currency. The Credit Derivatives Definitions provide that, if no currency is so specified, Specified Currency means the lawful currencies of any of Canada, Japan, Switzerland, the United Kingdom and the United States of America and the euro (and any successor currency to any such currency). The Credit Derivatives Definitions provide that these currencies may be referred to collectively in a Confirmation as the "Standard Specified Currencies".

[53] If no currency is specified, the Credit Derivatives Definitions provide that Domestic Currency will be the lawful currency and any successor currency of (a) the relevant Reference Entity, if the Reference Entity is a Sovereign, or (b) the jurisdiction in which the relevant Reference Entity is organized, if the Reference Entity is not a Sovereign. In no event shall Domestic Currency include any successor currency if such successor currency is the lawful currency of any of Canada, Japan, Switzerland, the United Kingdom or the United States of America or the euro (or any successor currency to any such currency).

[54] If Direct Loan Participation is specified as a Deliverable Obligation Characteristic, specify any requirements for the Qualifying Participation Seller here. If requirements are not so specified, the Credit Derivatives Definitions provide that there shall be no Qualifying Participation Seller, with the result that only a participation pursuant to a participation agreement between the Buyer and Seller will constitute a Direct Loan Participation.

[55] Specify maximum period to maturity from the Physical Settlement Date.

[56] Unless specified as an Excluded Deliverable Obligation, the Reference Obligation will, subject to the second paragraph of Section 2.20(b)(i) and Sections 2.32(a) and 2.33(a), be a Deliverable Obligation even though at the time of delivery it does not fall into the Obligation Category or lacks any or all Deliverable Obligation Characteristics.

[57] Include if the parties intend that the Partial Cash Settlement Terms are to be applicable in relation to Consent Required Loans.

[58] Include if the parties intend that the Partial Cash Settlement Terms are to be applicable in relation to Assignable Loans.

[59] Include if the parties intend that the Partial Cash Settlement Terms are to be applicable in relation to Direct Loan Participations.

[60] If necessary, specify the Offices through which the parties are acting for the purposes of the Credit Derivative Transaction.

Monoline insurers: additional provisions

[A.60] This ISDA form is available to download from the ISDA website (http://www.isda.org).

ADDITIONAL PROVISIONS FOR PHYSICALLY SETTLED DEFAULT SWAPS – MONOLINE INSURER AS REFERENCE ENTITY[1]
(published on May 9, 2003)

Additional Provisions

(a) Qualifying Policy. "Qualifying Policy" means a financial guaranty insurance policy or similar financial guarantee pursuant to which a Reference Entity irrevocably guarantees or insures all Instrument Payments (as defined below) of an instrument that constitutes Borrowed Money (modified as set forth below) (the "Insured Instrument") for which another party (including a special purpose entity or trust) is the obligor (the "Insured Obligor"). Qualifying Policies shall exclude any arrangement (i) structured as a surety bond, letter of credit or quivalent legal arrangement or (ii) pursuant to the express contractual terms of which the payment obligations of the Reference Entity can be discharged or reduced as a result of the occurrence or non-occurrence of an event or circumstance (other than the payment of Instrument Payments). The benefit of a Qualifying Policy must be capable of being Delivered together with the Delivery of the Insured Instrument.

"Instrument Payments" means (A) in the case of any Insured Instrument that is in the form of a pass-through certificate or similar funded beneficial interest, (x) the specified periodic distributions in respect of interest or other return on the Certificate Balance on or prior to the ultimate distribution of the Certificate Balance and (y) the ultimate distribution of the Certificate Balance on or prior to a specified date and (B) in the case of any other Insured Instrument, the scheduled payments of principal and interest, in the case of both (A) and (B) (1) determined without regard to limited recourse or reduction provisions of the type described in paragraph (d) below and (2) excluding sums in respect of default interest, indemnities, tax gross-ups, make-whole amounts, early redemption premiums and other similar amounts (whether or not guaranteed or insured by the Qualifying Policy).

"Certificate Balance" means, in the case of an Insured Instrument that is in the form of a pass-through certificate or similar funded beneficial interest, the unit principal balance, certificate balance or similar measure of unreimbursed principal investment.

(b) Obligation and Deliverable Obligation. Sections 2.14(a) and 2.15(a) are hereby amended by adding "or Qualifying Policy" after "or as provider of a Qualifying Affiliate Guarantee".

(c) Interpretation of Provisions. In the event that an Obligation or a Deliverable Obligation is a Qualifying Policy, the terms of Section 2.21(d) will apply, with references to the Qualifying Guarantee, the Underlying Obligation and the Underlying Obligor deemed to include the Qualifying Policy, the Insured Instrument and the Insured Obligor, respectively, except that:

    (i) the Obligation Category Borrowed Money and the Obligation Category and Deliverable Obligation Category Bond shall be deemed to include distributions payable under an Insured Instrument in the form of a pass through certificate or similar funded beneficial interest, the Deliverable Obligation Category Bond shall be deemed to include such an Insured Instrument, and the terms "obligation" and "obligor" as used in the 2003 ISDA Credit Derivatives Definitions in respect of such an Insured Instrument shall be construed accordingly;

(ii) references in the definitions of Assignable Loan and Consent Required Loan to the guarantor and guaranteeing shall be deemed to include the insurer and insuring, respectively;

(iii) neither the Qualifying Policy nor the Insured Instrument must satisfy on the relevant date the Deliverable Obligation Characteristic of Accelerated or Matured, whether or not that characteristic is otherwise specified as applicable in this Confirmation;

(iv) if the Assignable Loan, Consent Required Loan, Direct Loan Participation or Transferable Deliverable Obligation Characteristics are specified in this Confirmation and if the benefit of the Qualifying Policy is not transferred as part of any transfer of the Insured Instrument, the Qualifying Policy must be transferable at least to the same extent as the Insured Instrument; and

(v) with respect to an Insured Instrument in the form of a pass-through certificate or similar funded beneficial interest, the term "outstanding principal balance" shall mean the outstanding Certificate Balance and "maturity", as such term is used in the Maximum Maturity Deliverable Obligation Characteristic, shall mean the specified date by which the Qualifying Policy guarantees or insures, as applicable, that the ultimate distribution of the Certificate Balance will occur.

(d) Not Contingent. An Insured Instrument will not be regarded as failing to satisfy the Not Contingent Deliverable Obligation Characteristic solely because such Insured Instrument is subject to provisions limiting recourse in respect of such Insured Instrument to the proceeds of specified assets (including proceeds subject to a priority of payments) or reducing the amount of any Instrument Payments owing under such Insured Instrument, provided that such provisions are not applicable to the Qualifying Policy by the terms thereof and the Qualifying Policy continues to guarantee or insure, as applicable, the Instrument Payments that would have been required to be made absent any such limitation or reduction. [2]

(e) Deliver. For purposes of Section 8.2, "Deliver" with respect to an obligation that is a Qualifying Policy means to Deliver both the Insured Instrument and the benefit of the Qualifying Policy (or a custodial receipt issued by an internationally recognized custodian representing an interest in such an Insured Instrument and the related Qualifying Policy), and "Delivery" and "Delivered" will be construed accordingly.

(f) Provisions for Determining a Successor. Section 2.2(c) is hereby amended by adding "or insurer" after "or guarantor".

(g) Substitute Reference Obligation. Section 2.30 is hereby amended by adding "or Qualifying Policy" after "or as provider of a Qualifying Affiliate Guarantee" in the definition of Substitute Reference Obligation and paragraph (b) thereof. For purposes of Section 2.30(a)(ii)(B) and Section 1.14(b)(ii), references to the Qualifying Guarantee and the Underlying Obligation shall be deemed to include the Qualifying Policy and the Insured Instrument, respectively.

(h) Other Provisions. For purposes of Sections 2.15(a)(ii), 4.1, 8.2, 9.1 and 9.2(a) as well as Section 3(a)(iv) of the Novation Agreement, references to the Underlying Obligation and the Underlying Obligor shall be deemed to include Insured Instruments and the Insured Obligor, respectively. Any transfer or similar fee reasonably incurred by Buyer in connection with the Delivery of a Qualifying Policy and payable to the Reference Entity shall be payable by Buyer and Seller equally on the Delivery Date or Latest Permissible Physical Settlement Date, as applicable.

---

[1] The "Additional Provisions for Physically Settled Default Swaps – Monoline Insurer as Reference Entity", published on May 9, 2003, ("Additional Provisions") may be added to a credit default swap confirmation as a new paragraph to the relevant confirmation (immediately following "Settlement Terms "). Alternatively, the Additional Provisions may be incorporated into a relevant confirmation (including in electronic form) by wording in the document indicating that the Additional Provisions, published on May 9, 2003, are so incorporated by reference thereto.

The Additional Provisions are intended for physically-settled credit default swap transactions where (i) the Reference Entity is a monoline insurance company issuing financial guaranty insurance policies or similar financial guarantees, (ii) Borrowed Money (or a subset), as modified by the Additional Provisions, is selected as the Obligation Category, (iii) Bond or Loan (or a subset), as modified by theAdditional Provisions, is selected as the Deliverable Obligation Category, and (iv) the Credit Events are Failure to Pay and Bankruptcy.

[2] By incorporating this provision in a document, no inference should be made as to the interpretation of the "Not Contingent" Deliverable Obligation Characteristic in the context of limited recourse or similar terms applicable to Deliverable Obligations other than Qualifying Policies.

60-day cap side letter

[A.50] This ISDA form is available to download from the ISDA website (http://www.isda.org).

[Address of counterparty]

[   ], 2003

LETTER AGREEMENT RELATING TO 60 BUSINESS DAY CAP ON SETTLEMENT

Dear Sir/Madam:

We refer to the Credit Derivative Transactions between [   ] ("Party A") and [   ] ("Party B") (the "Subject Transactions") that are entered into pursuant to the Master Credit Derivatives Confirmation Agreement dated as of [   ] between Party A and Party B (the "Master Confirmation"), incorporating the definitions and provisions contained in the 2003 ISDA Credit Derivatives Definitions as supplemented by the May 2003 Supplement to the 2003 ISDA Credit Derivatives Definitions, as published by the International Swaps and Derivatives Associations, Inc. (together, the "Credit Derivatives Definitions").

Any references (a) to this "Letter" shall include the appendices thereto and (b) to an "Appendix" shall be references to an appendix to this Letter. Any terms not defined in this Letter shall have the same meanings ascribed to them in the Master Confirmation or in the Credit Derivatives Definitions.

In consideration of the mutual agreements contained in this Letter and with the intention to be legally bound by it, Party A and Party B agree that:

(a) the language set forth in Appendix I hereto is incorporated into the Master Confirmation between Party A and Party B where specified as applicable in Appendix II;

(b) for each Subject Transaction, the other provisions set out in the Master Confirmation shall remain in full force and effect; and

(c) for each Subject Transaction, the amendment made in accordance with paragraph (a) above will take effect from the date of this Letter.

This Letter may be executed and delivered (including by facsimile transmission) in counterparts, each of which when executed shall constitute an original but all the counterparts shall together constitute one and the same instrument.

This Letter shall be governed and construed in accordance with the law specified or referred to in the Master Confirmation.

The parties hereby indicate their agreement to be bound by the terms of the foregoing by signing in the space provided below.

[counterparty]   [counterparty]

By: _____   By: _____

Name: _____   Name: _____

Title: _____   Title: _____

Date: _____   Date: _____

Appendix I

Notwithstanding Section 1.7 or any provisions of Sections 9.9 or 9.10 to the contrary, but without prejudice to Section 9.3 and (where applicable) Sections 9.4, 9.5 and 9.6, if the Termination Date has not occurred on or prior to the date that is 60 Business Days following the Physical Settlement Date, such 60th Business Day shall be deemed to be the Termination Date with respect to this Transaction except in relation to any portion of the Transaction (an "Affected Portion") in respect of which:

(1) a valid notice of Buy-in Price has been delivered that is effective fewer than three Business Days prior to such 60th Business Day, in which case the Termination Date for that Affected Portion shall be the third Business Day following the date on which such notice is effective; or

(2) Buyer has purchased but not Delivered Deliverable Obligations validly specified by Seller pursuant to Section 9.10(b), in which case the Termination Date for that Affected Portion shall be the tenth Business Day following the date on which Seller validly specified such Deliverable Obligations to Buyer.

Appendix II

The language set forth in Appendix I is incorporated into the Master Confirmation between Party A and Party B where specified as applicable in relation to each Transaction Supplement entered into in connection with the Master Confirmation with the Transaction Type set forth herein:

Transaction Type	60 Business Day cap on Settlement
[Asia]	[Applicable] [Not Applicable]
[Australia]	[Applicable] [Not Applicable]
[Japan]	[Applicable] [Not Applicable]
[New Zealand]	[Applicable] [Not Applicable]
[Singapore]	[Applicable] [Not Applicable]
[European]	[Applicable] [Not Applicable]
[North American]	[Applicable] [Not Applicable]

Index

A

Aeroporti di Roma ....[8.30]
AFMA *see* Australian Financial Markets Association (AFMA)
Alumina Limited ....[2.140]
Anglian Water Services (UK) ....[8.20]
ANZ (Bank) ....[2.70]
APRA *see* Australian Prudential Regulation Authority (APRA)
Artemus ....[4.10]
Asahi Shinbun ....[3.360]
Australian Financial Markets Association (AFMA) ....[2.140]
Australian Financial Review ....[3.360]
Australian Prudential Regulation Authority (APRA) ....[2.290], [3.340], [5.90]
Australian Stock Exchange ....[8.80]

B

Bank for International Settlements (BIS) ....[2.270], [2.380], [3.590]
capital adequacy regulations *see* capital adequacy regulations
Banking Act 1959 (Cth) ....[2.330]
bankruptcy
  credit event, as ....[2.50], [3.340]
  definition of
    1999 Definitions ....[2.160]
    ISDA Master Agreement 1992 ...[2.160]
Basel Accord (Basel I) ....[2.380], [3.270], [3.580], [3.670]
Basel Committee ....[2.390]
Basel I *see* Basel Accord
Basel II (proposed) ....[2.380], [3.570], [3.600], [3.610], [3.670], [4.620]
BBA *see* British Bankers' Association (BBA)
Bernstein ....[4.150]
BioPharma Royalty Trust ....[7.10], [7.80]
BIS *see* Bank for International Settlements (BIS)
Bond Market Association (US) ....[2.390], [5.110]
British Bankers' Association (BBA) ....[2.380]
Brookland ....[4.150]

C

CAD3 *see* capital adequacy directive, third .... (CAD3)
Caiola case ....[3.450]
capital adequacy directive, third (CAD3) ....[2.380]
capital adequacy regulations
  Basel Accord
    (Basel I) ....[2.380], [3.270] [3.580], [3.670]
  Basel Committee ....[2.390]
  Basel II (proposed) .. [2.380], [3.570], [3.600], [3.610], [3.670], [4.620]
  CAD3 (capital adequacy directive, third) [2.380]
  CP3 (Consultation Document, The New Basel Capital Accord).............[2.380], [2.390]
  credit derivatives, and ....[2.390]
  internal ratings based approach (IRB) ..[2.380]
  QIS3 (Quantitative Impact Study) ....[2.380]
  synthetic securitisation, and   [3.570], [3.580]
cash bond market
  credit default swap market, distinguished from ....[4.30]
cash securitisation ....[1.20]
  copyright *see* copyright securitisation
  entire business enterprise *see* whole of business securitisation (WOBS)
  hedge fund *see* hedge fund securitisation
  life insurance *see* life insurance securitisation
  mechanics of ....[8.50]
  patent *see* patent securitisation
  trademark *see* trademark securitisation
  true sale of securitised assets ....[8.60]
  types of ....[1.20]

cash-flow securitisation *see* traditional securitisation
CAT bonds ....[5.20], [5.30]
  "insurable interest" ....[5.100]
  "insurance business" ....[5.90], [5.100]
    whether ....[5.110]
  insurance contract ....[5.90], [5.100]
    whether ....[5.110]
  insurance, in relation to ....[5.90]-[5.110]
  market, development of ....[5.20]
  principal-protected CAT bond ....[5.80]
  recharacterisation ....[5.90]
  transactions *see* CAT bonds transaction structure
CAT bonds transaction structure
  catastrophe, occurrence of ....[5.60]
  generic structure ....[5.40]
  payment triggers ....[5.70]
    "book of business" trigger ....[5.70]
    indemnity trigger ....[5.70]
    index trigger ....[5.70]
    modelled loss trigger ....[5.70]
    non-indemnity trigger ....[5.70]
    parametric trigger ....[5.70]
  principal-protected CAT bond ....[5.80]
  risk transfer agreement ....[5.50]
  tranching ....[5.80]
    principal-protected tranche ....[5.80]
catastrophe-linked securities *see* CAT bonds
catastrophic risk securitisation ....[1.30]
  advantages ....[5.30]
  CAT bonds *see* CAT bonds
  classes of risk ....[5.20]
  Hurricane Andrew (US) (1992) ....[5.20], [5.30]
  Kobe earthquake (Japan) (1995) ....[5.20]
  market, development of ....[5.20]
  Northbridge Earthquake (US) (1994) .....[5.20], [5.30]
  Tokyo Disneyland ....[1.30], [5.20]
  types of risk ....[5.10]
  Typhoon Mireille (Japan) (1991) ....[5.20]
  Vivendi ....[5.20]
  winter storms (Europe) (1990) ....[5.20]
CDO *see* collateralised debt obligations (CDO)
CDS *see* credit default swaps (CDS)
CFO *see* collateralised fund of hedge fund obligations (CFO)
Chalet   ....[3.100]
Cibeles I ....[4.150]
Circuit Layouts Act 1989 (Cth) ....[7.60]
Clearing House Electronic Subregister system (CHESS) ....[8.80]
CLO *see* collateralised loan obligations (CLO)
collateralised debt obligations (CDO) [1.40], [2.50]
  Asia-Pacific market ....[3.20]
  Australian market ....[3.30]
  CDO Evaluator ....[4.290], [4.300]
  CFO structure, distinguished from ....[6.30]
  global market ....[3.20]
  managed synthetic CDO *see* managed synthetic securitisation
collateralised fund of hedge fund obligations (CFO) ....[1.40]
  benefits ....[6.20]
  Diversified Strategies CFO ....[6.10], [6.120]
  funds of hedge funds *see* funds of hedge funds
  Investcorp Management Services ....[6.10]
  JP Morgan Chase ....[6.10]
  Man Glenwood Alternative Strategies CFO ....[6.120]
  structure ....[6.30]
    CDO structure, distinguished from ....[6.30]
    principal-protected tranche ....[6.40]
    total return swaps ....[6.50]
    tranching ....[6.40]
  underlying asset *see* funds of hedge funds

collateralised loan obligations (CLO) ....[3.710]
confidentiality
    credit derivatives ....[2.360]
    synthetic securitisation **[3.420]**, **[3.460]**-**[3.490]**
        blind pools ....[3.470]
        disclosure, levels of ....[3.490]
        portfolio disclosure ....[3.460]
        reference entities, disclosure of ....[3.480]
Conseco Inc ....[2.130], [2.180]
control issues (managed synthetic
    securitisation) *see also* manager
    (managed synthetic securitisation)
    categories of securities, definitions of ...[4.310]
        credit-impaired security ....[4.310]
        credit-improved security ....[4.310]
    eligibility criteria ....[4.280]
    introduction ....[4.270]
    liquidity facility ....[4.330]
    portfolio tests ....[4.290]
        coverage tests ....[4.290]
        profile tests ....[4.290]
        quality tests ....[4.290]
        verification ....[4.290]
    proprietary models ....[4.300]
        CDO Evaluator ....[4.300]
        Vector model ....[4.300]
    regulatory issues *see* regulatory issues
    (managed synthetic securitisation)
    surveillance ....[4.320]
Copyright Act 1968 (Cth) ....[8.90]
    s 10 ....[8.90]
copyright securitisation ....[1.30], [7.10]
    Bowie Bonds ....[7.10], [7.70]
Corporations Act 2001 (Cth)
    Chapter 5C ....[4.610]
    Chapter 2K ....[7.60]
    s 262(1)(a) ....[8.90], [8.100]
    s 262(1)(e) ....[8.90]
    s 262(1)(f) ....[8.100]
    s 262(1)(g)(ii) ....[8.80]
CP3 (Consultation Document, The New
    Basel Capital Accord) ....[2.380], [2.390]
Craegmoor (care homes) ....[8.20]
credit default swap market
    cash bond market, distinguished from ...[4.30]
    protection buyers, risks for ....[4.40]
credit default swap (CDS) .....[1.40], [2.10], [2.30]
    credit events ....[2.40], [2.50]
        bankruptcy ....[2.50], [3.340]
        credit event notice ....[2.70], [3.360]
        definition ....[2.160], [3.330], [3.350]
        failure to pay ....[2.50], [3.340], [3.360]
        moratorium ....[2.50]
        notice of PAI ....[2.70], [3.360]
        obligation acceleration ....[2.50]
        obligation default ....[2.50]
        repudiation ....[2.50]
        restructuring ....[2.50], [2.130], [3.340]
    documentation ....[4.450], [4.460]
        ISDA documentation ....[4.450], [4.480]
    introduction ....[2.40]
    obligations ....[2.40], [2.60]
        deliverable obligations ....[2.60]
        obligations, qualification as ....[2.60]
        reference obligations ....[2.60]
    settlement *see* settlement (credit
        default swap)
    simulation of credit transfer ....[3.190]
    unwinding ....[2.260]
    what happens in ....[3.190]
credit derivatives ....[1.40]
    capital adequacy regulations *see* capital
        adequacy regulations
    credit default swaps *see* credit
        default swap (CDS)
    Credit Derivatives Definitions
        1999 Definitions *see* Credit Derivatives
            Definitions 1999
        2003 Definitions *see* Credit Derivatives
            Definitions 2003
    credit linked notes *see* credit linked notes
    credit risk management, alternative for ...[2.420]
    credit spread transactions ....[1.40], [2.30]

documentation *see* documentation
    (credit derivatives)
drivers for ....[2.90]
    arbitrage ....[2.90]
    credit risk managment ....[2.90]
    portfolio diversification ....[2.90]
    "short" a bond, opportunity to ....[2.90]
legal framework *see* legal framework
    (credit derivatives)
multi-name swaps ....[2.30]
recharacterisation *see*
    recharacterisation (credit derivatives)
risks in ....[2.100]
    basis risk ....[2.110]
    counterparty risk ....[2.110]
    documentation risk ....[2.110]
    liquidity risk ....[2.110]
    market risk ....[2.110]
    regulatory risk ....[2.110]
    ultra vires ....[2.100]
total return swaps ....[1.40], [2.30]
types of ....[1.40], [2.30]
what are ....[2.20]
Credit Derivatives
    Definitions 1999 ....[1.40], [2.10], [2.120]-
        [2.160], [2.170], [2.190], [2.200],
        [2.210], [3.310], [4.480]
    Convertible Supplement ....[2.120], [2.150]
    Railtrack PLC ....[2.150]
    Restructuring Supplement
        (May 2001) ....[2.120], [2.130]
        Conseco Inc ....[2.130], [2.180]
        Mod R ....[2.130], [2.180], [4.490]
        Old R ....[2.130], [2.180], [4.490]
    Successor Supplement ....[2.120], [2.140]
        bankruptcy, definition of ....[2.160]
        National Power PLC ....[2.140]
    Credit Derivatives Definitions 2003 ..[1.40], [2.10],
        [2.70], [2.110], [2.160], [2.170]-[2.210],
        [2.220], [2.260], [2.370], [3.190], [3.310],
        [3.350], [3.410], [3.640], [3.700], [4.480]
    bonds or loans not delivered ....[2.190]
    effective date ....[2.210]
    guarantees, clarification of ....[2.200]
        qualifying affiliate guarantee ....[2.200]
        qualifying guarantee ....[2.200]
    Mod Mod R ....[2.180], [4.490]
    novation provisions ....[2.210], [2.260]
    physical settlement ....[2.210]
    scheduled termination date ....[2.210]
    user's guide ....[2.400]
    credit events ....[2.40], [2.50]
        bankruptcy ....[2.50], [3.340]
        credit event notice ....[2.70], [3.360]
        definition ....[2.160], [3.330], [3.350]
        failure to pay ....[2.50], [3.340], [3.360]
        moratorium ....[2.50]
        notice of PAI ....[2.70], [3.360]
        obligation acceleration ....[2.50]
        obligation default ....[2.50]
        repudiation ....[2.50]
        restructuring ....[2.50], [2.130], [3.340]
        selection of ....[3.330], [3.340]
        tailoring of ....[3.360]
    credit linked notes ....[2.30]
        documentation ....[3.410]
        equity tranche ....[3.200]
        tranching ....[3.200]
Credit Support
    Annexes (CSA) ....[2.100], [2.230], [4.510]
CSA *see* Credit Support Annexes (CSA)

D
Daiwa ....[2.70]
Deutsche Bank ....[2.70]
documentation (credit derivatives)
    credit default swaps, unwinding ....[2.260]
    Credit Derivatives Definitions
        1999 Definitions *see* Credit Derivatives
            Definitions 1999
        2003 Definitions *see* Credit Derivatives
            Definitions 2003
    Long Form Credit Swap Confirmation ...[2.120]

INDEX

Master Agreement *see* Master Agreement (ISDA)
Master Confirmation *see* Master
   Confirmation (ISDA)
  monoline insurers, additional provisions ..**[2.240]**
  physical settlement, 60-day cap on ......**[2.250]**
documentation (managed synthetic securitisation)
  credit default swap ....**[4.450]**, **[4.460]**
    format of documentation ...**[4.450]**, **[4.480]**
  credit events, selection of ....**[4.490]**
  credit linked note ......**[4.450]**, **[4.460]**, **[4.520]**
  credit risk ....**[4.510]**
  dealers, involvement of ....**[4.450]**, **[4.470]**
    gatekeeper approach ....**[4.470]**
    pre-agreed list ....**[4.470]**
    Robeco VII ....**[4.470]**
  principal reductions ....**[4.530]**
  redemption of notes ....**[4.560]**
  security package ....**[4.450]**, **[4.550]**
  settlement issues ....**[4.500]**
  waterfall ....**[4.540]**
documentation (synthetic securitisation)
  credit default swaps ....**[3.330]**
    credit events, definition of ..**[2.160]**, **[3.330]**,
                                                     '**[3.350]**
    credit events, selection of ..**[3.330]**, **[3.340]**
    credit events, tailoring of ....**[3.360]**
    settlement *see* settlement (credit
      default swaps)
  credit linked notes ....**[3.410]**
  traditional securitisation, difference
    from ....**[3.320]**

E
Enron Corporation .... **[1.10]**, **[3.150]**,
                                                  [4.130], **[4.440]**
Enterprise Act 2002 (Cth) ....**[3.560]**
entire business enterprise securitisation
  see whole of business securitisation (WOBS)
ESAF Navigator ....**[4.150]**
Euro Multi-Credit ....**[4.150]**

F
*Financial Services and Markets Act
  2000* (UK) ....**[2.310]**
Financial Services Authority (UK) (FSA) .....**[2.320]**,
                                                              [5.110]
Formula One ....**[8.20]**
FSA *see* Financial Services Authority (UK) (FSA)
funds of hedge funds
  diversification benefits ....**[6.70]**
    illusory ....**[6.80]**
  expensiveness of ....**[6.70]**
  hedge funds, access to ....**[6.70]**
  liquidity benefits
    hedge fund investments, increased
      for ....**[6.70]**
    illusory ....**[6.80]**
  structure
    advantages ....**[6.70]**
    disadvantages ....**[6.80]**
  underlying hedge funds, monitoring of ..**[6.70]**

G
GIC *see* guaranteed investment contract (GIC)
Golden Bar ....**[3.100]**
Golden Jade ....**[4.10]**
guaranteed investment contract (GIC) ....**[3.300]**
  liquidity facility ....**[3.300]**

H
Harrows ....**[3.100]**
hedge fund securitisation ....**[1.40]**
  collateralised fund of hedge fund
    obligations *see* collateralised fund
    of hedge fund obligations (CFO)
  introduction ....**[6.10]**
hedge funds ....**[1.30]**, **[6.10]**
  collateralised fund of hedge fund
    obligation *see* collateralised fund of
    hedge fund obligations (CFO)
  definition ....**[6.100]**
  expensiveness ....**[6.100]**

funds of hedge funds *see* funds of
    hedge funds
  investing in, rationale for ....**[6.90]**
  investment strategies *see* investment
    strategies (hedge funds)
  leverage, use of ....**[6.100]**
  limited liquidity ....**[6.100]**
  manager *see* manager (hedge fund)
  market ....**[6.100]**
  securitisation *see* hedge fund
    securitisation structure ....**[6.100]**
Hurricane Andrew (US) (1992) ....**[5.20]**, **[5.30]**
Hy-Fi ....**[3.500]**

I
Imperial II ....**[4.130]**
insider trading ....**[2.370]**
insolvency ....**[1.30]**
insurance
  CAT bonds in relation to ....**[5.90]**-**[5.110]**
  "insurable interest" ....**[5.100]**
  "insurance business" ....**[5.90]**, **[5.100]**
  insurance contract ....**[5.90]**, **[5.100]**
  securitisation *see* insurance securitisation
Insurance Act 1973 (Cth) .**[2.330]**, **[5.100]**, **[5.110]**
  "insurance business" definition of ....**[5.100]**
Insurance Companies Act 1982 (Cth) ....**[2.310]**
Insurance Contracts Act 1984 (Cth) ....**[5.100]**
insurance securitisation ....**[1.40]**
  advantages ....**[5.30]**
  catastrophic risk *see* CAT bonds;
    catastrophic risk securitisation
  insurance and reinsurance ....**[5.10]**
  introduction ....**[5.10]**
  life insurance *see* life insurance securitisation
  peak peril ....**[5.10]**
  reinsurance ....**[5.10]**
  retrocessionaires ....**[5.10]**
intellectual property rights
  finite duration ....**[7.40]**
  infringement of ....**[7.40]**
  introduction ....**[7.10]**
  licence of ....**[7.50]**
  originator's claim, validity of ....**[7.40]**
  securitisation *see* intellectual property
    securitisation
intellectual property securitisation ....**[1.40]**
  Circuit Layouts Act 1989 (Cth) ....**[7.60]**
  copyright *see* copyright securitisation
  Corporations Act 2001 (Cth) ....**[7.60]**
    Chapter 2K ....**[7.60]**
  distinguishing features ....**[7.30]**
  finite duration of IP rights ....**[7.40]**
  infringement of IP rights ....**[7.40]**
  legal risks ....**[7.40]**
  legislative requirements ....**[7.60]**
  licence of IP rights ....**[7.50]**
  originator's claim to IP rights, validity of **[1740]**
  patents, securitisation of *see* patent
    securitisation
  Plant Breeders' Rights Act 1994 (Cth) ....**[7.60]**
  software, securitisation of *see*
    software securitisation
  trademark, securitisation of *see*
    trademark securitisation
  what is ....**[7.20]**
International Swaps and Derivatives
    Association (ISDA) ....**[2.10]**, **[2.390]**
  bonds or loans not delivered ....**[2.190]**
  credit default swaps, unwinding ....**[2.260]**
  Credit Derivatives Definitions 1999 *see*
    Credit Derivatives Definitions 1999
  Credit Derivatives Definitions 2003 *see*
    Credit Derivatives Definitions 2003
  Credit Support
    Annexes (CSAs) .....**[2.100]**, **[2.230]**, **[4.510]**
  Long Form Credit Swap Confirmation ..**[2.120]**
  market practice working group ....**[2.120]**
  Master Agreement *see* Master Agreement (ISDA)
  Master Confirmation *see* Master
    Confirmation (ISDA)
  Master Credit Derivatives
    Confirmation Agreement ....**[4.660]**

monoline insurers, additional provisions **[2.240]**
physical settlement, 60-day cap on ......**[2.250]**
user's guide to 2003 Definitions ....**[2.400]**
investment adviser (managed
   synthetic securitisation) ....**[4.70]**, **[4.120]**
investment strategies (hedge funds)
   convertible arbitrage strategies **[6.130]**, **[6.150]**
   directional strategies ....**[6.120]**, **[6.160]**
   equity market neutral strategies **[6.130]**, **[6.150]**
   event-driven strategies ....**[6.130]**, **[6.150]**
   fixed income arbitrage
      strategies ....**[6.130]**, **[6.150]**
   flexibility of ....**[6.100]**
   introduction ....**[6.120]**
   long/short equity strategies .....**[6.130]**, **[6.140]**
   merger arbitrage strategies ....**[6.150]**
   relative value strategies ....**[5.130]**, **[6.120]**
ISDA *see* International Swaps and
   Derivatives Association (ISDA)

J
Jazz I and II ....**[3.100]**, **[3.660]**, **[4.160]**

K
Kobe earthquake (Japan) (1995) ....**[5.20]**

L
Latitude ....**[3.100]**
legal framework (credit derivatives) .**[2.270]**-**[2.420]**
   confidentiality ....**[2.360]**
   insider trading ....**[2.370]**
   Master Agreement (ISDA),
      integration with ....**[2.370]**
   recharacterisation *see*
      recharacterisation (credit derivatives)
   structured transactions ....**[2.350]**
legal issues (synthetic securitisation)
   capita selecta ....**[3.420]**, **[3.520]**-**[3.560]**
   insolvency ....**[3.560]**
   profits ....**[3.550]**
   redemption events ....**[3.540]**
   set-off ....**[3.530]**
   confidentiality *see* confidentiality
   recharacterisation *see* recharacterisation
      (synthetic securitisation)
   retail investors, issuance
      to ....**[3.420]**, **[3.500]**-**[3.510]**
      disclosure ....**[3.500]**
      Hy-Fi ....**[3.500]**
      Legio Lease ....**[3.510]**
      Nexus Bonds ....**[3.500]**
      risks ....**[3.510]**
      Robeco VII ....**[3.500]**
Legio Lease ....**[3.510]**
Leonardo ....**[3.100]**
LIBOR *see* London Inter Bank
   Offered Rate (LIBOR)
Life Insurance Act 1995 (Cth) ....**[5.130]**
life insurance policy *see* life insurance securitisation
life insurance securitisation ....**[1.30]**, **[1.40]**
   life settlement ....**[1.40]**, **[5.130]**
      structure ....**[5.130]**
   open block ....**[1.40]**, **[5.120]**
      structure ....**[5.120]**
   viatical settlement ....**[1.40]**, **[5.130]**
      structure ....**[5.130]**
London City Airport ....**[8.30]**
London Inter Bank Offered
   Rate (LIBOR) ....**[2.30]**, **[3.300]**

M
Mahonia case ....**[3.210]**
Man Glenwood Alternative Strategies CFO .**[6.120]**
managed arbitrage synthetic CDO *see*
   managed synthetic securitisation
managed synthetic CDO *see* managed
   synthetic securitisation
managed synthetic
   securitisation ....**[1.40]**, **[3.650]**, **[4.50]**
   Artemus ....**[4.10]**
   asset hybrids ....**[4.260]**
   cash flow ....**[4.340]**, **[4.380]**
   collateral manager ....**[1.40]**, **[3.650]**, **[4.50]**

   collateral risk ....**[4.340]**, **[4.360]**
   control issues ·*see* control issues
      (managed synthetic securitisation)
   credit risk ....**[4.340]**, **[4.350]**
   currency risk ....**[4.340]**, **[4.430]**
   disclosure ....**[4.620]**
      increased ....**[4.660]**
   documentation *see* documentation
      (managed synthetic securitisation)
   effective date ....**[4.170]**, **[4.190]**
   excess spread ....**[4.390]**
   Golden Jade ....**[4.10]**
   interest divergence ....**[4.340]**, **[4.420]**
   legal issues ....**[4.570]**-**[4.600]**
   market
      depth of market ....**[4.440]**
      development of ....**[4.10]**, **[4.630]**
   offsetting credit default swaps ....**[4.230]**
      additional risks ....**[4.230]**
      special requirements ....**[4.230]**
   open positions ....**[4.240]**
   opportunities ....**[4.220]**-**[4.260]**
   order of events ....**[4.170]**-**[4.210]**
   portfolio risk ....**[4.340]**, **[4.370]**
   post-reinvestment ....**[4.170]**, **[4.210]**
   ramp-up ....**[4.170]**, **[4.180]**
      investors' risks ....**[4.180]**
      risks, reduction of ....**[4.180]**
   ratings quality ....**[4.640]**
   regulatory issues ....**[4.610]**-**[4.620]**
   reinvestment period ....**[4.170]**, **[4.200]**
   risks and enhancements ....**[4.340]**-**[4.440]**
   Ruby Finance ....**[4.10]**
   securities lending ....**[4.250]**
   structure *see* synthetic arbitrage structure
   styles of management ....**[4.220]**
   summary ....**[4.670]**
   trading gains ....**[4.400]**
   trading losses ....**[4.410]**
   tranche-only CDOs ....**[4.650]**
   transactions, evolution of ....**[4.60]**
manager (hedge fund)
   investors, as ....**[6.110]**
   location ....**[6.100]**
   management fees ....**[6.110]**
   performance fees ....**[6.110]**
manager (managed synthetic securitisation)
   see also control issues (managed synthetic
   securitisation); investment adviser (managed
   synthetic securitisation); portfolio administrator
   (managed synthetic securitisation)
   appointment of ....**[4.50]**, **[4.70]**
   choice of ....**[4.100]**
   confidentiality ....**[4.590]**
   legal and regulatory issues ......**[4.570]**-**[4.620]**
   managed investments
      regulations ....**[4.570]**, **[4.610]**
   management fee ....**[4.90]**
   noteholder, conflict with ....**[4.570]**, **[4.590]**
   rating agencies
      consent to removal ....**[4.100]**
      review by ....**[4.80]**
   regulatory requirements
      in relation to ....**[4.570]**, **[4.620]**
   removal
      with cause ....**[4.100]**
      rating agencies, consent of ....**[4.100]**
      without cause ....**[4.100]**
   responsibilities ....**[4.80]**
   SPV, relationship with ....**[4.570]**, **[4.580]**
   trading requirements ....**[4.220]**
Master Agreement (ISDA) ....**[2.100]**, **[2.160]**,
      [2.230], **[2.370]**, **[3.260]**, **[4.480]**, **[4.550]**
   bankruptcy, definition of ....**[2.160]**
   protocol ....**[2.370]**
Master Confirmation (ISDA) ..**[2.220]**, **[2.230]**, **[2.250]**
   General Terms Confirmation ....**[2.230]**
   Transaction Supplement ....**[2.230]**
Master Credit Derivatives
   Confirmation Agreement ....**[4.660]**
Mod Mod R (restructuring regime) **[2.180]**, **[4.490]**
Mod R (restructuring
   regime) ....**[2.130]**, **[2.180]**, **[4.490]**

INDEX

N
National Association of Insurance
  Commissioners (US) ....[5.110]
National Power PLC ....[2.140]
Nexus Bonds ....[3.500]
Nihon Keizai ....[3.360]
1999 Definitions *see* Credit Derivatives
  Definitions 1999
Northbridge Earthquake (US) (1994) **[5.20]**, **[5.30]**

O
Old R (restructuring regime) ....[2.130], [2.180]
over-the-counter (OTC) ....[3.190]

P
PAI *see* publicly available information (PAI)
patent securitisation ....[1.30], [7.10]
  BioPharma Royalty Trust ....[7.10], [7.80]
Plant Breeders' Rights Act 1994 (Cth) ....[7.60]
portfolio administrator (managed
  synthetic securitisation) ....[4.70], [4.110]
publicly available information (PAI)
  notice of ....[2.70], [2.230], [3.360]

Q
QIS3 (Quantitative Impact Study) ....[2.380]

R
Railtrack PLC ....[2.150]
rating agencies
  managed synthetic securitisation
    credit risk ....[4.510]
    portfolio tests ....[4.290]
    proprietary models ....[4.300]
    trading gains ....[4.400]
  manager
    consent to removal ....[4.100]
    review of ....[4.80]
  synthetic securitisation ....[3.170], [3.430]
Really Useful Theatres ....[8.20]
recharacterisation (CAT bonds) ....[5.90]
recharacterisation (credit
  derivatives) ....[2.270]-[2.340]
  gaming ....[2.340]
  guarantee ....[2.340]
  insurance ....[2.280]-[2.330]
    Australian law ....[2.330]
    authorised insurers ....[2.290]
    insurable interests ....[2.320]
    jurisdiction ....[2.300]
    legal opinion ....[2.310]
recharacterisation (synthetic
  securitisation) ....[3.420], [3.430]-[3.450]
    beneficial ownership, transfer of ....[3.440]
    bond or loan ....[3.450]
      Caiola case ....[3.450]
    insurance ....[3.430]
    legal opinion ....[3.430]
regulatory issues (managed
  synthetic securitisation)
  Chapter 5C, *Corporations Act 2001* (Cth) [4.610]
    disclosure ....[4.620]
      increased ....[4.660]
    managed investment scheme ....[4.610]
    manager, requirements in relation to ....[4.620]
regulatory issues (synthetic securitisation)
  Basel II (proposed) .....[3.600], [3.610], [3.670]
    operational requirements ....[3.600]
  capital adequacy rules ....[3.570], [3.580]
  implementation "avant la lettre" ....[3.630]
  limited guidance ....[3.570]
  risk weights ....[3.610]
  super senior investor, risk transfer to ....[3.590]
    equity note ....[3.590]
  super senior swaps ....[3.620]
risk factors in synthetic
  securitisation ....[3.230]-[3.310]
    bullet maturity ....[3.310]
    collateral risk ....[3.270]
      addressing ....[3.270]
      collateral, investment in ....[3.270]
    credit derivatives definitions,
      evolution of ....[3.310]

guaranteed investment contract (GIC) ..[3.300]
    liquidity facility ....[3.300]
  originator credit risk ....[3.250]
    enhancement of ....[3.250]
    interposed bank ....[3.250]
  portfolio credit risk ....[3.240]
  prepayment risk ....[3.310]
  put option ....[3.290]
  repurchase agreement ....[3.280]
  settlement currency ....[3.310]
  termination risk ....[3.260]
    termination, events related to ....[3.260]
    termination provisions ....[3.260]
  total return swaps ....[3.290]
Robeco series ....[3.500], [3.660], [4.150],
                                                [4.470], [4.660]
Ruby Finance ....[4.10]

S
securitisation
  cash securitisation *see* cash securitisation
  copyright *see* copyright securitisation
  entire business enterprise *see* whole of
    business securitisation (WOBS)
  hedge fund *see* hedge fund securitisation
  insurance *see* insurance securitisation
  intellectual property *see* intellectual
    property securitisation
  life insurance *see* life insurance securitisation
  patent *see* patent securitisation
  synthetic *see* synthetic securitisation
  trademark *see* trademark securitisation
  true sale or traditional *see* traditional
    securitisation
  types of transactions ....[1.30]
  what is ....[1.20]
settlement (credit default swaps)
  cash settlement ....[2.80], [3.370]
    actual recovery *see* recovery
      of reference obligations
    market valuation ....[3.370], [3.380]
    preset of calculation method [3.370], [3.390]
  conditions to ....[2.40], [2.70], [3.360]
  credit event notice ....[2.70], [3.360]
  method and valuation ..[2.40], [3.370]-[3.400]
  notice of PAI ....[2.70], [3.360]
  physical settlement ....[2.80], [3.370]
    notice of ....[2.70]
  recovery of reference
    obligations ....[3.370], [3.400]
      calculation agent ....[3.400]
      cut-off date ....[3.400]
      obligation category and
        characteristics ....[3.400]
Shinbun ....[3.360]
Silk Road ....[4.50]
software securitisation ....[1.40], [7.10]
Tokimeki Memorial Game Fund .[7.10], [7.100]
Special Purpose Reinsurance
  Vehicle Model Act 2001 (US) ....[5.110]
special purpose vehicle (SPV) ....[3.40], [3.220]
  "insurance business" and ....[5.100]
  synthetic arbitrage ....[4.130]
SPV *see* special purpose vehicle (SPV)
super senior swap
  advantages ....[3.210]
  capital relief ....[3.210]
  cost efficiency ....[3.210]
  Mahonia case ....[3.210]
  regulatory issues ....[3.620]
  synthetic arbitrage securitisation ....[4.140]
  terms of swap ....[3.210]
Symphony II ....[4.160]
synthetic arbitrage
  ABS ....[4.150], [4.160]
  arbitrage transactions, what are ....[4.20]
  Asia-Pacific market ....[4.50]
  Australian market ....[4.10], [4.50]
  Bernstein ....[4.150]
  Brookland ....[4.150]
  Cibeles I ....[4.150]
  Enron Corporation ....[4.130], [4.440]
  ESAF Navigator ....[4.150]

213